Forgotten Elegance

Forgotten Elegance

The Art, Artifacts, and Peculiar History of Victorian and Edwardian Entertaining in America

Wendell Schollander and Wes Schollander

GREENWOOD PRESS
Westport, Connecticut • London

Library of Congress Cataloging-in-Publication Data

Schollander, Wendell, 1943–
    Forgotten elegance : the art, artifacts, and peculiar history of Victorian and Edwardian
entertaining in America / Wendell Schollander and Wes Schollander.
      p. cm.
    Includes bibliographical references and index.
    ISBN 0–313–31685–6 (alk. paper)
    1. Entertaining—United States—History—19th century. 2. Dinners and dining—United
States—History—19th century. 3. Victoriana in interior decoration. 4. Table setting and
decoration—History—19th century. 5. United States—Social life and customs—19th
century. I. Schollander, Wes, 1974– II. Title.
TX731 .S3295 2002
642'.4'097309034—dc21   2001016185

British Library Cataloguing in Publication Data is available.

Library of Congress Catalog Card Number: 2001016185
ISBN: 0–313–31685–6

First published in 2002

Greenwood Press, 88 Post Road West, Westport, CT 06881
An imprint of Greenwood Publishing Group, Inc.
www.greenwood.com

Printed in the United States of America

The paper used in this book complies with the
Permanent Paper Standard issued by the National
Information Standards Organization (Z39.48–1984).

10 9 8 7 6 5 4 3 2 1

Copyright Acknowledgments

The authors and publisher gratefully acknowledge permission to reproduce the following
material:

Some of the silver items shown are courtesy of Peter M. Braswell, who granted permission
for the use of his collection. Photographs were taken by David Reavis and reprinted with
permission. Figure 10.2 is reproduced by permission of Ray Doub. Figure 10.6 is
reproduced by permission of Robert Campbell and Monte Campbell. Figure 13.2 is
reprinted courtesy of Oak Alley Plantation.

Every reasonable effort has been made to trace the owners of copyright materials in this
book, but in some instances this has proven impossible. The authors and publisher will be
glad to receive information leading to more complete acknowledgments in subsequent
printings of the book and in the meantime extend their apologies for any omissions.

To Jayn Schollander, wife, mother, Stakhanovite of the household, and lady of grace and intellect. Not only is she the inspiration for this work, but its completion would not have been possible without her knowledge and help.

Contents

Contents

Acknowledgments

We would like to thank Debby Adams, who breathed life into this project, Susan Walker and Gina Brannock for typing and thoughtful suggestions, and Rene Wise for computer work. A special thanks to the librarians, too numerous to mention by name, at the following libraries: Forsyth County Public Library, Winston-Salem; Jackson Library, University of North Carolina at Greensboro; the Rakow Library at the Corning Museum of Glass; and the Tuxedo Park Library. Librarians are the nicest and most helpful people in the world.

Introduction

The origins of this book date back to a wedding present Jayn, the wife of one of the authors, received. Jayn had a slightly madcap aunt who was of the old school, and for a wedding present she gave us a small silver plate. Neither of us had any idea what it was to be used for. Jayn could not very well write to thank her aunt for the lovely "whatchamacallit," and one could never be sure if a gift from her was a proper etiquette item or some whimsical reflection of her bohemian side. So we started asking questions. The scions of what we felt to be a wealthy and cultured family lived in the apartment next door. They guessed it was a plate for collecting calling cards from those whom our aunt undoubtedly thought would be paying formal visits to us in the future. Another set of friends thought it was a plate for serving after-dinner mints. Other people had different ideas. We checked with jewelry and department stores without success. Finally, an elderly salesperson told us that it was merely a bread-and-butter plate made of silver to match Jayn's silver pattern.

Jayn had grown up in a place and time when well-to-do relatives picked a silver pattern for a little girl and gave her pieces when she had a birthday or for Christmas. These gifts of silver were unappreciated by an eight-year-old who wanted a doll, but they were much valued years later after she married and started to entertain.

This wasn't to be the last mystery gift that we would receive from that dear aunt. From time to time an unusual fork or spoon, the purpose for which we could not divine, would appear and more research would be necessary. Gradually we got to know where to go to find the information, and the search became interesting in its own right.

What had been researched for practical reasons, for writing thank-you notes and finding out the names of items Jayn owned, became a hobby. As with any hobby, the more we learned, the more we wanted to know. Having discovered how to identify pieces, it was a short step to figuring out how these various specialized eating utensils and different types of china were used during a meal or formal tea. And that spurred our interest in trying to put on such a meal.

This was a whole new challenge. Today we have only the vaguest knowledge of how our ancestors entertained in the Victorian era of the late nineteenth and early twentieth centuries. The literature of the era gives us dazzling images of long, leisurely, elegant meals put on with a sizable number of kitchen and dining room help. It describes flickering candlelight, sparkling crystal, glowing silver, and luminous china. Teas were formal with their own set of special rules and rituals. The majority of people did not live like that, of course, but those who could afford it lived in a very graceful style.

The first place we turned was old etiquette books, but they are maddingly nonspecific. It is only by cross-checking many books, one against the other, that the customs followed in Victorian entertaining are revealed.

This book then serves several purposes. If you are a collector of old items, or have an interest in how some people lived "only yesterday," then we hope you will find this book a useful and interesting resource for rounding out your knowledge of old silver, stemware, and china. If your bent is social history, you can follow the evolution of social habits and the material elements that accompanied them.

In the following pages you will discover how those elegant meals and teas were staged. You will even learn how you can entertain in proper Victorian style, with authentic menus, if you so desire. The text includes detailed information on what to use, and when and how to use it. If you should wish to put on such an entertainment, you will find very detailed information on what you, your guests, and helpers should do at each step. With a little extra work and planning, you can reproduce the form and spirit of these events, not for everyday life, of course, but for special occasions with friends who enjoy returning to those elegant days for an evening, or an afternoon, or even a few hours at lunch.

At this point, even if you find yourself fascinated with the idea of recreating this grand style of high dining for some special occasion, you may not take the notion seriously. You may think, "I don't know anything about which fork to use or have the specialized pieces necessary to carry it off."

Put your mind at ease. While it is true that many different items were made in the Victorian period, it is possible to quickly learn what is what. Included with the text are pictures of almost anything that you may encounter. Besides, we will let you in on a secret: many of these speciality items were not regularly used by the Victorians. The manufacturers produced them, but some of them were not popular with the buying public. Even at the height of the Victorian period there was a limited demand for crawfish knives or individual asparagus holders. In fact, some thought that too much reliance on specialized dinnerware showed that you were not really "old money." What was good enough for Queen Anne was good enough for them, and she most definitely did not use all those different plates and specialized silver. This fact also makes it easy for you and your friends to put on an authentic Victorian meal with what you have.

Even if you choose not to entertain in the different Victorian styles, you may find the information in this book useful in your life today. After reading through the information on one of these twelve-course (or more) meals, you will be able to meet the challenge of almost any formal occasion. It is doubtful that anyone will ever put out a fork that you will not have seen, nor will you worry quite as much about what wine to order.

Forgotten Elegance is the result of many years of research and trial and error. It is what we would have liked to have had access to when we started collecting old pieces of china and silverware, and thought about having dinners with the theme of the elegant meals served during the reigns of Victoria and Edward VII.

Whether you are reading this because you are a collector, are interested in the Victorian period, or want to put together a different kind of meal with some friends who are willing to get in the spirit of re-enacting a past way of life, we hope you enjoy the book. And should you be emboldened to stage such an event, it is our sincere hope you have a lot of fun doing so. Our family and our friends certainly have.

I

A Short History
of the Art of Dining

Chapter 1

A History of Formal Dining

The Victorian period lasted approximately sixty years, from 1837 to 1901, which corresponds to the reign of Queen Victoria, and is synonymous with the nineteenth century. The "Edwardian Period" is often referred to as the period from 1901 to 1914 although Edward VII ruled from only 1901 to 1910. The terms and concepts that became associated with the formal meals of this era did not arise in a vacuum; they were the outgrowth of dining terms and concepts that date back to the Middle Ages. To understand fully the how and why of Victorian formal meals, a quick history lesson is in order.

In Western Europe in the late Middle Ages, at great formal banquets, both the diners and the dinner were the show. The host and his special guests would sit along one side of a table set at the head of the great hall of the castle. This allowed the other diners to view the actions of the great and powerful.

At the head table, the most important people sat in the middle, at center stage as it were, and the lesser people toward either end. At some point down the table were placed great salt holders, or saltcellars. This evolved into a natural delineation of status among the diners at the head table. One was either above the salt, that is, close to the important people, or below the salt, with the hoi polloi.

In accounts of medieval dinners a great deal of attention is paid to who sat where. The host sat in the middle of the *high table*, so called because it was often placed on a platform. The table was set up on the stage so that others could watch what their "betters" were doing and how they behaved. This custom is still followed today in some of the college dining rooms at Cambridge University, England, and at public banquets.

The tables for the other diners were often placed at right angles to the main table. These people were so far off the social scale that they did not merit being ranked as above or below the salt. Women were even further off the social scale. At first, the wives of the nobles were not even allowed at great banquets and were relegated to a spectators' gallery. Later, they were allowed to sit at the table in a group well below the salt.

Entertainments were given between the "mets," a medieval term for a main course of a dinner. The entertainment might be short plays, songs by troubadours, animal acts, dancing, jesters, or juggling. Many dinners were for political show, and on really special occasions, pageants were performed. Several of these were so noteworthy that they are mentioned in some history books. One such dinner was the Banquet of the Vow of the Pheasant, given by the duke of Burgundy in 1453. Footmen brought out a pheasant for each knight in attendance and placed it before him. Each knight vowed by the pheasant and before God to abstain from whatever action his imagination conjured up—to sleep in a bed, to change his clothes, and so on—until Constantinople had been reconquered from the Ottoman Turks, who had captured it that year. This vow created a sensation as Constantinople had been thought to be impregnable, and all Christians were humiliated and terrified at the idea of the city in Muslim hands. Unfortunately for Christendom, the knights came to their senses in the days following the meal and did not try to take back Constantinople.

Guests were given light tidbits to eat while watching these shows. In time, such dishes came to be called *entremets*, literally, between the mets.

The dinner itself was full of pageantry to entertain and impress those in attendance. The food was brought in in a procession, often with flute players leading the way. The less important foods, called "entrees," came in and were laid out first, building up to the presentation of the *pièce de résistance*, which might be a full roasted ox or a roasted pheasant with its skin and feathers still attached.

In time, kings and other nobility found it wearisome to be on display. They just wanted to eat with other important people, their friends and allies, in privacy. These intimate meals moved from the great halls to the lord's private living areas. The table changed from a long, relatively narrow strip of wood with seating on only one side, to a square or oblong table where people could sit on all sides. Status was still gained, however, by sitting close to the lord or other notables, and the women were grouped either at another table or the end of the table away from the host.

The wider tables allowed more food to be put on the table itself. This in turn permitted far greater displays of food. The table would almost creak under the weight of joints of meat, fish, fowls, and side dishes. With diners on all sides of the table, however, it was not possible to bring each dish in after people sat down. The table had to be largely set before the diners arrived, which meant that the food would get cold while the diners filed in to take their places. Essentially, the nobles gained the ability to talk and dine intimately with their companions at the expense of hot meals. This was not as great a loss as it might appear to us today. Up until the nineteenth century, the cooking area was always set well away from the main part of the house lest a cooking fire get out of control and burn everything down. Thus the food lost a good bit of heat while being carried to the dining room.

Over time, what had started out as small private meals grew into pageants in their own right. This came about in the seventeenth century, when absolute monarchs ruled most of Europe. In keeping with the ethos of the era, every aspect of the king's life was made a display.[1] Vast and elaborate meals were one way to assert power, wealth, and status, and they once again moved back into public view. But, this time, women fully participated as the bold innovation of alternating men and women at the dinner table took hold. This practice arrived in England from Holland in the 1600s and was known as the Dutch style of seating.

The last ingredient in the evolution of formal Victorian dining came about in the early 1800s, as the combined weight of England and Russia was defeating the military genius of Napoleon. Ironically, even as the French were losing on the battlefield, they were about to emerge victorious on the culinary front. They had developed a sophisticated culinary style, drawing in large part upon what they had learned from the Italians. Italian cooks and courtiers came to France in 1533 when fourteen-year-old Catherine de

Medici of Florence, the great-granddaughter of Lorenzo the Magnificent, married the future king of France, Henry II. Their arrival helped transform French cooking and manners. They opened new vistas of taste and introduced new dishes: sweetbreads, truffles, artichoke hearts, and ice cream. Prior to this, the Italians had looked down on the French. Niccolò Machiavelli, the Italian political philosopher, had referred to them as the barbarians. Before Catherine's arrival, all the French had was raw military power. Afterward, they were on their way to *haute cuisine*.

Although the French developed sophisticated cooking methods, their style was not to everyone's taste. The English preferred fresh ingredients, simply cooked to allow the natural flavors to come out. Englishmen who undertook the Grand Tour, the tour of Europe that English nobles in the eighteenth century ventured upon to acquire polish, complained about the French cooks. One said: "For wholesomeness they are inferior to ours, most of their dishes being too highly seasoned, and some of them a perfect hodgepodge or according to the vulgar proverb, a medicine for a sick dog."[2] Another less flamboyantly observed that the French style of cooking was forced on them by the poor quality of their meat.[3]

All of that changed at the end of the 1700s. The French Revolution in 1789 broke the power of the French nobility, and many of their household cooks were thrown out of work. Some established restaurants, and others went to serve the aristocracies in England and Russia. These emigres introduced French cooking, and gradually a taste for it developed outside of France.

In 1811, during the Napoleonic Wars, the prince regent of England hired France's most renowned cook, Antoine Careme (1784–1833), "the cook of kings, and the king of cooks," to become his personal chef. Later, Careme served as cook to Tsar Alexander I of Russia. He also cooked for Talleyrand, the French diplomat, and Baron Rothschild, a leader of the rich international banking family. In addition, Careme was an author of books on cooking and food. He and Jean Brillat-Savarin (1755–1826), who was the philosopher of gourmandism, built the foundation for France's dominance of all things culinary during the nineteenth century. By the time of Queen Victoria's coronation in 1837 French cooking methods occupied a place of honor in international royal society, and their tradition of serving a meal in a few multidish courses held sway through most of Europe.

While the international cooking style became French, the standard method of presentation was still that of the late Middle Ages—to place all the food in the first course on the table before the diners came in to eat.

In the United States in the first third of the nineteenth century, food preparation and service were generally straightforward. French cooking was not the norm. This fit in with the American sensibility of being a republic, with the old Roman Republic being the guiding light. Before the decadence of the Roman Empire, Romans had lived straightforward lives of simplicity, and Americans, in theory, tried to do the same. Meals consisted of only two courses (plus a dessert of fruit), and the cooking was simple. Plain roasts of beef, lamb, or birds and simple platters of vegetables were the norm. To abandon this convention of simple, dignified living was frowned upon. In 1840, during the Van Buren administration, a meal served at the White House in the new French style became a political issue. A congressman attacked it and the royal style it represented, and the menu was placed in the *Congressional Record*. The meal, according to its critics, consisted of five courses and dessert. It committed two sins. In addition to being overly large, it was full of "French style" cooking. The menu is presented below:

First course:
Potage au tortue, Potage a la Julienne, et Potage aux pois.	Soup

Second course:
Saumon, sauce d'anchois, Bass pique a la Chambore.	Fish

Third course:
Supreme de volaille en bordure a la galee, Filet de boeuf pique au vin de Champagne, Pate chaud a la Toulouse.	Entrees

Fourth course:
Salade d'homard monte, Filets mignons de mouton en chevreuil, Cerveau, de veau, au supreme, Pigeons a la royal aux champignons.	Entrees & Joint

Fifth course:
Becassines, Canard sauvages, Poulet de Guinee piquee. Patisserie—Charlotte russe au citron, Biscuit a la vanille decore, Coupe garnie de gelee d'orange en quartiers, Gelee au marasquin, Gelee au Champagne rose, Blanc-mange; Sultane, Nougat, Petits gateaux varies.	Sweets & Game

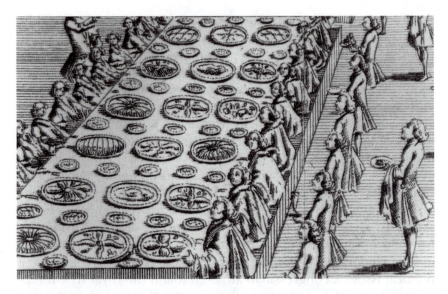

Figure 1.1 Table settings circa 1760. From *The Gentleman's Magazine, and Historical Chronicle*. London, v. 31 (1761) December. Plate following p. 548: A View of the Inside of Guildhall as it Appear'd on Lord Mayors Day, 1761. (Courtesy, The Winterthur Library: Printed Book and Periodical Collection.)

Dessert:
Fruits, et glace en pyramide, et en petits moules,   Fruit and Sweets
Toste d'anchois, Cafe et liqueur[4]

Van Buren lost the presidential election of 1840 to William Harrison, whose supporters boasted of his simple ways—living in a log cabin and drinking hard cider. Whatever its political implications, the meal shows that luxuries were starting to creep into the United States.

As is often the case when political rhetoric is involved, the story's presentation was a bit misleading. Let us look at a typical meal in the United States in the period just before the date of the 1840 meal at the White House.

From the pre-revolutionary period up to about 1830, dinners had been presented in two main courses, followed by a dessert course of fruits and sweets. When the guests came in to eat, they found food already on the table. The more food, the greater the display. As can be seen from Figure 1.1, a fully set table with all its footmen made an impressive display.

At the head of the table would be the soup tureen, or perhaps the shell of a West Indies sea turtle holding soup. The rest of the table was filled with lesser side dishes.

First the diners had their soup bowls filled by the hostess, and the bowls were then handed around by the servants. Next came the fish, quite often brought in in all its glory in a procession reminiscent of the Middle Ages—the larger the fish, the more impressive the display. It was carved by the host and handed out by the servants. While all of this was going on, diners were filling their plates from the side dishes already on the table. These side dishes were referred to as the "entrees" in recognition of the old treatment of minor dishes that in the Middle Ages had been brought in to the diners first. It was considered polite to fill the plate of those seated close to you or to send an unusually good tidbit to a friend at another part of the table.

After the soup and fish had been eaten, the tureen and fish platter were removed, and main dishes of beef, lamb, and other meats took their place. These main dishes were called "removes," as they removed the tureen and fish platter. The entrees were also sometimes removed and replaced by other side dishes. The replacement dishes were referred to as "flying dishes" as they were not on the table when the meal began, but were carried in from the serving area.

Figure 1.2 depicts a chart taken from a housewife's manual from the mid-eighteenth century showing how the main courses of a dinner would be placed on the table.

After the first course of soup, fish, meats, and side dishes, the dishes and tablecloth were removed. Another tablecloth would already be in place under it, and a second course comprised of birds, game, and more side dishes was placed on the table.

Quite often several items on the table during one of the two courses would need carving. This was the duty of the host, hostess, or a guest sitting near the food. Thus, the ability to carve was an important part of every gentleman's and gentlewoman's education. The ability to carve gracefully while remaining seated was much esteemed. The carved meat would be put on a plate and passed to guests by other diners or servants.

Many times a diner, hesitant to bother others, and unable to catch a footman's eye, would eat only those foods that were in his or her immediate reach.

Then, the second tablecloth was removed and dessert was

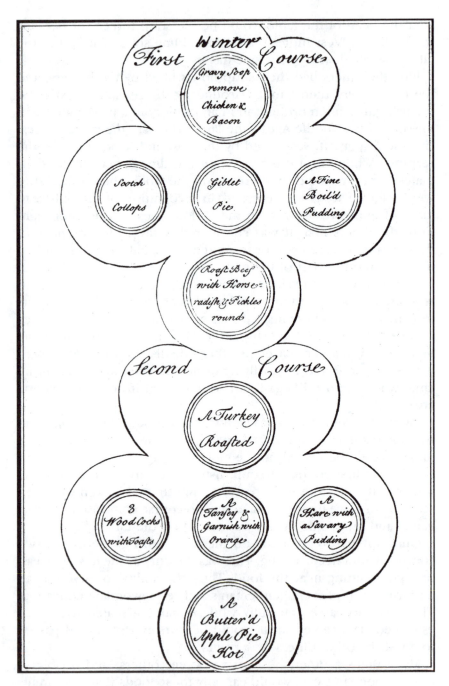

Figure 1.2 Chart showing the two main courses of dinner *à la Francaise* circa mid-1700s.

placed on the bare table, or diners moved to another table set up for dessert. The word "dessert" comes from the French term *des-servie*—"to clear the table." The dessert consisted of sweet dishes, often called "sweet breads," and fruit. In England, after the dessert, the women went to the withdrawing room (now shortened to the drawing room) and left the men to their port or sherry and often rather drunken and boorish masculine conversation. On the Continent, the men and women all drank coffee and liqueurs together in a separate room and behavior was more genteel.

No one was expected to eat all the choices placed before him or her. The whole point of entertaining was to make a lavish display, earning status by showing how much the host could afford to place before a guest. Its spirit was close to that of an an elaborate buffet.

The French style of dining, when it began to be adopted by the Americans in the 1840s, made a few important changes to this system. Under the old "English" style used in the United States up to that time, the first course had soup, fish, entrees, and joints. The second course would consist of game, more entrees, and some sweets. The third course, the dessert, consisted of fruit and more sweets. This was, however, not always the case. For example, the following dinners à la Francaise were recorded in diaries and letters:

Where:	Savannah, Ga.	Albany, N.Y.	Plantation, Coastal S.C.
When:	1822	1827	1832
First course:	Cod	Ham	Turtle soup
	Southern bacon	Roast ducks	Leg of boiled mutton
	Ducks	Roast beef	Turtle steaks & fins (2)
	Oysters (2 ways)	Boiled mutton	Pie of macaroni
	Bread	Beans	Two small dishes of oysters
	Onions	Turnips	Boiled ham
	Beets	Potatoes	Haunch of venison
	Boiled rice		Roast turkey

	Irish potatoes (2 ways)		
Second course:	Cherry pie	Bread pudding	Bread pudding
	Cranberry pie	Biscuits	Jelly
	Quince, orange, and other preserves	Cheese	High glass dish of ice cream
	Salad	Sweetmeats	Madeira
	Cheese	Peaches	Sherry
	Butter	Plums	Champagne
	Pineapple cream	Melons	
		Grapes	
Dessert:	Oranges		Bananas
	Plantains		Oranges
	Raisins		Apples
	Walnuts		Hermitage
	Cordials		Madeira
	Wine		Cordials[5]

The "French" style, in addition to breaking the first two courses into four courses, typically put fewer dishes on the table for each course, as can be seen in Figure 1.3. The first course was the fish and soup with a few side entrees. Then, came a course of nothing but entrees. The third course consisted of the joints with a few entrees. The fourth course was the game, sweets, and more entrees. These four courses were followed by the dessert course of fruits, ices, and nuts.

To people used to two courses, the new system sounded as if more food was being served. The anti–Van Buren partisan capitalized on this confusion when he attacked the White House dinner. He also misrepresented the soup and fish as being separate courses. He made it sound as though the meal hit a new extreme in gluttony. He also played on the fact that the cooking was in the French style, rather than "good old American" (and English) basic cooking.

The French style also imposed new rules on the order in which food was served. This was a result of the theories of Careme and Brillat-Savarin, who said that the foods' relation-

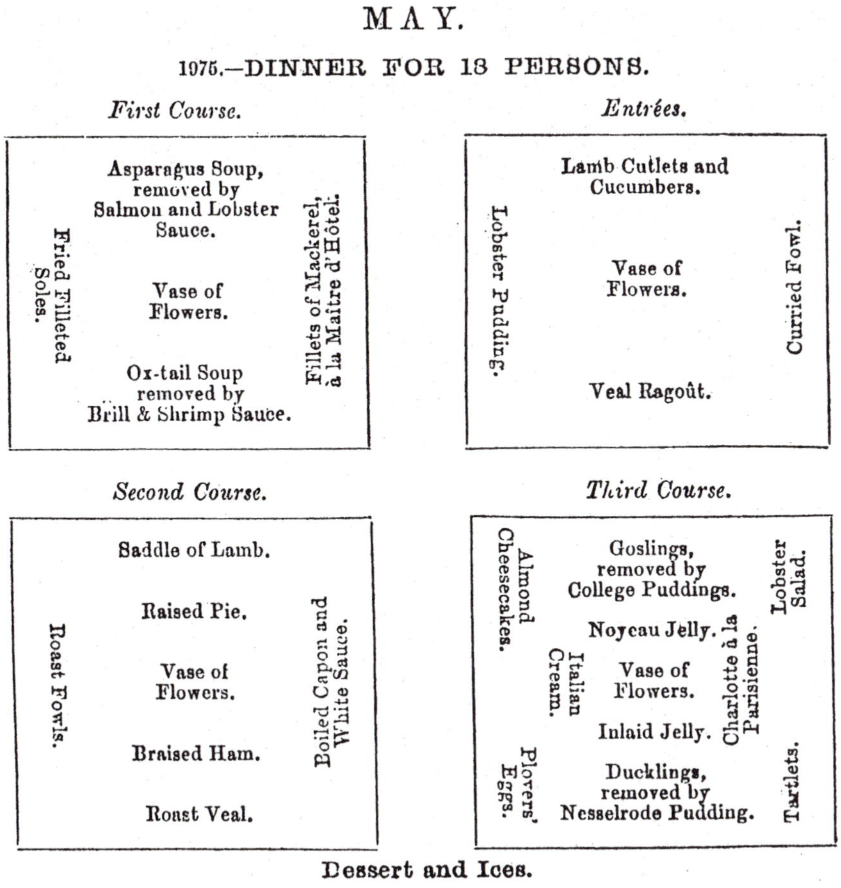

M A Y.

1075.—DINNER FOR 18 PERSONS.

First Course.

Asparagus Soup,
removed by
Salmon and Lobster
Sauce.

Vase of
Flowers.

Ox-tail Soup
removed by
Brill & Shrimp Sauce.

Fried Filleted Soles.

Fillets of Mackerel, à la Maître d'Hôtel.

Entrées.

Lamb Cutlets and
Cucumbers.

Vase of
Flowers.

Veal Ragoût.

Lobster Pudding.

Curried Fowl.

Second Course.

Saddle of Lamb.

Raised Pie.

Vase of
Flowers.

Braised Ham.

Roast Veal.

Roast Fowls.

Boiled Capon and White Sauce.

Third Course.

Goslings,
removed by
College Puddings.

Noyeau Jelly.

Vase of
Flowers.

Inlaid Jelly.

Ducklings,
removed by
Nesselrode Pudding.

Almond Cheesecakes.

Italian Cream.

Plovers' Eggs.

Charlotte à la Parisienne.

Lobster Salad.

Tartlets.

Dessert and Ices.

Figure 1.3 Chart showing the courses offered at a dinner *à la Francaise* circa 1861. Note the extra course and the dessert course.

ships to each other were an important element of the dining experience. Accordingly, they believed food should be served in this order: soup, fish, meat, game, sweets, and fruits. The side dishes and everything else, whether called entrees, *entremets*, or hors d'oeuvres, supplemented these main items.

In the United States this method of service was used until shortly after the Civil War, when it was supplanted by service *à la Russe*. This method is said to have been introduced to France in 1811 by the Russian ambassador to Napoleon, Prince Aleksandr Borosovich Kurakin, but it was not commonly used until the 1860s and 1870s. This change, so revolutionary at the time, has today become the norm for formal dining, and it is hard for us to realize that any other system could have been followed. The old method survives only in family meals and Thanksgiving or Christmas feasts where close community is the norm.

This new method was often described as "serving from the side." When the diners arrived, there was no food on the table. A dish, a soup tureen, or a platter with carved meat was presented to each diner for his or her selection. Another servant followed with side dishes or condiments. The meat or fish was carved on a sideboard by a footman or waiter. The diners no longer did any of the work in cutting the meats or passing the food to each other. "The food appeared like magic and all we had to do was enjoy ourselves," one writer of the period enthused. Another noted that without having to have all the food ready at the same time, or to prepare elaborate presentations of the food, a dinner became a mere amusement.

Service *à la Russe* accomplished several things. First, it cleared almost all the food off the table. Rather than cover the table with meat and other dishes, it could be adorned with flowers or other decorations. The guests were surrounded by "the most delicious atmosphere of fruit and flowers instead of being stupefied with the fumes of meat," wrote one early diner. The art of table decorations came into its own, and will be discussed in chapter 11. Second, it strung out the presentation of the food. Rather than all the food being placed on the table at one time, the food was presented one dish after another as separate courses throughout the meal. Third, it placed on the waiters the responsibility for carving the meat and passing the food.

The years 1865 to 1880 were a period of transition. People were turning to the new Russian method, and there was uncertainty about how the table should be set, what foods should be served, and how much food represented a proper display of hospitality and status.

The earlier English and French styles had measured bountiful hospitality by the number of items on the table. This "more-is-better" tendency carried over to the Russian method. In the beginning, some hosts went overboard. Consider this menu, suggested in the late 1870s:

Oysters

Soups

Hors d'oeuvres (cold)

Fish

Hors d'oeuvres (hot)

Removes (Roast)

Roman punch (Iced punch)

Entrees (Side dishes)

Entremets

Game

Salad

Cheese

Entremets (sweet)

Ice cream and ices

Dessert

Coffee with biscuits (that is, cookies).[6]

This is far from the 29 courses often said to have been served during this period. It may be in reaching this count people were counting vegetables, often served separately, as a course. A more likely explanation lies in the odd number 29. The 29-course figure is in several books, but its origin appears to be a newspaper story by Emily Briggs, one of the first society reporters in the country. In a story dated March 18, 1870, she said a dinner at the White House ran to 29 courses. This should be taken with a grain of salt as two weeks later she reported that tea for a tea party in Washington, D.C. was brought by a U.S. Navy warship from Japan after a trip made specifically to collect tea for this one party. She also said it was reported that after the tea party the Japanese tea master, who had come from Japan with the tea committed hari-kari as his work here was completed. Clearly what she wrote should not be read too literally.[7]

In an effort to encourage her countrymen to cut down on the amount of food they served, Mary Henderson, the same American writer who had set out the above menu, suggested that the following menu was good enough in Europe and should be sufficient for any meal in the United States:

Oysters on the half shell

Amber soup (beef consomme)

Salmon with sauce hollandaise

Sweetbreads and peas

Lamb chops, tomato sauce

Fillet of beef with mushrooms

Roast quails with Saratoga potatoes

Lettuce salad

Cheese, celery, wafers

Charlotte Russe (sweets)

Chocolate, ice cream

Fruit

Coffee[8]

Basically the number of side dishes that surrounded the main dishes of the meal was reduced. This was to encourage people not to equate the number of different dishes with generous hospitality.

Even this "reduced" menu seems enormous today. But, it must be remembered, that a diner often did not partake of every course, and there is no way of knowing how much of each dish was eaten. Today, if someone were to write down every type of food offered to guests at a buffet, it might seem like an equally incredible amount of food. Most guests, however, take only small samplings and may skip some items altogether.

Computations from diaries and food records show that all social classes ate large amounts of food in the nineteenth century. However, three points must be kept in mind when thinking about the eating habits of that period. First, life required a great deal more physical activity in those days. Records of the tasks necessary to run a home or an office show how time and energy consuming these chores were compared to the twenty-first century with its labor-saving devices. The very wealthy did not put forth much more physical activity than we do today. But, even they were influenced by the norms of their society, and those norms called for more food as the great majority of people were faced with more physical labor. Second, views of what made for good health and proper eating habits were different. Some medical experts in the 1870s said it was unhealthy to eat more than one food at a time. It made the digestive system work too hard. The logical solution was to have many different one-item dishes at a meal. Rather than have meat and potatoes on the same dish, diners would eat the meat alone and then have a separate course of just the potato.

Some went so far as to not mix lettuce and vegetables in their salads. Third, the Victorian idea of physical beauty was different. Viewed in the light of history the modern idea of a physically attractive person is much thinner than in the past. Certainly the beauties shown in the frescos of Pompeii and in the masterpieces of Rubens were overweight by today's standards. Before the 1890s, it was considered socially desirable to have ample girth. Books told readers how to become fat, and tonic medicines that promised to make you "as fat as a pig" were sold.[9] America in this way fulfilled the emigrant's dream of a land of plenty.

In the 1880s and 1890s, the menus slimmed down a bit as the extra entrees were left out. A variation in the cheese course also appeared. The French ate the cheese course with fruit because often the two taste especially good together, and the cheese was thought to aid digestion. The English, on the other hand, moved the cheese course up to follow or accompany the salad. This difference caused confusion in the United States, as its citizens looked to both France and England for guidance on graceful living. So, in some American meals the cheese course would follow the French pattern and in others the English one.

The following is a typical formal menu from the period 1885 to 1895, in this case for a state dinner at the White House in 1891:

Blue Point oysters (Hors d'oeuvres)

Potage Tortue a L'anglaise or *Consomme Printaniere Royale* (Soups)

Canape a la Russe or *Timbales a la Talleyrand* (Side dishes, hot)

Saumon, sauce hollandaise (Fish)

Selle d'Agneau or *Filet de Boeuf* (Roast)

Ris de veau a la Perigeux, Cotelettes d'Agneau, and *Terrapin a la Maryland* (Entrees)

Punch Cardinal (Punch)

Canvasback duck (Game)

German asparagus or *Petite Pois* (Entremets)

Gelee au Champagne, Pudding *Diplomate* (Entremets, sweets)

Fruits (Dessert)

Coffee.[10]

It can be seen that the writers who criticized meals with too many courses as being too showy were successful, and many of the side dishes common twenty years earlier had been eliminated.

As the turn of the century approached, learned opinion began, more and more, to advise against overeating. In addition, there was a general movement to the idea that a shorter meal was better. Etiquette writers began to complain about the evils of spending several hours over dinner. This is a definite contrast to the earlier idea that a meal was a work of art and that gourmands should take their time and savor every bite.

A meal can be shortened in two ways: by serving it faster or dispensing with a course or two. Both were tried. Mrs. Stuyvesant Fish, one of the queens of Newport and New York society, was famous for her footmen (private homes have footmen, restaurants have waiters) snatching a diner's plate away after only a few minutes, so the dinner could keep moving at a dizzying speed. Her guests ate fast at one of her meals or went hungry. Also, private formal banquets increasingly tended to leave off the game course. With this change, the long march toward today's grazing and nouvelle cuisine began. Of course, problems with the supply of game in the East's crowded cities doubtless contributed to this trend. Canvasback duck, a staple for the game course for years, was being hunted almost to extinction. Passenger pigeons and even quail were becoming rarer.

By 1922, Emily Post described the following meal as the norm for the last twenty years:

Hors d'oeuvres

Soup

Fish

Entree

Roast

Salad

Dessert

Coffee.[11]

Whether or not this had been the norm since the turn of the century, as Mrs. Post asserted, is open to debate. Mrs. Post, like most of the great etiquette writers, was not above passing off her personal views as the accepted and proper way to do things. Many menus for formal private dinners and public banquets at that time still show a game course. But World War I did mark a watershed in formal meals. The war broke the old social conventions, and household help of any type was harder to come by. The servants of Europe and America, who escaped being sent to the trenches, were pulled into factory work during World War I. Many liked the freedom of industrial work and did not return to household service after the war. In addition, a youth cult followed the end of the war. Young people of the 1920s were not interested in the leisurely formal meals of their parents and grandparents, and social acceptance no longer depended on being able to give and to look good at one. In fact, the formal meal that had been at the heart of entertaining since the Civil War started to be viewed as stuffy and old-fashioned. Books and the new movies made fun of this type of meal.

By her 1929 edition, Emily Post had combined several courses, resulting in something much closer to our modern pattern of meals. The new standard was:

Soup or hors d'oeuvres

Fish or entree

Roast

Salad

Dessert and coffee

After World War II, the salad was moved to the beginning of the meal. This change seems to have resulted from a combination of two factors. This order for serving courses started in California and was picked up by restaurants as a cheap way of keeping diners busy while the food was prepared. In addition, the growing shortage of wait staff in private homes and restaurants created a tendency to put as much of the meal as possible on one plate. The entree (in the traditional sense of the word) dropped away, resulting in our present pattern of salad, meat, dessert, and coffee.

NOTES

1. A king's closest advisors were called the privy counsel.
2. Christopher Hibbert, *The Grand Tour* (New York: G. P. Putnam's Sons, 1969), p. 48, quoting Mr. (Sir Thomas) Nugent, *The Grand Tour*, 1749.
3. Ibid., citing Henry Thrale's statement to Dr. Johnson, p. 48.
4. *American Heritage Cookbook* (New York: American Heritage Publishing Co., 1964), p. 287.

5. Feay Shellman Coleman, *Nostrums for Fashionable Entertainments* (Savannah, GA: Telfair Academy of Arts and Sciences, 1992), Appendix III.

6. Mary Henderson, *Practical Cooking and Dinner Giving* (New York: Harper & Brothers, Publishers, 1877), p. 348. See also, DeB Randolph Keim, *Handbook of Official and Social Etiquette and Public Ceremonials at Washington*, 3d ed. (Washington, DC: DeB Randolph Keim, 1889), p. 216.

7. See Emily Edison Briggs, *The Olivia Letters* (New York: The Neale Publishing Company, 1906), pp. 204–205, 210.

8. Henderson, *Practical Cooking and Dinner Giving*, p. 351.

9. *The Economist*, September 20, 1997, p. 68.

10. Janet Halliday Ervin, ed., *The White House Cookbook* (Chicago: Follett Publishing Company, 1964), p. 20.

11. Emily Post, *Etiquette* (New York: Funk & Wagnalls Company, 1922), p. 189.

Chapter 2

Understanding the Food in a Victorian Meal

One of the main points of a formal meal has always been to impress others. Dinners *à la Francaise* and *à la Russe* met this goal. They both required extensive household help and experienced cooks or chefs. In addition, the main courses served at these dinners tended to be status foods. This concept is apparent when examining the classic French multicourse meal, developed out of the French ideal of what foods should be eaten and in what order. It is set up for service *à la Russe*, but the foods were served in both the French- and Russian-style meals.

CLASSIC MENU FOR FRENCH CUISINE

English	French
Cold appetizer	*Hors d'oeuvre froid*
Soup	*Potage*
Hot appetizer	*Hors d'oeuvre chaud*
Fish	*Poisson*
Main course	*Releve*/Joint
Intermediate course	*Entree*
Sorbet	*Sorbet*
Roast, salad	*Roti, salade*

Cold roast	*Roti froid*
Vegetable	*Legume*
Sweet	*Entremets*
Savory	*Savoury*
Dessert	*Dessert*

COLD APPETIZER

The first course, the cold hors d'oeuvre, consists of small tidbits to whet the appetite. In England, a punch was often served. In France, anchovies, canapes, or caviar was common.

During the nineteenth century Americans often began their meals with oysters, a local peculiarity that reflects the strong hold oysters had on the American menu. Oysters were not really a status food. They were plentiful and cheap and were used as a filler. Cookbooks of the period would call for more oysters if the cook could not afford beef or another meat. They were so much a part of American meals that people almost expected them at any dinner. European oysters are said to have a slight copper taste and thus were not served as much.

SOUP

The soup course at an English or American meal was very often turtle soup. The turtles used in this soup usually came from the Caribbean. In the 1700s, the English discovered they could ship Caribbean live sea turtles back to the United Kingdom if they were kept in barrels of sea water. This was both exotic and expensive—the perfect status dish. In the United States those who could not afford turtle soup often served mock turtle soup (made of calf's head), or ox-tail soup. (In fact, Campbell's Soup, aimed at a middle-class market, had an ox-tail soup before it had tomato soup.)

HOT APPETIZER

The third course was the hot hors d'oeuvre course. It was a hot tidbit to whet the palate. This course derived from the flying dishes of the older French-style service. These were dishes that were not placed on the table at the start of the meal. Rather, the waiters offered them to each diner as the meal progressed. They flew around the table rather than being more or less stationary like the major dishes. They might be morsels on toast, or light pastry filled with meat. This course in its heyday could be quite rich and complex. Foie gras, croquettes of fish or game, or patés with the same ingredients were common dishes.

Toward the end of the Victorian period, this course often consisted of just celery, almonds, and olives. The olives would often be stuffed with anchovy butter or with anchovies. These replaced the foods that in earlier years were served as cold hors d'oeuvres. The celery, olives, and so on were served with, or just after, the soup course. This was a shift in the order of the classical meal, and was done in an effort to speed up the meal.

Celery comes as a bit of a surprise since we think of it today a tasteless diet food. It was not so in the past. Prior to the late 1800s and early 1900s celery took a great deal of hand labor to raise and then blanche. Later agribusiness developed a stalk of celery that was easier to grow and was self-blanching, making it far more available—and, one suspects, less tasty.

The hot hors d'oeuvre course was one of the first to drop away as the Victorian meals became shorter. In a thirteen- or fourteen-course meal, there was not much need for an appetizer. A truncated remainder of this course, celery and olives served with the fish, lasted into the 1940s.

FISH

The next dish was almost always fish. The preferred fish were salmon or sturgeon. On rare occasions in the United States, it might be terrapin. Whatever it was, the goal was for it to be bigger and better than everyone else's.

In the pre–Civil War era, fish was displayed whole at the other end of the table from the soup. Status was gained by having the largest possible fish. After it was paraded around the table for the guests to admire, it was placed on the table for carving. A well-known anecdote relates how a host had two very large sturgeon, and he wished to show them both off. He racked his brain for a way to do so in the course of the meal. Finally, he had an idea. He ordered both fish cooked and elaborately dressed, each on its own serving dish. He instructed the staff on just what to do.

When the proper point in the meal came, the second largest fish, very large in its own right, was brought out and marched around the hall for all to admire. Then after everyone had closely examined it and it was being taken back to be carved, one of the footmen was seen to stumble. The fish fell off the plate and on to the floor. Cries of horror came from the guests and they all commiserated with the host on his loss. After a few minutes of this, things quieted down. Then the host commented, "Bring in the other fish."[1]

In service *à la Russe* the food is carved on the sideboard. Thus, there is no real chance to show off the size of the fish. But, on major occasions, the dressed fish was still marched around the room to show its size before being placed on the sideboard.

JOINT COURSE

In the French classical tradition of food service the "joint" course followed the fish course. As the name implies the piece brought in from the kitchen could be a large cut of any animal. Most of the time this was beef.

There are several reasons for this. The first is the simple fact that grazing large animals such as cattle takes a lot of land. In poorer areas this land would be devoted to producing a larger crop of rice, wheat, or potatoes. The United States has so much land and is so wealthy that people forget that in earlier times serving beef was in itself a form of conspicuous consumption. Maybe the best analogy today is to serve Kobe beef, the beef from Japan where the farmers do not let the animal move, feed it alcohol in the form of beer or saki, and massage it every day to keep it tender and well marbled. It is so expensive that it is almost never seen in the United States.

In England, up to the eighteenth century, beef was a rare food. In the United States in the colonial period and up to the opening of the midwestern plains to cattle production by the westward expansion of the railroads following the Civil War, beef was also an expensive product. Pork, often salted, was the food of common people. Beef, as a fairly expensive food, was a proper status food in the late 1700s and 1800s when the make-up of a formal meal was being set. In time beef in both countries ceased to be an unusual delicacy, but by then its place in formal meals was fixed.

INTERMEDIATE COURSE OR ENTREE

The next dish was the entree. It is a puzzle how this secondary dish came to be known as the main course of American meals in modern usage.

At first, the entrees were small cooked meats—lamb chops, the cheek meat of an animal, or meat-filled pastries, sweetmeats, and so on. In service *à la Francaise*, these were meats of minor importance, placed on the table more or less as fillers. When service *à la Russe* became the norm, the entree course was fairly elastic, that is, it could consist of one dish; but, on the other hand, at grand meals it could be composed of several of these minor meat dishes served one after another. This was done because in the early days of service *à la Russe* there was still a carryover of the idea that the more food put on the table the more impressive the meal.

In the later 1880s and 1890s, as the richest Americans began employing master chefs, the concept of the "man-made" portion of the meal developed.

The idea was that just cooking a fish, meat, or soup really did not give the chef a chance to show what could be done with food. The chefs began to develop elaborate and visually appealing dishes. Pheasant breasts in a towering aspic mold were a common dish. Victorian writers often romanticized this course as being more than merely cooked food—the entree showed what modern man's skill could create. It became a symbolic representation of the other marvels—such as the railroad, the telegraph, and medical advances—that Victorian man had by his intellect and skill created. The entree became referred to as the "high-water" mark of the meals. The artificial, man-made creations reflected modern man's advance in dining. Any savage could have cooked meat or fish— only the most progressive and skilled peoples could have created the complex entree.

The use of the term "entree" for secondary dishes is confusing as today it refers to the main dish of the meal. The stress on the entree course in the United States explains why what started out as a course of small tidbits came to be the American term for the main part of the meal.

In the 1870s and early 1880s, in the English-speaking world, the entree course was moved to the position of the first course after the fish. In books written in the late nineteenth and early twentieth centuries, the term "entree" is defined as "the first dish after the fish course."

While this shift in placement was occurring, the movement away from serving so many courses continued. The many side dishes had already dropped away; the next to go was the game course. Then as the pace of Americans grew faster and more informal the entree course was dropped. This left a meal of basically just soup, fish, meat, and salad. Yet with so much intellectual and emotional investment in the importance of the entree course, there lingered in the general mind the idea that the entree course, the first dish after the fish course, was important. After all, it was the high-water mark of the meal. It was just a short step to applying that term to the main course of the meal—whether it be meat, fish, or pasta.

PUNCH

Next came the punch course, a way to clear the palate for the game course, which for many years was the most important, and highest status, point in the meal. Since the game was so important, it was natural for some special little ceremonies to grow up around it. First, it was necessary to clear the palate so as to be able to experience every bit of the taste. Another idea was to try to make sure the diner had an empty stomach to enjoy the treat.

The punch was normally a drink of crushed ice, lemonade, and some form of liquor (about the consistency of a frozen daiquiri, or a smoothie). The most common was "Roman Punch," which had rum as its liquor. The theory was the lemonade cleared the palate and the rum cleared a hole in the stomach. The purists objected to rum as they felt the rum dulled the taste buds. They preferred a liqueur for the alcoholic portion of the drink.

Today in France, gourmets still take calvados, an apple brandy made in the Normandy area, to create what is called a "Norman hole." It is thought to revive the diner and encourage him or her to go on. The alcoholic kick in calvados is powerful as it is a form of applejack and can have the kick and taste of moonshine liquor.

One outgrowth of this punch course is the American custom of serving sherbet at the midpoint of the meal. This course today is often referred to as the intermezzo. This shift from an alcohol-based course to a non-alcoholic course was an outgrowth of the temperance movement in the United States, which resulted in Prohibition. First by choice for many, and later by law for all, rum and other liquors were done away with. Without the alcohol the liquid could freeze, and so there was a move away from a drink of smoothie consistency to a solid food that one ate with a spoon.

GAME OR ROAST

The game course was the highest status course of the meal, and as such was the high point of the meal. It takes a lot of land for game to run free to be hunted as well as labor to manage the land and the animals, and to keep poachers away year round.

In highly populated areas, land was a scarce commodity and it was expensive to keep land unproductive and at the same time have it manned by gamekeepers to provide game a habitat. In addition, starting in the Middle Ages, hunting was a pastime limited to the nobility. By law, tradesman, farmers, and merchants, no matter how wealthy, could not hunt. Poaching was a capital crime. By the Victorian period the laws against non-nobles hunting had been repealed, but the status connotation of hunting game remained. Thus, to serve deer, grouse, pheasant, and so on was a visible sign of wealth and status.

In the United States things were, of course, much different. Deer was what "wild Indians," frontiersmen, and settlers ate. It was not a status meat. In place of deer, grouse, or pheasant, canvasback duck became a staple at American formal meals. It had two advantages. Duck hunting then, as now, was a sport for the fairly well-to-do so it, albeit somewhat subtly, spoke of status. Also, duck was easy and fairly cheap to buy at the local eastern markets as the duck flyways ran down the East Coast.

Toward the end of the Victorian period, the game course began to drop off the menu of formal dinners. This probably was the result of a combination of things: the general desire for faster meals, and the increasing unavailability of duck and other game as overhunting took its toll.

COLD ROAST

This course was a chance to start winding down the meal. It often consisted of cold cuts of a different game animal than what had been featured in the roast course: deer, if the game course had been a game bird, or cutlets of pheasant or another game bird if the main game course had been deer. In spite of the course's

name, cold foie gras was often served. This course was one of the first to disappear from formal meals.

VEGETABLE

In modern times a vegetable does not seem to convey much status as frozen foods and fresh vegetables are shipped in year round. However, prior to the development of the railroad and refrigeration, or even canning, one could only eat vegetables at certain times of the year. The first canning took place during the Napoleonic Wars (champagne bottles were used to store the preserved vegetables), and canning was not fully developed until the middle of the nineteenth century. The extensive complex of railway tracks and refrigerated freight cars necessary for shipping fresh vegetables was not in place until after the U.S. Civil War. Prior to these developments, if one was to serve a vegetable out of season it had to be grown in a hot house. The expense of this made the product far beyond the reach of the average person.

In Victorian meals in the United States, the vegetable course was often omitted or lettuce was served. In the Edwardian period, iceberg lettuce, which had become commercially available in the 1890s, was often served. It was a tremendous breakthrough at the time as it was the first lettuce that could stand the stress of being shipped from California, where it could be grown almost year-round, to the East Coast.

SWEETS

The sweet course offered one last chance to impress guests. The serving of anything sweetened with sugar bespoke wealth. Up to the Napoleonic period, sugar was quite expensive, and sugar growing was a source of great wealth. There was so much money to be made from growing sugar that in 1667, Holland traded New York in part for the sugar-producing area of Surinam in South America. A century later, in 1763, the French gave up their claim on Canada for two small sugar-producing islands in the Treaty of Paris. One example can show why these trades were made. In 1761, England received £600,000 worth of profit from sugar exports from one sugar island, Guadeloupe, and only £14,000 in products from all of Canada. Sugar was so expensive it was often kept under lock and key.

The price of sugar began to fall in the late 1800s as more sugar-growing areas were developed and as chemists discovered how to extract sugar from beets. By 1812, Napoleon declared sugar independence from the British, who controlled a great deal of the very profitable world sugar production, and were putting economic pressure on France. With the drop in the price for sugar, the British need for slaves to grow sugar decreased, and in 1807 the British outlawed the slave trade.

With sugar no longer incredibly expensive, sweets made with sugar were no longer a statement of wealth. Another way to show status as part of the sweets course had to be found. This was ice cream.

From colonial times onward part of the sweet course was often ice cream. Today with our ubiquitous refrigeration it is easy to produce, buy, and store ice cream. But in colonial times one needed ice to cool the liquid cream and sweeteners into ice cream. This was not a problem in the North during the winter. But ice was not easy to come by in the summer or in the South. Ice blocks would be cut out of lakes and stored in special ice houses dug into the ground. There was a great deal of expense involved as the labor and shipping costs had to be paid, as well as having the land and money to build a specialized building for storing the ice. Then to produce the ice cream, a good deal of this expensive ice had to be used in the cooling process. As the Victorian period progressed, the harvesting and shipping of ice became more industrialized and more common. (New England ice was even shipped as far afield as India.) But, it took a long time for ice cream to lose its special status; so ice cream, albeit increasingly served in more specialized ways, continued to be a part of formal meals.

SAVORY

The savory was seen as the last chance to whip up the jaded appetite for the end of the meal. It consisted of some extremely tasty food served as a sort of appetizer before the last course of the meal—the dessert course.

This course was normally dropped from American Victorian meals, which instead featured two types of sweet foods. The sweet course was often a pudding or cake. Then ice cream was served as the savory. The English moved this course to the end of the meal, following the dessert. They often served anchovies, which seems very odd to Americans today who are used to ending a meal on a sweet note. The French often served cheese as their savory course, or would combine the cheese with the fruit of the dessert course.

DESSERT

Dessert in the French tradition meant fruit. Fruit for many years was one of the few sources of a sweet taste. By the seventeenth century sugar from sugarcane was available, although at a high price, but the tradition of serving fruit at the end of the meal remained common.

With fruit becoming more common and less important as a source of sugar, the method of showing status in the dessert course changed. Upper-class Victorians gloried in serving fruit in winter. This serving of fruit out of season showed that the host had gone to the expense of buying fruit shipped in from southern areas (which in the early days before refrigerated box cars and ships bespoke expense because of the large waste due to spoilage) or grown in local hot houses. To serve grapes, oranges, and so on while the snow laid high on the ground outside was a sign of wealth and taste. The tsars often showed their wealth and power in this way. But, even the wealth of the tsars had limits. One American young woman, given the honor of dining at the tsar's table, was very embarrassed when she clipped off a grape stem with some ten or twelve grapes. Everyone else was careful to take only two or three. She received many hard looks from the other ladies for her greed.

NOTE

1. Colin Clair, *Kitchen and Table* (London: Abelard-Schuman, 1964), pp. 83–84, citing Dumas, *Dictionaire de Cuisine*.

Chapter 3

Wine and Other Beverages

HISTORY AND FOOD MATCHES

For years wine has been an important part of most elegant meals. How it is served has changed over the course of history. Surprisingly, for such a seemingly highbrow and esoteric subject, economy and sheer chance have played a large part in determining the popularity and choice of what wine is served. Our current practice of drinking specific vintage wines with certain foods is largely a product of the nineteenth century. In the early 1800s, the idea of matching an aged wine with a particular dish or food was unknown. The change in how wine was served and drunk, which took place over the nineteenth century, the Victorian age, was the result of the interplay of custom, technology, and political economics.

The fact that the Victorian era saw a radical change in how wines were served with meals can make choosing a wine today for an authentic Victorian meal troublesome. Add to this the uncertainty that grips many of us when facing a wine list at a restaurant or store, and it is tempting to forgo wine altogether (which, as will be seen, is a viable option). The subject of what wine to serve with a meal is, or can be, a very complex and inexact art. Bookstores and libraries have shelf after shelf devoted to this one subject, so a complete treatment of wine is more than can be covered in this one chapter. The goal here is more modest. It is, first, to assure readers that they are not alone in their uncertainty about wine and to examine what forces create this uncertainty. Second, it is to give a historical context to what wines were drunk at meals by Victorians and why, as well as to examine whether there really are correct wines for a given food. Third, it is to examine how Victorians matched wines with food. For those not familiar with the different wines, the latter part of this chapter gives a history of the main wines the Victorians drank and some brief comments on American wines. If uncertain about the difference between a burgundy, a hock, and a claret, read it first.

History

Historically, the key factor in determining the wine that people drank was geographic location: wine was a fragile bulk product and was hard to move. Because of poor roads, a bulk product, such as wine, could only be shipped a few miles unless a boat was used. Because of this, people tended to drink wines grown locally or ones that could be shipped in by water. Almost all the historic wine-producing areas are either next to a seaport or a river. Wines often had a high alcoholic or a high sugar content as this made them more stable and thus easier to ship undamaged. Up through the middle of the nineteenth century, producers thought nothing of adding brandy and other higher alcohol content wines to what they produced.[1] This was even done in the Bordeaux area, today the home of delicate, light, and expensive wines. The process was known as "Hermitaging" as the heavy Hermitage wine of South France was often used for this purpose.[2]

The Greeks and Romans kept their wine in clay pots. Toward the end of the Roman Empire, Romans picked up the habit of using wood barrels to store and transport wine. That custom was followed after the fall of the empire. Wine was put in a wood cask at the vineyard and shipped in that cask through several middlemen to the consumer. With this method of storage, for reasons that were not discovered until the middle of the nineteenth century, wine went bad within a year or two of being produced; therefore, it was drunk young—normally in the year following its harvest. (The wine was taken out of the cask while young and carried to the table in carafes or bottles.)

Technological innovations changed all this. First, strong glass bottles had to be developed. This occurred in the middle third of the seventeenth century. England was running out of wood and entrepreneurs turned to coal to produce the heat necessary in making glass. The resulting bottles were stronger and cheaper than any heretofore produced.

The coal imparted a brown or dark green color to the glass, and this was soon accepted as a sign of its quality and strength. Later, it was learned that the dark color had the added advantage of protecting the liquid by keeping out light. The period from 1700 to about 1900 saw a revolution in how wine was stored. It was discovered through trial and error, during the course of the eighteenth century, that the interplay between air and bottling the wine with corks affected the aging process. For reasons that will be discussed later, preserving wine depended on putting wine in bottles sealed with corks and storing the bottles on their side. The cork sealed the bottle, and storing the bottle on its side had two advantages. The cork came into contact with the wine, and its moisture kept the cork from deteriorating. With the bottle on its side the air pocket moved away from the cork and thus came into contact with more of the wine. In 1700 the standard wine container was designed to sit upright, but a century later the norm was to have it lie on its side with the wine in contact with the cork.[3] As people began storing wine in bottles, they discovered that some wines improved with aging. Then they learned that some areas and certain years produced wines that aged better than others.

This change can be seen in cellar wine lists kept over the course of the Victorian period. Early in the Victorian era, wine tended to be described generally; for example, as claret, light claret, Pontac, or sherry. As the century wore on, wine lists increasingly included the name of the wine, the vineyard, and for French wines, the year. Sherries were classified by type: Manzanilla, Amontillado, and so on.

The middle years of the Victorian period also saw a clearer scientific understanding of the role that oxygen plays in the aging of wine. In 1863, Louis Pasteur, at the request of Napoleon III, emperor of France, undertook a study to determine why so much French wine went bad while being shipped to the consumer. Far from aging well, much French wine did not even last long enough to get to the store to be sold. Pasteur found that too much oxygen allowed the rapid growth of bacteria, which create vinegar as a byproduct. This is why old wine can taste like vinegar. But, one could not merely put wine in an airtight container and pump all the air out. A slight amount of oxygen allows wine to mature and develop the complex tastes that wine connoisseurs love. Pasteur also found that the wood in the wine barrel or cask, while giving special flavors to wine, also allowed more air to reach the wine, and its oxygen-breathing bacteria, and thus sped the aging process. How fast the wine in a barrel was affected depended on the thickness of the planks, the type of wood, whether or not the wood was painted, and how encrusted the wood was.

The answer to controlling aging is extremely complex and is still being studied. For the Victorians a major step toward producing vintage wine, capable of being stored for a long time, came from reducing the length of time the wine spent in wooden casks. They learned to leave it in the cask just long enough for the wine to pick up flavors from the wood. Then they would drain the wine into bottles that were sealed with a cork. Bottling largely stopped the contact with air, slowing the process by which wine turned into vinegar.

Economics had an impact on what wines people drank. Taxes, in the form of import duties, played a major role in determining what wine was consumed during different periods. For much of the Middle Ages the English drank wine from the Bordeaux region of France as the English ruled this area for some three hundred years. Considered part of the same country, there were no import taxes. This is more fully explained in the section on claret. The English were driven out of Bordeaux in 1453, but by then the habit of drinking claret was established.

Then in 1662 Charles II, the king of England, married the sister of the king of Portugal. As a result of the ties created by this marriage, and the need to band together against growing French military and political power, the two countries signed a treaty in 1703 that favored Portugal's wines and heavily taxed French, Spanish, and German wines. This was an act born of desperation. The royal family of France, the strongest and most aggressive military power, in 1703 inherited the Spanish throne. Spain was the largest empire in the world. Together they posed a terrifying threat to Portugal, England, and other European countries, most of whom promptly went to war to try to stop this union. The result was the War of Spanish Succession, which left both France and Spain crippled.

Because they were cheap and could be shipped easily by sea, Portuguese wines, especially port, became a mainstay on the English table. As a net result of the tax pattern caused by these political and diplomatic developments, the English tended to drink the lightly taxed port with their meals throughout the 1700s, and by habit on into the Victorian age. These wines were both sweet and highly alcoholic, and a taste for this type of wine became common.

Sherry, a product of Spain, was also hit with the 1703 tax. But sherry became popular again after the Napoleonic Wars, just in time to become a common Victorian drink.

An 1845 cellar book for the Duke of Richmond and Gordon lists 2,077 bottles of Spanish and Portuguese wines, with the sherries outnumbering the port. The cellar also held 1,091 bottles of French wine and twenty-three bottles of German wine. A less aristocratic household, where money was more of an issue, would have held fewer French and German wines.[4]

At an 1847 dinner and dance given by the duke, the eighteen diners drank two bottles of port, ten bottles of sherry, and only one bottle of claret.[5] Early Victorian writers stated flatly that sherry was the dinner wine, just as the late Victorian etiquette writers were equally firm that champagne was the dinner wine.

This state of affairs lasted until 1860, when England's Chancellor of the Exchequer, and future prime minister, William Gladstone, reduced the taxes on French and German wines. This was done in part because of Gladstone's belief in free trade and in part to make wine a cheaper alternative to gin. Historically gin, the curse of the English working class, had caused widespread drunkenness. Some at the time said the English naturally preferred the heavy (high alcohol) and sweet wines of the south over the "light" French wines. However, when French and German wines became cheaper, their consumption in England soared. This created a shift to serving French and German wines with Victorian meals.

Matching Wine to Food

The concept of systematically matching certain wines with certain foods developed alongside the change in how food was served at formal meals, the switch from service *à la Francaise* to service *à la Russe*, as noted in chapter 1. This switch occurred gradually between 1850 and 1870.

With service *à la Francaise* many different foods and wines were placed on the table at the same time. Diners would then match their wine with their food according to personal whim. It was not the general custom to try to match certain foods with certain wines as is done today. For this reason, the well-dressed table presented relatively few wine glasses during the first twenty or thirty years of the Victorian period, when service *à la Francaise* was the norm.

With service *à la Russe* and its emphasis on serving food by courses, it became logical to serve a particular wine with each course. In short order, a protocol of food/wine combinations developed for formal dinners. This, in turn, led to a proliferation of the types and numbers of wine glasses the dinner guest had to negotiate.

Basic Rules

A lighter wine precedes a heavier wine. A drier wine precedes a sweeter one. The wines in the meal should build up to the best wine, thus the earlier wines should be of lesser quality than the latter ones. The idea is, if at all possible, to serve the best wine last—whether it is a burgundy or a bordeaux. Some feel that not every wine served should be a great wine. The first wines served should be of a lower quality to more clearly set off the great wine at the end of the meal.

Burgundy is a heavy wine of power and complexity. It is traditionally matched with meats of powerful flavor, such as game. The red bordeaux are favored for their delicate taste. A classic match for a red bordeaux is lamb.

Dry white wines are normally matched with fish, which is considered to have a light, delicate taste. Sweet wines are often served with the portion of the meal that offers sweet food, or just before these foods to set the palate for the sweet food to follow.

However, tastes change over time. The Romans added spices to their wine to give it a bite. The Victorians often liked sweet wine, a carryover from their days of drinking port and sherry. They often served sauternes with the fish course.[6] During the seventeenth and early eighteenth centuries it was considered coarse to drink wine undiluted with water.[7] Up to the end of the nineteenth century hostesses were told to be sure to have servers offer ice for wines throughout the meal.

Wines of the Victorian period were mostly French and continental wines. The United States had a wine industry, but American wines were not common at elegant meals for several reasons. The

California wine industry was minor during this period. American wines, as grown in the East, were based on native American grapes. European vines would not grow in the eastern United States because of a thylloxera, a tiny louse, which grew on vine roots. This louse ate and killed the roots of the European grapes, but the American vine stock had over the centuries developed resistance to the louse. Unfortunately, native American grapes produced a wine with a distinct taste that many found unpleasant. Often it was described as "foxie." Needless to say, the taste did not go well with the delicate French cooking then in vogue. In addition, trends in taste and dining were set by the French and English, who, of course, used French and continental wines. This is not to say that the United States did not have a significant wine industry. In 1914, Americans drank over 50 million gallons of wine, and most of it was produced domestically. Much of this was New York sparkling wine, first introduced in the United States about 1860. (The champagne method of developing effervescence in the bottle somehow kills the foxie taste.)

Further complicating the situation, the English, the French, and the Americans all drank slightly different wines at different points in the meal. What, then, did the late Victorians drink with the different courses of their meals? When one examines old Victorian books on serving dinners, it is surprising what they felt went with what course. For example, as noted above, a great deal of sherry was consumed with red meat and fish during the early Victorian period.

When dinner *à la Russe* became common, the Victorians moved to drinking specific wines with specific foods. The chief chef of Delmonico's, the high temple of American fine dining during the Victorian period, showed the following wines being served at different points in the meal:

Oysters	Chablis
Soup	Sherry
Hot hors d'oeuvre	Sherry
Fish	Hock or Graves
Removes	Champagne
Entrees	Champagne
Roast	Burgundy

Foies gras	Spatlese
Hot *entremets*	Claret
Dessert	Madeira

Mrs. Henderson, an etiquette writer for the middle class of the 1870s, frowned on serving too many wines with dinner. She called for the following pattern:

Oyster	White wine, or hock
Soup or Fish	Sherry or Madeira
Removes	Champagne
Game	Claret or other red wine
Dessert	Sherry, port, burgundy, or other fine wine.

Most noteworthy about both of these wine menus is that they include champagne as part of the main meal.

These general patterns were not followed by all Victorian writers. Because of the vagaries of time and personal taste, and the clash of the American and European wine protocols, a wide range of guidelines were found in these books. The following chart shows what a few wine etiquette writers in different years suggested should be served with different foods.

	1848	1876	1887	1890	1893
Oysters	White Burgundy	Sauterne Hock		Chablis Sauterne	Chablis
Soup	Sherry	Sherry Madeira	Sherry		Sherry
Fish	Hock		Chablis Hock	Dry white wine	Hock
Meat	Claret	Champagne	Claret Champagne	Claret Burgundy	Champagne
Entrees		Champagne	Claret Champagne	Claret Burgundy	

	1848	1876	1887	1890	1893
Game		Claret	Claret Champagne	Claret	Burgundy
Hot Desserts				Champagne	Burgundy
Dessert	Champagne	Sherry Port Burgundy	Sherry Claret Burgundy	Port Tokay	Madeira

This chart shows just how much disagreement there was over the years about what wine should be served with what food.

In the United States, during the late Victorian period, champagne was the general dinner beverage served with most of the meal, while on the Continent it was reserved for dessert. The Victorian use of champagne seems odd today. Diners now have gotten used to the French pattern of drinking a red wine with red meat, and having a white wine with most fish. With their one dish and a salad, Americans, much like the early Victorians, do not think of serving different wines at a meal of several courses.

For those wishing to host a Victorian dinner complete with several different wines, consider using the European wine protocol set out below, if the American practice of drinking champagne with red meat seems too strange:

Oysters	Dry white wine
Soup	Medium-dry sherry
Fish	Hock
Meat	Claret
Entree	Claret
Game	Burgundy or other red wine
Sweet	Sweet champagne

Other Beverage Options

Finally, there is one other option: One can omit wines altogether when recreating a formal Victorian banquet. During the Victorian period the temperance movement was gaining force and many Victorians chose to completely forgo alcoholic beverages at their meals. The wife of President Rutherford Hayes (1877–1881) would not allow wine to be served in the White House. She simply served water or lemonade at her meals. (She was known, but not to her face, as Lemonade Lucy.) The etiquette books of the period are full of advice on how to behave if one is a guest and does not wish to drink alcohol; whether or not a teetotaling hostess should serve wine; and how the abstaining host and hostess should react if wine-drinking guests should toast them.

Today a common option is to serve iced tea or coffee rather than wine. Some people prefer a cola with their meal.

WINE TYPES

Claret

The most common wine drunk in England during late Victorian times was claret. The term "claret" is a corruption of the Latin word for clear. As used by the Victorians the term had two slightly different meanings. Primarily, it meant dry red wines from the Bordeaux region of France. But, it also meant generally any light red wine—rather like the term "cola" is used for any carbonated soft drink. It is doubtful if many of the proper Victorians, while drinking Claret, gave a thought to why it was such a common wine.

Bordeaux wines became popular throughout England because of Eleanor of Aquitaine. During the twelfth century (the Middle Ages), she was the rich and headstrong heiress to the Duchy of Aquitaine, which encompassed the southeastern quarter of France. At a young age, she was married to Louis, soon to become the king of France, but the marriage was an unhappy one. He thought she was unfaithful, and she said he acted like a monk. After 15 years, the marriage was annulled on the grounds of incest because they were third cousins. Eight weeks later she married Henry Plantagenet, Count of Anjou. With her help and money, they consolidated their vast possessions and Henry became king of England. Two of their eight children are well known today—Richard the Lionhearted and Prince John of Robin Hood fame. Their descendants ruled England and the Bordeaux region of France for 300 years, from 1152 to 1453.

For these 300 years the sale of Bordeaux wines was naturally favored in England as the two areas were part of the same country. Bordeaux wine was cheaper than wine grown in England and its importation drove English and Welsh winegrowers out of business. The ability to ship the wine by water played a major part in this popularity. Even after the two areas broke apart, the deep ties formed by this long association meant that claret continued to be shipped to England. Even the increase in import duties passed on French wine by England in 1703 and the hard feelings caused by the many wars between the two countries between 1703 and 1815 did not wholly stop this trade. The rich continued to buy some through normal trade channels and from smugglers. Reducing the import duty on these wines in 1861 caused the sale of claret to take off. Claret became a staple of the late Victorian dinner table.

Bordeaux today has the distinction of producing some of the finest and most expensive red wines in the world. The imprimatur of quality was created for the Bordeaux wines by a classification system in 1855 for the Paris World Exposition.

The classification which guides so many even today came about because businessmen need a good visual for a marketing display. As originally planned, the exposition dealt mainly with technological advancements. The Bordeaux Chamber of Commerce saw that they could also advertise their wine in the display space allocated their region. Each winery donated a few bottles of wine for the display, and a map of the Bordeaux area was set up behind the table to provide a focal point.

The map showed the location of the different chateaus that had produced the bottles of wine. Then the project director decided to rank the wine producers shown on the map. Time was short so the chamber of commerce requested that the local brokers' union, which included wine buyers, provide the rankings. This was done under the leadership of Charles-Henri-Georges Merman, who may or may not have consulted with anyone. It is not known how much thought went into the ranking system. There was no tasting at all; he, or they, apparently just assigned a ranking based on what prices were paid for different wines over the last few years. (Although if price lists and rankings are examined over the hundred years or so prior to 1855, the rankings are roughly the same.)

Since the map was a project of the Bordeaux Chamber of Commerce, no effort was made to show or rank wines that were grown in nearby areas and were shipped from other ports. This is why some wines thought of today as Bordeaux wines were not rated.

The whole display process at the exposition was hardly impartial. Some of the chateaus were trying hard to build a better name for themselves and to declare their independence from the wine buyers and their set purchase system with its pre-established pricing points.

To this end they started lobbying the managers of the exposition for their own display space and their own ranking system. Now more than a display map was the issue. The whole economic relationship between buyers and sellers was in doubt. The chamber of commerce and buying merchants also began backstage lobbying in favor of the wine rankings, issued in such speed, as an adjunct to the display map. A testing was arranged with a panel.

The panel consisted of the chief taster of the Paris police, two wine buyers, the director of the Paris wine tasters, and two merchants. Their main focus was the fabrication of wine. They were busy as they judged wines from all over the world so little time could be spent weighing the relative tastes and merits of individual wines of just one region.

The results were issued when the panel and the lobbying were finished, and the panel's ranking was exactly the same as the list put together by the Bordeaux wine buyers. Whether this was a result of tasting or lobbying is unknown. The list named four premier growths—Chateau Lafite Rothschild, Chateau Latour, Chateau Margaux and Chateau Haut-Brion. (After decades of complaining and lobbying Chateau Mouton-Rothschild was added to the list in 1973.[8])

Of course, there are more to the clarets than the first growths. The 1855 classifications also included growths two through five, each one progressively cheaper. Over the years many wine connoisseurs have hoped to beat the system—that is, to find a lower classification wine that has superb taste and obtain it at the lower price dictated by its classification. But this "top 10" list, short and fairly easy to remember, made it convenient for consumers, who wanted to serve the best but were not wine connoisseurs, to know what to serve.

Bordeaux's wines first became popular in the United States following the Revolution when Lafayette served them to his American army comrades. He had set sail for America from the Bordeaux region and he had brought with him enough claret to share. American trade with France flourished following the Revolution, and it was natural for Americans to drink the Bordeaux wines they had been introduced to by Lafayette. But, the drinking of claret really took off in the United States after it became common in England in the 1860s. The country still took its social guidance from the British Empire.

The Bordeaux region also produced two famous white wines—Graves, which is rather dry and light, and sauternes, which is covered in the next section. During much of the Victorian period, in the United States, dry white wine from the Bordeaux region was often referred to as sauterne, without the final "s." Today more exact terms for the local region are used—Graves, Entredeaux-mers, and so on. On the other hand, the term "sauterne" could also refer to the sweet wine we now call "Sauterres" (with the final "s"). The late Victorians retained a taste for sweet wine from their early days of drinking port and sherry with dinner, and they often drank a sweet Sauterres, such as Chateau d'Yquem, with their fish. All of this makes it very hard to know if a meal featured a dry Graves or a sweet Sauterres at a given point in the meal if the wine was not specifically named in the menu. None of the dry white wines of Bordeaux were included in the classification of 1855. Therefore, it was hard to remember the officially approved top brands of this type of wine, and they did not get much notice during Victorian times, being largely overshadowed by German white wine—the so called hocks (which are covered in more detail later).

French Sweet Wines—Sauternes

Sauternes is an intensely sweet wine. It is made by letting a mold form on the grapes—the so-called noble rot. This has the effect of pulling water out of the grape. The shriveled grape has a higher concentration of sugar, which is kept in during the fermentation process. It also has a high alcohol content, which makes it easier to transport over long distances. The most famous of the sauternes is Chateau d'Yquem, and it was well known even before the classification scheme of 1855. Thomas Jefferson, when he returned to Virginia after serving as U.S. minister in Paris, brought 250 bottles of Chateau d'Yquem with him.[9]

No one knows when the area first began producing sweet wine. One local legend has it that the first sauternes were made at Yquem as late as 1847. It is said that in the 1830s a Monsieur Fock traveled to Germany and brought back the secret of the noble rot. He gave this information to the Comte de Lur-Saluces of Chateau D'Yquem.

There is some question as to whether or not this legend is true as there are earlier references to sweet wines from the area and to the production methods used in producing sweet sauternes. This story also raises the question of whether Jefferson's bottles contained plain white wine or a sweet dessert wine. Other stories have the discovery of noble rot taking place when a nobleman was delayed at the court of Louis XIV and the wine harvest could not start until he returned.

Burgundy

Probably the most famous of the French red wines are the burgundies. Because of accidents of history and geography, the rise to fame of the wines of Burgundy come late in French history.

When Charlemagne's empire was divided among his grandsons in 843, part went to France and part to other powers. The area that produces burgundies lay close to the border. Over the centuries the area was either independent or quasi-independent of Paris authority. It was also part of, or very close to, areas that were, because of marriages and wars, controlled by powers opposed to the French throne. All of this interfered with the long-term peaceful production of wine for the Paris market.

But, perhaps the largest bar to burgundy becoming a celebrated French wine was that the area lies along the Sabne, a river that feeds into the Rhone River, which in turn flows into the Mediterranean Sea. It is a long overland road journey from the Burgundy area to Paris. Given the terrible road system in France up to the nineteenth century, and the problems of transporting a bulk product overland, little Burgundy wine reached Paris. The natural outlet for this wine was downriver to the Mediterranean Sea. Some went north on old cloth trade routes to what is now Belgium and Holland, areas ruled by Burgundy in the Middle Ages. A salesman's sample book from the early 1700s that has cloth swatches in the front and a wine list in the back still exists.[10]

Areas closer to Paris produced the celebrated French wines of the Middle Ages and early modern period. Because of the forces of economics, many of the well-known vineyards of the Middle Ages are now planted in low-quality, high-producing grapes used for the production of ordinary table wine.

By the time of the Sun King, Louis XIV (1638–1715), conditions were ripe for change. The borders of France had been moved eastward through luck, wars, and diplomacy. In addition, the internal transportation system in France had been improved. Roads were upgraded, and more importantly, canals were dug. A canal linking the Rhone River system and the Seine River system (the river that flows through Paris) was completed in 1600.[11] It was during this period that burgundies started replacing the red wines of the Champagne area as the standard red wine. Some feel that this change took place because the Champagne area was too far north to compete with the same kind of grapes grown in the warmer Burgundy area. The burgundies became really fashionable at the beginning of the eighteenth century when Louis XIV's doctors ordered him to drink it in his old age. And soon, thereafter, the Champagne area turned to producing a different product—the effervescent wine known today as champagne.

The subject of Burgundy wine is extremely complicated with references to regions, villages, and microclimates. There are far more top wines, *Grand Crus*, in the Burgundy region than in the Bordeaux region. Probably the best known burgundy is Chambertin, which gained popularity when Louis XIV adopted it as his favorite. Chambertin is said to have also been Napoleon's favorite wine. This wine originated in vineyards tended by monks as part of their monastery. During the French Revolution the church holdings were broken up, and today a fairly large number of different families share the vineyards. Because of differences in skill and the wine-making philosophy among the various proprietors, the wines called Chambertin can vary from one bottle to another, depending on who produced it. This tends to create confusion among the general public, while allowing wine connoisseurs to exhibit their knowledge.

The white burgundies did not receive very much notice from the Victorians. Most of the wine-growing areas in Burgundy produce at least a little white wine, but two areas specialize in white wine: Chablis and Maconnais. The latter produces the well-known and very popular Pouilly-Fuisse. Out of an area that produces mostly red wines comes a very well respected white burgundy called Montrachet. The Victorians, when they thought of white burgundies, thought primarily of Montrachet and Chablis. Both Chablis and white burgundies such as Montrachet were dry wines, suitable for fish and oyster courses.

Champagne

The wines of the Champagne area were well known and well thought of in the Middle Ages. However, the wine the area produced in the Middle Ages was a regular red wine similar to burgundy. It was not until the mid-1600s that the Champagne area started producing sparkling wine with bubbles. As sparkling champagne is "brewed" in bottles, it needs cheap, mass-produced bottles that are very strong and corks to hold the champagne down. These became generally available in the 1600s.

The monk Dom Perignon is said to be the man who "invented champagne." What Dom Perignon probably did was perfect the blending of different grapes (and vineyards) to make a better tasting product, and work systematically to develop the fermentation of wine in its bottle. This is the heart of the production of champagne. He also pioneered the use of corks to seal the bottles, which is key to fermenting wine in the bottle. Before this period, the closures were not strong enough to withstand the pressure that built up in the bottle during fermentation.

Dom Perignon must have done something important because champagne became very popular among the lascivious French nobility during the French Regency period, 1715–1725, which was right after his lifetime. It was connected with a period of adulterous affairs and exuberant drinking parties.

Champagne would be associated with beautiful women and the bon vivant life from that point on. In the begining it was very expensive to produce and therefore was available only to the the very wealthy. This was because the art of bottling champagne was not perfected and the bottles, strong as they were, were very likely to explode. Losses from explosion often ran between 15 percent and 40 percent. In one particularly bad year, 1828, 80 percent of the bottles broke.[12] With this rate of loss few bottlers wanted to trust their livelihoods to the product, and sparkling champagne was produced as more of a speculative sideline. During the eighteenth and early nineteenth centuries, the Champagne area produced more regular red wine than sparkling champagne.

Studies undertaken about 1840 into the relationship of sugar to carbonation in sparkling champagne, and the invention of a way to measure the sugar in the wine, resulted in the champagne that is known today.

The loss from bottle explosions dropped dramatically, and bottlers started producing more sparkling champagne instead of still red wine. As a consequence the price dropped. When the product became cheaper sales to the vast middle class were opened up as they also wanted to take part in the lifestyle represented by drinking champagne. Champagne became, for the balance of the century, the main wine to serve with dinner.

The sale of champagne became very important economically to the French. They took their champagne so seriously that the word "champagne" was protected and limited to French wines by the Treaty of Versailles, which ended World War I. (For good measure the French also protected the word "cognac," and by treaty Germany could use neither of these names for its wines.) By treaty the term "champagne" was reserved for wines from the region just north of Paris; everyone else must use the term "sparkling wine." (The French are still tenacious, and they are fighting hard within the European Union to limit the term "champagne" to their product. Meanwhile, the Americans cheat a bit by using the word "champagne" with a modifier—New York champagne or California champagne.)

Depending on the amount of sugar in the mix, sparkling champagne can range from dry to sweet. The English and the Americans preferred dry champagne, the French a sweeter version, and the Russians a very sweet drink. Before the Russian Revolution of 1917, a special version of champagne, so sweet that no one else would drink it, used to be shipped to Russia.

Traditionally, in the Victorian period, the French drank their champagne as a sweet wine with dessert at the end of the meal. The English had their port and the Americans Madeira for their desserts, so they drank their dry champagne with the main part of the meal. Until about 1850 almost all the champagne produced was sweet. The concept of dry champagne is credited to Venve Pommery, who reasoned that sweetness masked the lively, delicate taste of champagne.[13]

In the United States champagne was seen as the drink of the formal meal; it became the main wine served with the joint and the entrees.

At times, people went so far as to drink nothing but champagne at a meal. This may have been because they wanted to create a festive, celebratory ambiance for the meal or because they did not feel they were knowledgeable enough to risk serving different wines with different foods.

During the Victorian period the English would buy particular vintages of champagne and age it. This allowed them to have champagne of a particular quality with their meals. This custom was not generally followed by dealers in the United States, much to the dismay of visiting Englishmen. The British system of vintages and aging disappeared during the period of wild shifts in the relative value of the pound and the French franc following World War I. Today the idea of aging champagne is largely an alien one.

A general rule of thumb is that *brut* is a dry champagne and *sec* is sweet. Surprisingly extra dry is sweeter than *brut* and *Demi-sec* is sweeter still. *Demi-sec* is the sweetest champagne normally seen by consumers. An even sweeter champagne, Doux, is produced but it is rather hard to find in the United States.

Today a sweet champagne has about fifty grams of sugar per liter and there are about 15 grams of sugar in *brut*. By comparison, in the mid-1800s the French drank a champagne that had about 165 grams of sugar, Americans drank champagne with between 110 and 165 grams of sugar, and the English champagne had twenty-two to sixty-six grams of sugar. The special sweet champagne made for the Russians had a range of 250 to 330 grams of sugar per liter.[14] It stopped being produced when the Russian Revolution of 1917 closed down the Russian market for Champagne.

Hock

Hock is the English term for Rhine wine—just as claret is the general term for red bordeaux. The name is said to come from the town of Hocksheim, a wine-shipping port on the Rhine River.

Rhine wine was widely drunk in England during the Middle Ages. Again, the ability to ship it directly to England by boat was very important; but the drinking of Rhine wines fell out of favor when the British government began taxing them heavily during the 1700s. German Rhine wine again became popular in England during the Victorian period because it was a favorite of Queen Victoria, and because taxes on it were decreased in a general effort to encourage the drinking of wine in place of gin. It is said that Victoria's German husband, Albert, had a great deal to do with developing her taste for Rhine wines, but Victoria also came from a family that had its roots in Germany.

The term "hock," as used by the Victorians in the United States is usually taken to mean wine produced in the Rheingau region.

This is the section of the Rhine River where it turns west for some twenty miles. The hills that border the right bank of the river face south and are able to catch more hours of sunlight—an important consideration for wine growers in this northern climate.

Perhaps the best known hock is from the Johannesberg vineyards. According to tradition, Emperor Charlemagne first ordered vines planted there. He is said to have noted, from a palace in Ingelheim across the river, that snow melted sooner there than elsewhere along the river. By 1100, the vineyard belonged to the Benedictine monks. During the Napoleonic Wars the fortunes of battle gave the French control of this region and under French anti-church influence the property was taken away from the monks in 1801. At the Congress of Vienna in 1815, it became the personal property of the emperor of Austria, who in turn gave it to Metternich, his Machiavellian chancellor. For over a hundred years this property was controlled by the Metternich family, and they paid tithes to the Habsburg family for the gift.

Almost all German wine is white. Since the Germans produce almost no red wine, they do not tend to have red wine with red meat and game, which is common in France and England.

During the Victorian period Rhine wines were generally of a dry nature. It was only later that they came to have more of a sweet flavor, which is why they were taken with the fish course.

German Sweet Wines

Germany also produced a sweet wine using the noble rot. The Johannesberg vineyard is said to be the birthplace of Spatlese wine—the German sweet wine, their counterpart to the French sauternes.

The term "Spatlese" means "late picked." Legend has it that in 1775 there was a bit of a mix-up among the monks who owned Schloss Johannesberg. They were not allowed to harvest the grapes until the abbot gave his permission. In 1775, the abbot was away at a synod. When the grapes started to ripen early, and even to rot, a rider was sent to ask permission to harvest, but of course it took some time for the rider to go out and come back on horseback. By the time he returned many of the grapes in the field were covered with rot, but the monks went ahead and harvested and produced the wine. To their amazement the wine was extremely good. Thereafter, they tried to replicate this happy accident and the Spatlese-style wine is the result.

Madeira

Madeira was an extremely popular wine for many centuries. Once the island of Madeira was settled by Europeans in the early fifteenth century, vines brought from Crete were planted. A brisk trade with France and England developed.

In 1665, England, under Charles II, decreed that the American colonies could only import goods through English ports using English ships, but since Charles was married to Portugal's Catherine de Braganza, an exception was granted for Portugal's Madeira Island. Madeira was permitted to trade directly with the colonies and the Caribbean. Ships, often slavers, sailing to Africa stopped in the Madeira Islands for water and provisions and while there also loaded a few casks of Madeira. They then carried them to Africa or India and back home. This made Madeira far cheaper than other wines in the colonies, and, as a bonus, shipping the wine through the heat of Africa, India, or the Caribbean improved its flavor. The British upper class discovered the quality of this new-style Madeira shipped through tropical heat when serving in the British Army in the colonies during the American Revolutionary War.

Madeira lost popularity during the latter part of the Victorian era. The poverty of the South following the Civil War limited one of the wine's best markets. A host of other factors may also have contributed to its fall in popularity. There were several different blights that hit the grapes on the island between 1860 and 1900, and Madeira never seemed to recover from them.

Another factor may have been the replacement of sailing vessels by steamships. The combination of heat and the gentle rocking motion of a sailing ship seems to have had a positive effect on Madeira. Some merchants even sent their Madeira on a round trip to India before shipping it to England or the United States, as this gave it a greater exposure to heat and the rocking motion of the sailing ships. In many cities in the United States, it was the custom to hang a barrel of Madeira in a common area or a hall and everyone who walked by gave it a little push. This further rocking was felt to improve the wine.

It is noteworthy that in the pre–Civil War period connoisseurs of Madeira classified it not by the producer, but by the ship that brought it. This was because every voyage had a different combination of heat and wave action, depending on where it went and what type of weather it ran into. Madeira can be artificially heated, as it is today, but the rocking motion caused by a sailing ship at sea is almost impossible to replicate.

The final blow to the Madeira tradition in the United States came with Prohibition in 1920. During the Prohibition years Americans got out of the habit of drinking Madeira, and since traditionally the United States was the major consumer of Madeira, this was a major blow to the island. Following Prohibition Americans adopted a European pattern of what they drank and Madeira never caught back on in the United States.[15]

Madeira like sherry can range from dry to sweet in taste. A dry Madeira is traditional with terrapin. A sweet Madeira might be served with fruit or walnuts as dessert.

Calvados

Calvados is a brandy made from the fermented juice of crushed apples. It is the traditional drink of the Normandy area of France. The area of Normandy that produces calvados got its name from the Spanish Armada ship *El Calvador*, which wrecked on the area's coast in 1588. In French cuisine, a glass of calvados is often drunk at mid-meal. Traditionally, this creates a "Norman hole" in the stomach, which allows the diner to eat more and finish the meal. Calvados is a cousin of apple jack and as such is quite potent. Roman Punch, which contains rum or amaretto, can be substituted for calvados at a Victorian meal as calvados was not often served at American Victorian meals.

Tokay

Tokay is a sweet wine that was highly thought of by the Victorians. It is produced near the Carpathian Mountains of northeastern Hungary. Tokay can range from dry to sweet, but the best known, although not the most common, form of Tokay is Aszu. In fact, the term "Tokay" is widely used to mean Aszu Tokay. Aszu Tokay is a wonderful sweet dessert wine with high alcohol content. Even in Victorian times it was a bit hard to acquire as the Austrian emperors, the tsars, and the popes acquired most of it.

Aszu Tokay has its own legendary beginnings. In 1650, the area's wine producers, fearing an attack by the Turks, who ruled most of Hungary at that time, delayed the harvest. This delay allowed the noble rot to begin to grow on the grapes.

Whether this is true or not, Tokay does seem to be the oldest of the sweet dessert wines. Tokay was a great favorite of the Sun King, Louis XIV, and Peter the Great. Peter used to have armed soldiers guard his yearly shipment of the wine to Russia.

It was possible to ship Aszu Tokay far from its point of origin, even over bad roads, because its high alcohol and sugar content made it more stable than regular wine.

As a princely gesture, the Austrian Emperor Franz Joseph began sending Queen Victoria Tokay Aszu wine on her birthday—a dozen bottles for each year of her age. Unfortunately for him, it turned out that both he and Queen Victoria were among the longest reigning rulers in the history of Europe—so year after year more and more bottles of this rare wine went to London. By the year 1900, the total was up to 972 bottles.

Following the Communist takeover of Hungary, the quality of Tokay is said to have gone down as the collective mentality was not conducive to producing great wines. However, with the fall of the Iron Curtain, the situation is changing, and expertise and investment is flowing into Hungary and improving the product. Perhaps to distinguish the post-Communist product, the wine today is called "Tokaji"—its original spelling. Under either name, Westerners can again enjoy the "Wine of Kings."

The sweetness of the wine is graded by how many baskets of specially picked grapes with the noble rot are added to a cask of normal wine. The more the better. The Hungarian word for basket is *puttonyos*. The bottles are labeled by how many *puttonyos* they have. The highest grade is a six *puttonyos* wine.

Port

Port, the most famous of all the dessert wines, is sweet and has a high alcohol content. It is produced in northern Portugal and shipped from the town of Oporto—hence its name. It is a fortified wine, meaning it has alcohol added to it to keep it from going bad in shipping. The mellow rounded taste of port is due to its being aged—either in oak casks or its own bottle.

The name "port" has been copied so much that the Portuguese

have taken to renaming their product Porto to distinguish it from all the copies.

Port has been shipped to England since the 1670s. In the 1700s shippers began fortifying the port with brandy to help preserve it while being shipped north. It is the brandy, added during fermentation, that causes port to be sweet and gives it its high alcohol content. Most port is aged in wooden casks and is classified as either Ruby Port or the lighter-colored Tawny Port, which is more expensive (and presumably better tasting). There is also Vintage Port, which can be held in bottles for a long period of time to improve its taste.

The Vintage Ports are considered the very best, assuming the shipper was correct in declaring the harvest to be a vintage year. Traditionally, English parents of a certain class buy port—a bottle or a crate depending on their pocketbook—to be held until the newborn child turns twenty-one. This produces a fully matured Vintage Port, and a suitable toasting beverage for the young adult's twenty-first birthday.

Economics has played a large part in the rise to popularity of port. Beginning in the seventeenth century for political reasons, England placed a heavy tax on French wines. As part of a treaty of friendship with Portugal in 1703, which until this point had been a friend of France, the tax on Portuguese spirits was lowered to about one-eighth that of French and German wines.

Port became much cheaper than other wines and fortified wines, and the English love affair with port began. Port is an interesting example of how there are no "right" wines to be drunk with any particular food. In English-speaking countries port is a dessert wine or a wine to be drunk at the end of the meal. The French, on the other hand, drink port as an aperitif before their meals.

When served, port is poured from a decanter that is placed before the host. The host fills the glass of the man on his right and then his own glass. The port is then passed around to the left. It is a grave solecism to pass it to the right—a sure sign a person is a cad and perhaps even a blackleg. However, in certain circumstances a "backhander" is allowed. This is the pouring of a drink for the man on one's right. There are no hard and fast rules on when this is allowed.

The word "man" is used here deliberately because in England only the men drank port, and in Georgian times (1714–1830) as often as not got drunk on it after the women withdrew to the drawing room. One wit said the custom arose because the men wanted to keep all the port for themselves.

Port produced in the United States can be made with any grape and basically by any method. One should be very careful when buying an American wine labeled "port" or California Port. It may be a fine wine, but it may not be a true port-type drink.

Sherry

Sherry, the tipple of little old ladies and Oxford dons, occupied a major place at most Victorian meals. The traditional sherry is a product of the hot south of Spain. Its name is said to be an English corruption of the name of its major shipping port—Jerez. Sherry was called "sack" in Elizabethan times—a corruption of the Spanish word *sacar*, meaning export. The early Victorians drank a great deal of sherry and port throughout their meals.

Sherry ranges from very dry to quite sweet. There are many complex steps in producing sherry, involving the presence or absence of yeast. For the beginner interested in Victorian dinners only three terms need be remembered. Fino is a dry sherry, Cream is a sweet sherry, and Amontillado is a medium-dry sherry. (These terms are not technically correct, but are given the meaning that was in common use during the Victorian period.)

It was Amontillado that was typically served with turtle soup or consomme. So common was this usage that the term "Amontillado" was often synonymous with sherry in the Victorian period. Cream Sherry is served as a dessert wine competing with port and Madeira.

The sherry drunk by little old ladies and dons is normally a dry Amontillado. The Fino is often served as an aperitif.

American wines

The approach to wine in the United States is quite different from that of Europe. The U.S. laissez-faire traditions meant that the country did not control how wine was produced as is common in France and the rest of Europe. And perhaps more importantly, there was not a government-sponsored ranking of wines as in France. At its most exacting, American law is content to have the bottle state what grapes went into it, who produced it, and where most of the wine was grown. It is up to the buyer to know what he or she likes and what wine is better than another.

The American laissez-faire tradition caused several problems for the casual wine drinker between World War II and the 1980s. To begin with, the terms "burgundy," "Chablis," and so on did not have the same meaning as in France. But use of these terms to mean specific styles of wines, made with certain fine grapes in a prescribed way, as was done in Europe, was not applicable to U.S. wines. If a wine maker wanted to call his or her wine, however made and with whatever grape, a Chablis he or she was free to do so. For a long time wine producers put whatever name they wanted on the label. It is said there have been cases where the same batch of wine was labeled burgundy for one market and claret for another to take advantage of what sold best in a given area.

Today most fine wine sold in the United States is labeled by the type of grape used to make it—zinfandel, merlot, and so forth.

NOTES

1. Hugh Johnson, *The World Atlas of Wine* (London: Mitchell Beazley Publishers Limited, 1971), p. 16.

2. Dewey Markham, Jr., *1855, a History of the Bordeaux Classification* (New York: John Wiley & Sons, 1998), p. 185.

3. Johnson, *World Atlas of Wine*, p. 16.

4. William Younger, *Gods, Men and Wine* (Cleveland, OH: World Publishing Company, 1966), p. 404.

5. Ibid., p. 412.

6. Alec Waugh, *Wines and Spirits* (New York: Time-Life Books, 1968), p. 101.

7. Margaret Visser, *The Rituals of Dinner* (New York: Penguin Books USA, 1991), p. 253.

8. See generally Markham, *1855, a History of the Bordeaux Classification*.

9. Felipe Fernandez-Armesto, *Millennium: A History of the Last Thousand Years* (New York: Scribner, 1995), p. 344.

10. Hugh Johnson, *Hugh Johnson's Story of Wine* (London: Mitchell Beazley Publishers Limited, 1996), p. 277.

11. James Trager, *The Food Chronology* (New York: Henry Holt and Company, 1995), p. 109.

12. Johnson, *Hugh Johnson's Story of Wine*, p. 338.

13. Harold J. Grossman, *Grossman's Guide to Wines, Beers, and Spirits*, 7th ed. (New York: Macmillan, 1983), p. 74.

14. Johnson, *Hugh Johnson's Story of Wine*, p. 340.

15. Trager, *The Food Chronology*, p. 430.

II

The Accoutrements

Chapter 4

Silver

Glittering silver is an integral part of an elegant meal. A handsome array of silverware glowing by candlelight sets the mood for the meal to follow.

Silver has an emotional pull that is absent with most other products. Rare and fairly costly, it is still inexpensive enough to be used as dinnerware or coins. It has become part of people's thought processes, for example, being "born with a silver spoon" is a statement of wealth.

For centuries, the rich and noble had dinner items made of silver to impress visitors and friends. In the era before banks, this was a practical way to store wealth. Labor was cheap and silver expensive. In the 1470s silver cost about $800 per ounce in today's dollars. (Today, following New World silver strikes, it is about $6.00 per ounce.) In a time of crisis, the silver could be melted down or cut up into coins. For example, in 1646, during the English Civil War, Charles I had his dinner plates and dishes cut up into rude coins to pay his soldiers. After all, the only difference between a silver coin and a cut-up bit of a silver dish was the engraving on the coin. Over the centuries many nobles, when faced with less public financial crises, did the same thing, or melted down their plate, or simply sold it.

Early in English history a division of silver types developed. The grandiose chargers, dinner plates, goblets, and dishes represented family wealth and were the property of men. Women, by law, could not own property with one exception. Daughters and wives were allowed to own a class of property known as "paraphernalia." This consisted of personal items such as clothing, jewelry, and silver eating utensils. This property was the only thing women had to leave their heirs. This is why, even today, the set of silver knives, spoons, and forks have the initials of the woman on them, and why the family silver flatware often passes from mother to daughter or perhaps to a favored niece of the woman.

The use of silver in eating utensils is very old. Greeks and Romans had silver spoons, although they ate a great deal with their hands. Knives are as old as history. Forks were not widely used in Europe until the seventeenth century where they moved across Europe from Italy to France and then to England. The diary of Samuel Pepys, an invaluable guide to life in the mid-seventeenth century, notes that he bought his first set of that "new refinement," forks, in 1664. But, as late as 1779, John Adams was criticized as being anti-democratic by some Americans for using forks. Forks normally had steel or iron tines with handles of bone, silver, or other metals. Eating utensils of silver were still rare at the beginning of the nineteenth century. Up to the 1840s, forks and spoons were hand forged and shaped, as well as very expensive. A workman could only make twelve or so pieces a day.[1]

In the mid-nineteenth century, several developments came together to bring silver utensils within reach of those below the rank of nobility or the very wealthy. Mechanical power was introduced into what had been a handcraft, and dies were developed to use the mechanical power. No longer did each item of tableware have to be handmade by pounding it out with a small hammer, shaping it with a hand saw, and filing it. Now the piece could be stamped out, cut, and polished using machine-driven grinding wheels. The greater pressure, made possible by the ever improving dies, allowed for deeper designs on the silverware. Near the close of the nineteenth century silverware designs changed from simple, largely flat designs to more complex and three-dimensional designs.

The other factor that led to the wide use of silver flatware was the discovery of vast deposits of silver in Virginia City, Nevada. In 1860, 116,000 ounces of silver were produced in the United States. By 1900, the annual production was 57 million ounces. The increase in supply drove the cost down. Then, in 1873, the United

States and Germany stopped using silver in coins. This combination of supply and demand exerted a powerful downdraft on price. Such was the drop in price that the 1880s saw a mining depression and Virginia City, the main silver-producing center of the United States, almost became a ghost town.

By the 1880s, it was possible to produce vast amounts of silverware, and the economics were right to allow great numbers of middle-class people, created by the wealth of the expanding industrialization of the United States, to buy the output.

Falling silver prices cut into the profit margins of silversmiths and manufacturers. They responded by changing the emphasis on what they sold. Prior to the 1870s and 1880s, silverware was sold by weight and the pattern was relatively unimportant. Changes in the design of silver were infrequent. Because silver was expensive and the design unimportant, a common way for a housewife to buy silverware was by weight. Only a small price premium was paid for the design element. Because of the expense, women who wanted a new design would turn in their old silver to have it melted down and made into a new pattern.

A newspaper story in 1897 reported that Mrs. Cleveland, wife of President Grover Cleveland, had decided in 1895 to have the White House silver spoons and forks melted down to make new silverware. The silver to be melted down dated back to the days of Dolley Madison. Apparently Mrs. Cleveland did not like the silver's size or design. Efforts were made to try to save the Dolley Madison silver because of its historical value. At least one company offered to buy it for a handsome price, but Mrs. Cleveland would not hear of it. She sent the old silver to the U.S. mint and had it melted down to silver bars. The silversmiths making the new silver were required to sign affidavits that only the silver bars from the mint had been used in making the new silver. What is remarkable is that Mrs. Cleveland would even think of doing such a thing, and that no one was able to stop her.

The middle class in the Victorian era placed great emphasis on specialization. They were escaping their upbringing where everyone lived in a few rooms and wore the same clothes every day. To them, the spread of wealth and progress meant specialization in all aspects of life. They started building homes with sitting rooms, dining rooms, libraries, breakfast rooms, and so on. Special dress was expected for tea, for dinner, for riding. The same specialization showed up in silver.

The first reaction today of one who hears that fifty or sixty different silver eating utensils were once used is that someone in the past must have known all about them, perhaps at the courts of Louis XIV or Queen Victoria. But, one searches the records of those courts in vain and finds that this hyper-specialization was a product of the high Victorian age. Further, it seems to have been primarily an American development driven by aggressive marketing programs in the United States.

The American silver manufacturers competed fiercely among themselves. Part of this competition took the form of developing new and different patterns. Even in the Victorian period people wanted a modern-looking pattern. A study of the number of patterns introduced by Gorham Silver Company between 1830 and 1970 shows that the most new patterns were introduced in the decades between 1870 and 1910.[2] Then, when a company found a winning pattern, it was not satisfied with a customer having just a knife, fork, and spoon. The manufacturer realized it could expand its sales if it could persuade people they needed special instruments for corn, for terrapin, for oranges, and so on. When one examines the time at which different items of individual silverware were introduced, one gets the impression that in the first fifty or so years of the nineteenth century items were introduced naturally to fill a specialized need. After that, introduction was driven more by manufacturers trying to push product line extensions.

At the beginning of the nineteenth century, there were very few types of individual silverware. Old sets had a dinner fork and knife. Tea, soup, and dessert spoons, together with marrow spoons, were also used. A smaller knife and fork set was often added to collections for use in the dessert course. The dessert silver often did not match the pattern used for the rest of the meal. Then, as the nineteenth century wore on, specialized pieces became more common in America.

Listed below is the approximate period for the introduction of different specialized items of individual silver flatware:

1810s	spoon—egg
1820s	knife—pickle
1830s	fork—individual pickle, fish;
	knife—fish
1840s	fork—oyster;

	spoon—demitasse;
	knife—tea
1850s	fork—tea
1860s	nut pick;
	fork—pie
1870s	forks—berry, melon, cocktail, pie;
	spoons—individual salt, 5 o'clock tea;
	knife—melon
1880s	forks—ice cream, pastry, salad;
	spoons—fruit (or orange), round soup;
	knife—orange
1890s	forks—fruit, lemon, lobster, ramekin, escargot, terrapin, individual cheese;
	spoons—bouillon, chocolate, grapefruit, iced tea (or lemonade), sherbet, chocolate muddler/soda water, cafe parfait;
	knives—individual butter, crawfish, individual duck (or game), individual cheese;
	tongs—individual asparagus;
	food pusher for children
1900 and after	forks—mango, corn, individual duck (or game);
	spoon—iced tea, lemonade spoon/sipper.

Not everyone went along with the push toward specialization. Some established families saw no need to have a special-shaped fork for eating pie, or berries, or even salad, viewing this as something of a parvenu fixation. Their ancestors at the time of King Phillip's War, the French and Indian War, the American Revolution, or whatever golden age they traced their fortune to did not use these many different forks, and neither would they. These established families inherited their silverware, and they rather looked down on the *arrivistes* who had to buy their silver. Further, even the people who bought their silver in complete sets were often not acquiring the very specialized forks and spoons. An analysis of the large special silver sets made by Tiffany and the large silver sets sold by the main silver manufacturers shows an absence of many of the very specialized pieces.

Established people, the ton, did not screen newcomers by their lack of knowledge about silverware or bar social advancement as is often claimed. The ton did not care that much about different specialized pieces and this would not have been a very effective method anyway. In a normal meal as long as the newcomer knew enough to choose the fork or spoon furthest to the outside there was unlikely to be a gaffe. It is hard to imagine a situation where many different items of silverware were placed jumbled on a table and an initiate was ordered to pick up and identify a given piece. The dread of not knowing what item to use is largely a self-imposed fear, aided perhaps by advertising companies in the 1920s and 1930s to market etiquette books.

Still there was a wide range of utensils to master, as can be seen by looking at two of the larger sets of silver sold to the general public at the turn of the century. One large set had eighteen pieces of each of the following:

Forks: dinner, salad, pastry, ramekin, ice cream, fish, oyster, caviar, and fruit. It also had 36 breakfast forks.

Spoons: Soup, dessert, chocolate, bouillon, iced tea, orange, egg, and sorbet. It also had 36 teaspoons.

The knives were more limited, being dinner, dessert, fruit, fish, game, butter, and breakfast knives. In addition, there were lobster and nut picks, and individual asparagus tongs. The balance consisted of some forty-four different serving items—many having two or more items of each type.

A 197-piece set for sale in 1898, limited itself to twelve each of the following:

Spoons: chocolate, orange, iced tea, soup, 5 o'clock tea, table, dessert

Forks: ice cream, oyster, salad, dessert, and dinner

Knives: butter spreader, tea, fruit, duck, fish, dessert, and medium dinner.

The balance of the set consisted of some thirty-three serving pieces consisting of twenty-six different items.

Both of these large sets had idiosyncrasies. Caviar and lobster forks are very rare, and it is odd the second set does not include a fish fork. Neither set has a berry (strawberry) fork, but this may reflect the tendency to give such forks as a boxed set.

Completely absent are such specialty items as crawfish, orange, and melon knives; individual cheese knives and forks, corn, mango, and pie forks; and grapefruit, lemonade, and cocktail spoons. Marrow scoops had come and largely gone before these sets were produced. Other special table items such as sauce spoons were not yet in evidence.

But, the sellers of etiquette books and silver manufacturers did a good job. The fact remains that fear of specialized silver did enter into the American conscious. Even today, the surest way to befuddle someone is to seat him or her at a table with a lot of different silverware. It is still a staple of comedy to show someone faced with an unknown fork. On the other hand, there is a bit of delicious pleasure in working one's way through a complicated meal with different eating pieces successfully mastered.

Thus, this chapter will look at the different utensils that have been developed over the years, and a later chapter will show how these fit into a high Victorian meal.

Photographs of the items are to scale as size is an important feature of each piece. Some authors in order to make a point of how complicated silver usage was during the Victorian period show drawings of many different items and ask the reader to identify them. The normal reader, of course, fails. It is unfair to show drawings of several different items, none in scale with the others, and ask the reader to identify them. In real life, one is unlikely to confuse a lettuce fork with an ice cream fork, as the lettuce fork is too large to put into your mouth. Distinguishing between the two is harder if the two appear to be of the same size and one is asked to identify by shape alone.

The photos that follow are mostly of place pieces as most people fear using the wrong eating instrument.

The silver belongs to the Chantilly setting as it is one of the most popular patterns in American history. It was developed during the period when having many different pieces was a normal part of life—and a normal way for companies to extend their product line. The large base of Chantilly customers allowed for the introduction of many specialized items. In addition, its long history shows how changeable the names of a particular shaped eating instrument can be. The golden age of specialization in silverware ended in 1925, when the silver companies, under the guidance of Herbert Hoover, who was then secretary of commerce and pushing for efficiency in American industry, cut the number of items offered for sale. Under his prodding, manufacturers made a pact whereby the number of items that would be produced in any pattern was limited to a total of fifty-five place and serving pieces. Today about twenty items are offered by manufacturers.

In looking at the Chantilly examples bear in mind that the same piece in another pattern might have a different shape. Design considerations let different manufacturers create different shapes for a given item. The collector often cannot tell what a given item is unless he or she has an old catalog to check it against. This is the bane of modern collectors and leads to much fraud today. The user may know what the shape is meant to be in one pattern, but this does not necessarily hold true in another pattern by the same manufacturer. At times, because of considerations of design and economics, a given manufacturer might not make forks and spoons of the same shape, and for the same purpose, in different patterns. So, even if the collector knows what a given shape is called in one pattern, it might not serve the same function in another pattern. Confusion about what fork is used for what is almost inevitable.

FORKS

Figure 4.1 shows some of the many different forks produced in the Chantilly pattern over the years.

Dinner Forks

Viewing from left to right, the first two forks seen are dinner forks. These forks, of course, are used for the meat course. These come in several slightly different sizes. The first one pictured is one of the largest. Chantilly offered dinner forks in two different weights. The one with the most silver is often referred to today as a banquet fork. Next to it is a more normally configured and lighter-weight dinner fork.

Place Forks

The third item is a place fork. This is more common as it was cheaper than the dinner fork and is the fork young couples just starting out often elected to use. It was an all-purpose size and is often the only fork found in silver collections.

Figure 4.1 Forks. Top row (left to right): Dinner (banquet), dinner, place, lunch/dessert, pie, fish, corn, salad, bird, fruit, youth/tea/breakfast, dessert (barred). Bottom row: Dessert (barred), pickle, pastry, ice cream, cheese, oyster/seafood, caviar/oyster, terrapin, ice cream/sherbet, ramekin, lemon, strawberry, nut pick.

Lunch or Dessert Fork

Next comes the lunch fork. This is a fairly rare fork as many households could not afford separate silverware just for use at lunch. On the other hand, some brides chose this size in place of the large dinner fork as they liked the smaller size that fit more readily into a woman's hand. This is the first example of how manufacturers called the same item different names in an effort to increase sales. In the early catalogs this fork was called a dessert fork. When a separate fork for this course lost favor in the 1920s, it was renamed the lunch fork. This new usage allowed manufacturers to keep on using their expensive dies.

Pie or Cake Fork

The next item is a large pie fork, sometimes called a cake fork. It was used to eat pies with thick shells—thus the extra thick tine. Not many were sold so it is quite rare. The public evidently did not see much need to have a special fork for pies, and when they did, they often bought the smaller pickle fork, which had the same shape.

Fish Fork

To the right of the pie fork is the fish fork, which has thickened tines on both the left and right sides. Fish forks came into use in the 1830s, and were one of the first examples of the nineteenth-century tendency to develop specialty items for food and drink.

Corn Fork

Next is the corn fork, an experiment that failed. Corn on the cob, even today, is not a normal item at a formal meal—it is too messy. Yet, some Victorian hostesses did serve corn on the cob. There were several ways of handling corn on the cob. One was to use the silver cob holders shown in Figure 4.2. These worked exactly like the plastic cob holders the fastidious use on picnics today.

At least one 1880s etiquette book favored serving corn on the cob, noting, "A lady who gives many elegant dinners at Newport causes to be laid beside the plate of each guest two little silver-gilt spike-like arrangements. Each person then places these in either end of the corn-cob and eats his corn holding it by two silver handles."[3] Some etiquette writers advised people to use a knife to cut the kernels off the cob and then eat the loose kernels with a fork.

The corn fork reflects another approach. The center portion of this large fork was designed to be used in scraping the corn kernels from the cob. The fork could then be used to eat the loose kernels. As a design, it was a success, the scraper worked quite well. However, it was a product for which there was no real market. Few diners wanted to go to that much trouble for corn so the fork sold very poorly and today is almost impossible to find.

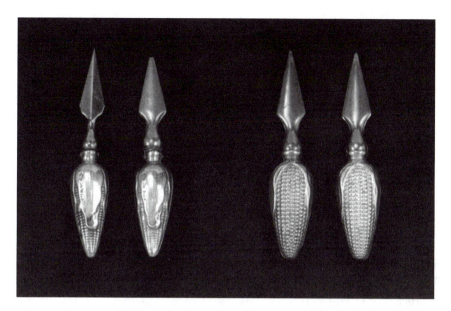

Figure 4.2 Corn holders.

Salad Fork

Next is the salad fork. This is a common piece, often one of the first expansion pieces young brides purchased or received. The left tine is slightly thickened to allow the fork to cut lettuce or other salad items. The salad fork is also referred to in old catalogs as a small fish fork. This is another attempt to boost sales by giving the same item different names.

Bird Fork

The bird or game fork is shown next. This fork and its accompanying knife allowed diners to carve the individual birds (squib, pigeon, etc.) often served at Victorian meals. It is shaped like a scaled-down version of the carving sets used for carving larger birds.

Fruit Fork

A fruit fork or avocado fork is pictured next. A small but intriguing mystery is why Chantilly did not have a fruit fork as part of its pattern in Victorian times, given that a fruit course was a standard part of Victorian meals. It certainly was as common as a cheese course featuring ramekins. And of course, there were any number of Chantilly fruit knives made over the years. There are rumors that a fruit fork was produced around the turn of the twentieth century, but they must not have had a long run as they do not show up in any of the catalogs. The one shown in the illustration probably dates from the late 1970s when an avocado fork and fruit knife were offered by mail order.

Clearly this is a modern item, made by adding a fork tine to a hollow handle. Many pieces that do not aspire for historical accuracy show up attached to a hollow handle. However, in this case the shape is appropriate. During the Victorian period, many fruit sets were sold separately from patterns, and had ivory or mother-of-pearl handles. The fruit fork is 6⅝ inches long, while the bird fork (to its left) is 6⅞ inches long. It is hard to tell the difference between the two if they are not right next to each other as the bird fork has a shape very much like that of a fruit fork.

Youth, Tea, or Breakfast Fork

The youth fork, which is next, was also marketed at different times as a breakfast fork and as a tea fork. It was a smaller version of the dinner fork to allow children to become adept at proper dining. The old catalogs refer to this shape as a tea fork. Following World War I, women's pace of life did not leave time for afternoon teas. This left manufacturers with expensive dies for an item that was no longer in vogue. The concept of designating this size as either a breakfast or a youth fork proved a neat solution.

Both had precedence in history. In the 1840s, the idea of smaller utensils for young people had been introduced. Some silver services at the turn of the century had included items designated as breakfast knives. Some Chantilly catalogs put out in the 1920s refer to youth forks and other catalogs call them breakfast forks.

Dessert Fork

The next item is a dessert fork. This fork with the bars across the tines is merely a very unusual variety of the more commonly found four-tine dessert fork. The barred fork was manufactured primarily before the 1920s. In Chantilly's sister pattern, Strasbourg, the manufacturer had this shape serve as three different types of forks—a fish, a salad, and a pastry fork. This shows that shape alone does not control what type of fork a given piece is called. This fork is shown at the end of the top row and as the first item on the second row, so the size of the forks in the two rows can be kept in perspective.

Pickle or Pie Fork

Next to the barred dessert fork on the second row is what old catalogs refer to as an individual pickle fork. There is another pickle fork that is a serving piece that looks completely different. In the days before widespread canning, the best way to preserve many foods was to pickle them. This is why a pickle fork was one of the first specialized items developed. Today, people do not eat many pickled foods, dill pickles eaten with the hands are the extent of most people's concept of pickling. This fork was referred to as a pie fork by dealers when there was no longer a market for a pickle fork. But calling this item a pie fork left the real, larger pie fork without a purpose. So, to avoid confusion, it was then referred to as a cake fork. The Victorians did not really have a special fork just for eating cakes. The pictured item is typically referred to today as a pie fork.

Pastry Fork

Next to the pickle fork is what is often called the pastry fork. The old catalogs refer to this as a dessert, small fish, or small salad fork. Again, the manufacturer was attempting to expand sales by citing different uses for the same item.

Ice Cream Fork

Next is the ice cream fork, or what today might be called a spork. Its shape reflects two historical factors. First, in Victorian times, ice cream was often cut off from well-frozen ice cream blocks. The blocks looked much like today's sheet cakes. The teeth on the fork helped cut off a piece from the hard ice cream sheet served to each diner. Eating from this block of ice cream was a different operation from skimming off a bit of relatively soft ice cream. The second factor was that in Victorian times there was a great insistence on using a fork wherever possible. One common joke was that the really fashionable people took everything but tea with a fork. This item is relatively unusual; it is a nice piece to have on a table and is almost always a subject of conversation. It is an item in high demand and the unscrupulous have met it by creating "new" ice cream forks by cutting down tea spoons. It is very hard to tell the difference between a real ice cream fork and a cut down tea spoon.

Cheese Fork

An individual cheese fork comes next. This two-tined piece was introduced in 1895. Since cheese served at the cheese course is normally, and historically was, eaten with the fingers or on a bit of cracker, this was not a big seller. It may reflect an effort to move to a more refined mode of eating just as the first forks replaced fingers in centuries past. Or it may be that the manufacturers desired to have another product to sell by extending their product line.

Oyster or Seafood Fork

Next comes the oyster or seafood fork; the name will vary depending on the manufacturer. The basic shape is always the same—a long thin handle with small tines. One or both outside tines are usually thickened.

The Victorians almost always referred to these long thin forks as oyster forks. In later years, as other types of seafood, such as shrimp, became more popular, the name was changed to a seafood or cocktail fork.

Caviar Fork

The caviar fork is a very rare item. True caviar lovers would not hear of caviar touching silver. The two are thought to set up a chemical reaction that affects the delicate taste of the caviar. They typically eat their fish eggs off gold-plated or mother-of-pearl instruments. One caviar gourmet even went so far as to use the wooden tongue depressors made for doctors to look down a person's throat. This man cares far more about taste than elegance. The average Victorian, when he or she ate caviar, was more interested in elegance, and would suffer the slight loss of pure taste to have a handsome eating utensil. Tiffany Silver Company called a similar shape, in at least one pattern, an oyster fork.

Terrapin Fork

Terrapin, a fresh water turtle, at one time found in large numbers in Chesapeake Bay, was considered a delicacy by the Victorians, who over time hunted them to near extinction. They were served mostly as an entree (which at that time meant an especially nice treat between the main courses of the meal). Terrapin was also sometimes served as a substitute for the fish course.

The terrapin fork is another very rare item. It is so hard to find that it has become something of the Holy Grail among Chantilly collectors. A terrapin fork is not shown in any of the known Chantilly catalogs but it is known that some were produced because of cost computations for a "terrapin spoon" in the Gorham manufacturer's financial records.[4]

The terrapin fork in other patterns is much like an ice cream fork (or spork, if you will) only with four tines instead of the three found in ice cream forks. Figure 4.3 shows the shape of a terrapin fork in another pattern.

The normal way to serve this entree was to serve it in a broth. To allow the diner to eat the broth the terrapin fork was a cross between a fork and a spoon.

Ice Cream or Sherbet Fork

The next fork is a small ice cream fork. This item is also known as a sherbet fork. The gold color has no effect on the name of the fork. Since eggs, salt, and other materials will stain silver, it was common to gold plate the bowl of silver pieces that would come into contact with these food items.

Ramekin Fork

The ramekin fork, which is shown next, is also a rare item. Ramekin forks in other patterns do not always have the little cutouts in the body as are shown here. No matter what pattern, the ramekin fork is always smaller than a regular dinner fork. The practice of eating ramekins (a type of souffle) during a dinner was already starting to die out by World War I. There was a social trend away from serving so many entrees, one of which was the ramekin course of the high Victorian period. The Chantilly ramekin fork is perhaps one of its most handsome forks. Ramekin forks sold today are sometimes made up by cutting down tea spoons.

Figure 4.3 Terrapin fork (on the left)
and marrow scoop.

Lemon Fork

A lemon fork is shown next. A lemon fork is normally considered
a serving piece. One is shown here because once ice tea became
a common drink with meals in the South, many silver sets included
a lemon fork for each person at a meal. This custom died out when
air conditioning became common in the South.

Berry or Strawberry Fork

The berry fork, often called a strawberry fork today, is next. This
shape is ubiquitous across almost all silver patterns, although in
some there are two tines. It is perfect for rolling a berry in powdered sugar.

Nut Pick

The last item shown in Figure 4.1 is a nut pick. Nut picks were not often found in one's pattern, but were individual items bought in addition to one's silver. Once a common Victorian piece of silverware, they are now almost unknown. Chantilly, since it had most everything else, did offer a nut pick to match the rest of the silver.

During the Victorian period nuts were a common part of the meal, eaten as part of the fruit course. Walnuts were the classic accompaniment with port. Regardless of gender, one of these nuts came at the end of the meal, which is the basis for saying about a complete meal—from soup to nuts.

The shells of the nuts were normally broken in the kitchen with a mallet and the loose nuts were taken into the dining room by the servants. The diner could use the nut pick to pick out the meat of the nut. Figure 4.4 shows a large nut spoon and nut picks.

KNIVES

Knives present their own special problems in identifying and matching. There are relatively few different types, but many variations of each type. Some are found in flat, others in hollow, handle versions, and over the years the style of the blades has changed. The shape of the blade can be used to roughly date the age of the knife.

The four shapes, as shown in Figure 4.5, are the blunt, French, new French, and modern blades. The blunt blade was used into the 1920s. The blunt shape of the knife is attributed to Cardinal Richelieu, who, depending on the story, ordered the sharp points of dinner knives ground down to prevent bloody knife fights at dinners, or to stop people from picking their teeth with the knife points. The blunt shape made it possible to place the knife in the mouth with relative safety—a common occurrence when polite society ate many foods such as vegetables from a knife rather than a fork.

During the late 1920s and up to about World War II, the shape of the knife blade changed twice. First came the French style and then the so-called new French blade. The modern shape came into use about World War II and has held sway since the 1950s. This allows a rough dating of when a given knife was produced. Another

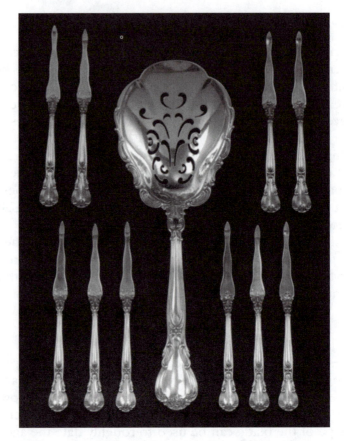

Figure 4.4 Nut picks and nut spoon (center).

guide is whether or not the blade is stainless steel. Stainless steel was patented in the United States in 1911, but the first stainless steel flatware was produced only in the early 1920s. The addition of chromium to steel (in proportion of about 12 percent) stops rust and the interaction of the steel with foods. This meant that no longer did fish, salad, and other knives have to be silver or silver plated.

Dinner Knife

Turning now to Figure 4.6, and viewing from left to right, the first knife shown is a dinner knife. The dinner knife is the largest of the knives, although the size of the steel blade can differ.

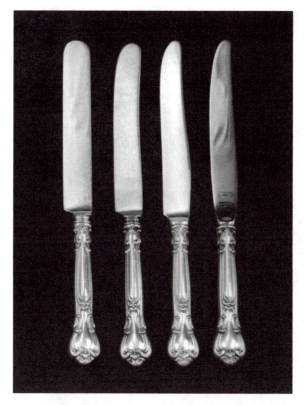

Figure 4.5 Different knife blade shapes. Left to right: blunt, old French, new French, modern.

Steak Knife

Two versions of steak knives are shown next. Steak knives were not offered until after the Victorian era. They first became common in the United States after World War II. This is another item where the shape of the steel blade changed over time. The first knife is the standard shape, and the second is a specialized blade that was only offered for a short period of time in the 1950s.

Fish Knife (Steel Blade)

Next is a modern fish knife with a stainless steel blade. The fish knife comes in at least three variations: flat blade, stainless blade, or silver blade.

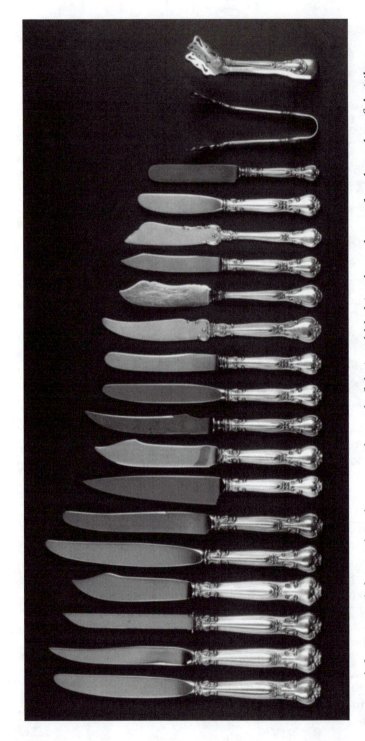

Figure 4.6 Knives (left to right): dinner, steak, steak, fish (steel blade), place, dessert/lunch, melon, fish (silver blade), game, tea/youth/breakfast, orange, tea, pickle, fruit, fish (small), butter, baby, individual asparagus tong (top and side views).

Most fish knives, whatever the pattern, have a similar shaped curved blade with a hump on the back. The blade is not used to cut the fish, but rather to separate its delicate flesh, and if necessary to lift bones for easy removal.

From their introduction in the 1830s, until the 1920s, blades were almost always silver. Metal blades, available for knives until the 1920s, were thought to interact chemically with lemon and fish oils to impart an off-taste to the fish. Because of this, etiquette demanded silver blades on fish knives. With the introduction of stainless steel in the 1920s, this practice was no longer followed. Fish knives were made of stainless steel and the manufacturer's profit margin fattened.

Place Knife

The next knife shown is the place knife. It is a smaller, slightly less expensive version of the dinner knife. It does not show up in Victorian catalogs and was probably introduced after World War I in order to offer a slightly less expensive product. Note how a longer blade has been used to mask the fact the silver handle is smaller.

Dessert or Lunch Knife

Next comes the lunch knife. This started out being called a dessert knife, but its name was changed when people stopped buying a special knife for desserts. Because the knife blade was blunt or French when this style knife was being sold as a dessert knife, and had the new French or modern shape when it was being sold as a luncheon knife, it is often felt that the shape of the blade determined whether a given piece was a dessert or luncheon knife. This, except indirectly, is not true. The name change was simply an effort to sell more product by renaming the utensil when the way people used their silver changed. It was only coincidental that the shape of the knife blade was changing over the same period.

Melon Knife

A melon knife is shown next. This sharp knife allowed the diner to cut a half or quarter of a melon into smaller pieces for easier eating. This item is not featured in Victorian and Edwardian silver catalogs and may be a modern adaptation.

Fish Knife (Silver Blade)

Next is an all-silver fish knife with a silver blade and handle. To keep costs down the silver blade is fastened to a smaller handle. Sometimes a knife such as this would be called a salad knife as well as a fish knife. Because of problems in the Victorian period with off-taste from using steel blades with salad many people either used silver-bladed knives or did not use a knife with salad. Most salads can be cut with a fork so a dull knife such as this one would work fine.

Game Knife

The game knife is a specialty item that was found in few homes. Its purpose was to allow the individual to carve his or her individual bird, or at least to be ready to, even if pre-carved pieces of duck or other game courses were served. The game knife seems to have dropped out of production fairly early. It was probably done away with in the simplification pact of the mid-1920s. The game knife was probably necessary because the old blunt knife would not allow one to cut meat off an individual small bird. A separate tool was necessary. The curved shape is common in most patterns.

Tea or Youth or Breakfast Knife

The next knife is the youth knife, breakfast knife, or tea knife. This size knife began its life as a tea knife and when the taking of tea became less common after World War I, the manufacturer changed its name to youth knife or breakfast knife to find a way to continue selling this item.

Orange Knife

The next item is an orange knife. Orange knives were another fairly uncommon specialty item. The shape shown is the more typical, although a blade that more resembles a blunt saw is found in other patterns. Oranges were normally served at breakfast so this item would not be found on a formal dinner table where cutting an orange would have been too messy.

Tea Knife

The next knife, with the slightly curved blade, is a tea knife. This was made in the Chantilly pattern in the 1890s. A larger knife with a similar blade, a dessert knife, was also produced in this pattern in the 1890s. This style knife did not sell well enough to justify its high cost of production, and in 1904 the hollow-handle tea knife was introduced to replace it.

Pickle or Butter Knife

The next knife was first used as a pickle knife in the 1890s, when the Chantilly pattern was introduced. The eating of pickled foods began to die out at the end of the nineteenth century when it became possible to ship fresh vegetables to northern cities in the winter. This naturally cut into the sales of pickle knives as well as pickle forks. Gorham silver began to reclassify this shape as a small master butter knife, as the only difference between it and a master butter knife was the location of the notch at the right side of the blade.

Fruit Knife

The fruit knife is an old piece that has enjoyed fairly constant production. There were a limited number of them produced as they were a fairly specialized item. As is the case with most knives, the steel shaft has varied slightly over the years. Many early fruit knives had silver blades to avoid the steel used at the time, which gave an off-taste to the fruit.

Small Fish Knife

The next knife is a small flat fish knife. The pattern offered two different sizes of flat, all-silver fish knives at one point. The smaller one is sometimes called an individual trout knife today.

Butter Knife

The butter spreader also comes in several styles, depending on the pattern and when it was produced. The sample shown here is the standard hollow-handle version.

Baby Knife

The next item is a baby knife with its very small handle and blade. It is often referred to as a canape knife. This is a fairly rare piece as apparently most people did not think it was a good idea to give a baby a knife. The blade is not necessarily rounded in an effort to protect the child, but is the shape of the blunt-style knife blades of the period.

Individual Asparagus Tongs

The individual asparagus tongs (side and top views) shown next are 4⅝ inches in length when laid on its side. A side and a top view are shown. It is another rare item that has appeared occasionally in other patterns. The old etiquette books note that it is perfectly proper to eat asparagus with one's fingers. The problem is the slightly moist (even slimy) feel of cooked asparagus. The individual tongs were an effort to add class to the eating of asparagus. It apparently failed because the tongs could not reliably hold the varying sizes of the asparagus spears.

SPOONS

Figure 4.7 shows the many different spoons developed by the Victorians and Edwardians. They are described, starting with the top row and working from left to right.

Chocolate Muddler

The first item is a chocolate muddler. This was made to stir chocolate in the tall, narrow chocolate pot. This shape was also called a soda water or soda fountain spoon. Today it is sometimes referred to as a sundae spoon as it is the right size to go with a tall ice cream sundae or ice cream float.

Lemonade Spoon

The next item shown is what is often referred to as a bar or lemonade spoon. The name bar or lemonade spoon comes by analogy to other patterns. These have appeared in fairly high number in the last few years and are often offered under the designation

Figure 4.7 Spoons. Top row (left to right): chocolate muddler, lemonade, iced tea, dessert/oval soup, place, sauce, soup/gumbo, soup/cream soup, grapefruit, orange/fruit. Bottom row: orange/fruit, cafe parfait, ice cream, tea, youth/breakfast, five o'clock, four o'clock/p.m., bouillon, egg/sherbet, chocolate, demitasse, individual salt.

of parfait spoons. This length is actually more useful in eating to-day's tall parfaits or sundaes than the true parfait spoon, which is about 5⅛ inches long.

Iced Tea

The iced tea spoon, almost universally used in the Old South (where it is often called an ice tea spoon in spite of what the Northern catalog named it), is just right to stir sugar in the tall glasses of iced tea that went with almost every meal before air conditioning came into use. Iced tea first became widely popular as a result of the 1904 St. Louis World's Fair. Although references exist to the drinking of iced tea some thirty or forty years prior to this, the fair introduced the idea to the public. More importantly, by that time plants for manufacturing artificial ice were in general use throughout the United States. This spoon is also often used as a parfait spoon. If a pattern has such a spoon, it is almost always in this configuration.

Dessert or Oval Soup Spoon

Next shown is the dessert spoon. In Georgian times, silver sets had both dessert and soup spoons. Both were in the oval shape shown. During the high Victorian period a round spoon became popular as a soup spoon. This allowed for more specialized spoons—a concept loved by the Victorians. The oval shape was used for the dessert spoon.

Then, following World War I, fashion changed and there was no longer a call for a special dessert spoon—especially one that was so large. The oval shape was renamed the soup spoon. Because of the existence of the round spoons, these newly designated soup spoons are often said to be for eating clear soups. The old round soup spoons were re-christened cream soup spoons.

Place Spoon

During the hard economic times between the world wars, a smaller-sized oval soup spoon was introduced—the place spoon. This seems to have been caused by two factors. The regular oval soup spoon was perceived as being too large to eat with and the smaller size, which has less silver, was cheaper and yielded a higher profit to the manufacturer.

Sauce Spoon

The next item shown is a sauce spoon. This flat item is used to scoop up thin sauce and pour it over a piece of fish or meat before eating. The use of this spoon was largely limited to continental Europe, and its use, when found in America at all, probably oc-curred after World War II when French cooking was in vogue. This piece does not appear in Victorian catalogs. Probably only one per-son in a hundred knows what this spoon is for; and when given one with a fish or meat course, diners inevitably leave it on the table rather than risk using it incorrectly.

Soup or Gumbo Spoon

The round soup spoon came in two sizes. The larger size shown first is today often called a gumbo spoon. It is referred to as a gumbo spoon by dealers as a way of differentiating it from its smaller version. There is no basis in fact for this name. The Victorians did not have a special spoon for eating gumbo, which was a regional dish largely unknown outside of Louisiana.

Soup or Cream Soup Spoon

The round soup spoon is just what its name implies. This shape is common across almost every pattern. In some it was the only soup spoon produced. Today, they are referred to as cream soup spoons—a clear error. The Victorians did not have a special spoon for cream soup. As noted above, this name came about when the large dessert spoon started being used for soup. This meant there were now two soup spoons in dealers' stock, so the old soup spoon, which was losing popularity, was renamed the cream soup spoon.

Grapefruit Spoon

In 1914, the Chantilly pattern had an orange spoon and a grapefruit spoon. The grapefruit spoon is shown first. As can be seen, the grapefruit spoon had a wider bowl than the orange spoon (to its right). This shape is common to almost all patterns.

Orange or Fruit Spoon

When the eating of oranges became common in America, they were most often Seville oranges, which are rather bitter. Oranges were eaten like grapefruit today, cut in half with sugar added. The sharp point is to dig out the pulp.

As sweeter oranges were introduced into the American larder, the style of eating oranges changed. The orange spoon no longer had a function and was re-christened a fruit spoon.

The orange spoon is shown at the end of the first row and at the beginning of the second row to allow comparison of size between spoons in the two rows.

Cafe Parfait Spoon

Cafe parfait spoons were produced for use with parfait desserts popular in Victorian and Edwardian times. Their stems are shorter than those of an iced tea spoon. The shorter stem matched the relatively short parfait glass. This is another specialized item that now is in short supply, presumably because most people saw no need to have a special parfait spoon when an iced tea spoon would do almost as well.

Ice Cream Spoon

The ice cream spoon is interchangeable with the ice cream fork. It is sometimes referred to as a sherbet spoon. It is another common shape across most patterns.

Tea Spoon

The tea spoon is perhaps the most common place piece existing. Almost every set had these in their basic sizes, whether the bride chose dinner-, place-, or lunch-sized knives and forks. Over the years the weight of these was slightly adjusted to cut or further increase company profit margins. In 1914, Gorham offered four different weights of silver content for the tea spoon.

Youth or Breakfast Spoon

The next spoon is a smaller, lighter version of a standard tea spoon. It is referred to as a youth or breakfast spoon to match the youth and breakfast knives and forks being marketed by manufacturers.

Five O'Clock Spoon

The small, or five o'clock, tea spoon shown next, was fairly unusual even in the days of afternoon teas, as the regular tea spoon was often used. The size difference was merely a matter of personal preference on the part of the buyer.

Four O'Clock or P.M. Spoon

A smaller version of the five o'clock tea spoon was also made. This is referred to by collectors as a four o'clock tea spoon and is shown next. Many patterns had three sizes of spoons for tea. A regular tea spoon, a small tea spoon, and a four o'clock or P.M. spoon. Calling one size a five o'clock spoon and the other a four o'clock spoon facilitates distinguishing between the two sizes in price lists and when talking over the phone. In much the same way, a large-size round soup spoon is called a gumbo spoon. It is very doubtful the Victorians had different spoons depending on whether you drank your tea at four or five o'clock. Victorian etiquette books pay little attention to different types of silverware and their usage, a sure sign that it was not an important screening device. It is therefore hard to know if these different sizes reflect personal preference on the part of the buyer. It should be noted that the normal time for the nursery tea for children was four o'clock. It may be the four o'clock teaspoon is in effect a child's tea spoon.

Bouillon Spoon

The bouillon spoon is shown next. These are designed to be used in the smaller bouillon soup bowls often used at lunch. The shape is a very common one for this function.

Egg or Sherbet Spoon

Egg spoons were designed to eat a boiled egg out of its shell, which is held in an egg cup. These are fairly hard to find, as the use of egg cups is more an English and continental custom than an American one. Gorham tried to expand the sales of this spoon by also calling it a sherbet spoon. The egg spoon, when used with an egg cup, is perfect for serving a bit of sherbet between courses as an intermezzo to cleanse the palate for the main course. If a pattern has this unusual piece, it is normally in the bulbous bowl shape. Figure 4.8 shows a sherbet spoon in another pattern next

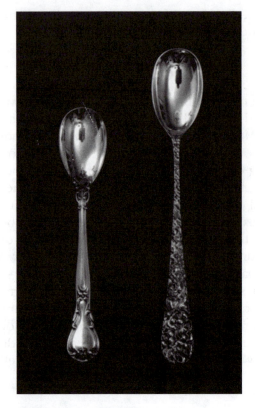

Figure 4.8 Sherbet spoons.

to the Gorham egg/sherbet spoon. The larger size is the true sherbet spoon.

Chocolate Spoon

The small chocolate spoon (measuring only $4\frac{3}{8}$ inches) was used with the smaller chocolate cup. They are fairly hard to find as chocolate parties were never really that common in the United States.

Demitasse Spoon

Demitasse spoons are fairly easy to locate. The formal dinner ended with coffee in the drawing room, so a demitasse spoon was a necessary accompaniment to those who aspired to the gracious life. Old catalogs refer to this as a coffee spoon.

Individual Salt Spoon

The final spoon shown is an individual salt spoon. They are individual spoons that go with individual salt containers. The salt was taken from the salt container with the little spoon and sprinkled on the food. It is a bit of an art if you are not used to doing this.

The use of individual salt spoons, rather than shakers, seems to have increased and waned throughout the seventy-five years of the Victorian and Edwardian periods. The bowls of these spoons are often gold washed, as this prevents the salt from pitting the silver. The round bowl shape is common.

OTHER EATING UTENSILS

Marrow Spoon or Scoop

A marrow spoon or scoop is pictured in Figure 4.3, along with a terrapin fork. Its shape is low and narrow for digging marrow out of the center of bones. The eating of marrow was largely an English custom of the late eighteenth and early nineteenth centuries. By the end of the nineteenth century eating marrow, even in England, was considered old-fashioned.

Marrow, when served, was often presented as a savory—that particularly English custom of serving a bit of meat, marrow, or anchovies at the end of the meal after the sweets and before the dessert of fruits.

Marrow spoons, when found, are usually of English manufacture, although a few American patterns included them as late as the early twentieth century.

Escargot Fork

Several different escargot forks are shown in Figure 4.9. The escargot fork did not appear in the known Chantilly catalogs before World War I. Indeed, while escargot was not unknown as a Victorian food item, it played a relatively minor part in Victorian dinners. Because of the strong taste of garlic in many of the escargot recipes, escargot was not a normal part of *haute cuisine* meals.

The eating of specially grown snails has a venerable history. The Romans enjoyed snails and had a special small spoon, the *coch-*

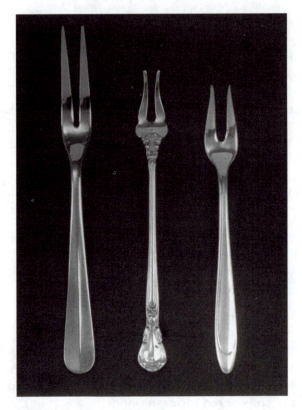

Figure 4.9 Escargot forks.

learia for eating them. (Its size was about the same as the chocolate spoon shown in Figure 4.7.) At least one Victorian era cookbook gave recipes for escargot, and noted they were eaten with a silver skewer from their shells. While some people used nut picks as the silver skewer, the more common approach was to use a narrow two-pronged fork to dig out the snail from its shell.

Lobster Fork

Figure 4.10 shows several different types of lobster forks. Lobster was a popular food among the Victorians. It was not normally served out of the shell but rather as a separate meat in aspic or as a sauce. Because of the mess, it would have been very unusual to serve lobster in the shell at a formal meal. For this reason there does not seem to have been a classic shape for a lobster fork. The first three items are English and American lobster picks. The next

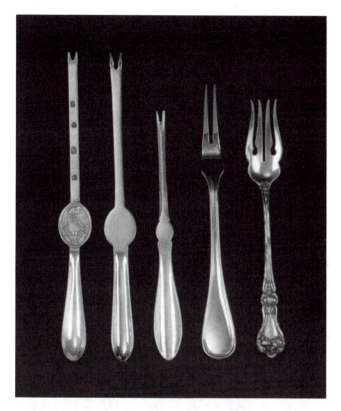

Figure 4.10 Left to right: lobster picks (3), lobster forks (2).

fork is a Christofle lobster fork that looks like an overgrown es-cargot fork. The fork next to it is a fork from another pattern that is referred to by silver dealers as a lobster fork. Without the pat-tern's catalog it is impossible to know if this is a trade name—like the so-called gumbo spoon—or if the pattern carried what would have been a very rare fork. Other patterns had lobster forks with two tines shaped like lobster claws, but these never really caught on and these forks are very hard to find today.

Crawfish Knife

Crawfish are small animals that look like miniature lobsters. They are considered a great delicacy in the Deep South and es-pecially in New Orleans. When the Victorians ate crawfish they nor-mally ate the meat, out of the shell, in an aspic. However, in the

Figure 4.11 Crawfish knife (left) and dinner knife.

Deep South crawfish were, and still are, served in the shell. The diner removes them from their shells and eats the meat.

Today people take great pleasure in eating crawfish in an animalistic way. The shell is broken with the fingers and the meat is popped into the mouth. This would have horrified the proper Victorians. They used the small crawfish knife to slit open the crawfish shell and then ate the meat with a fork. A crawfish knife is shown in Figure 4.11 next to a regular dinner knife to give an idea of its size.

NOTES

1. James Trager, *The Food Chronology* (New York: Henry Holt and Company, 1995), p. 219.

2. Number of Gorham patterns introduced in different decades:

1830	1
1840	4
1850	3
1860	17
1870	29
1880	56
1890	43
1900	33
1910	50
1920	9
1930	22
1940	5
1950	19
1960	15
1970	4

3. Florence Howe Hall, *Social Customs* (Boston: Estes and Lauriat, 1887), p. 78.

4. This is probably the correct shape for this fork as a terrapin fork in this same shape is shown in a 1910 Strasbourg catalog. Strasbourg is Chantilly's sister pattern and normally the shape of forks and spoons in the two patterns was the same. See "Catalogue of Strasbourg" (1910–1911; reprint, Cincinnati, OH: Eden Sterling Company, 1997), p. 162.

Chapter 5

China

When describing the china used for elegant Victorian meals, writers were referring to porcelain. Not many think of the romantic history of these rather everyday items, but porcelain was once a mystery— so rare that it was set in gold or silver holders and collected by kings. At one time, porcelain was made only in China, and like so much else that originated in China, the art of its production was a closely guarded state secret.

Porcelain is said to have been developed in the T'ang dynasty (A.D. 618–906).[1] Unbelievably, during the Middle Ages, some of these fragile items came to Europe overland or by sea around India. The treasury of San Mareo in Venice holds a thirteenth-century porcelain vase—once the city's pride. A blue and white porcelain cup is shown in Mantegna's 1490 painting, *Adoration of the Magi*, as one of the treasures offered the Christ child.[2]

Royalty avidly collected these rare, expensive, and beautiful items. Porcelain is listed in the inventories of Emperor Charles V, King Henry VIII, and Queen Elizabeth I in the 1500s.[3]

As early as the 1570s, Europeans were trying to produce their own porcelain, but the process was so complex that they failed until 1708. Meanwhile, vast amounts of Chinese porcelain were brought to Europe, first by the Portuguese and then by the Dutch. Between 1602 and 1657, the Dutch alone shipped more than three million pieces of Chinese porcelain to Europe. These items found a ready market among the rich and powerful.

Porcelain is hard and resists the cut of even a steel knife. Having a hard, tight surface seal, it can hold all types of liquids for long periods of time. It feels pleasant and takes hand-painted decoration beautifully. Its translucency is very appealing, and it is this characteristic that gives it its name. Marco Polo called it *porcellanta*, the Italian word for the cowrie shell, as he thought it had the same translucent glow. The two resemble each other in color and texture.[4]

Part of the problem of making porcelain lies in the special materials that must be used—kaolin clay (a French derivative of *kaoling*, which means high hill, where the material was first found) and petuntse clay (a French derivative of the Chinese term *Paitun-tzu*, which means white-stone-[for]-porcelain). French terms are used because a French missionary to China, Father d'Entrecolles, in 1712 first sent home a good general description of how Chinese porcelain is made. Kaolin and petuntse are purified, and then combined and aged for about eight weeks. The mixture is fired at a very high temperature (1,300–1,400 degrees Celsius) to certain highly technical specifications. The entire process requires a large factory-type system and a team of workers. It was almost impossible for a lone developer, even with access to the right types of clay, to produce the right mix in the correct sequence. No wonder the Chinese state kept its secret for 300 years after contact by European mariners.

With kings collecting porcelain, and paying any price for their hearts' desire, money drained out of Europe. Riches would be earned by the European entrepreneur who could produce porcelain. All sorts of people tried. "Medici porcelain" was made in Florence in the 1500s, later Delftware was produced by the Dutch, and "soft porcelain" by the French and others. These were all inferior products as only the surface was hard. Once chipped, the softer material underneath would not hold liquids or crumbled easily.

The first true European porcelain was produced in Saxony, today a region of eastern Germany, but then an independent state. Augustus the Strong, the Elector of Saxony and king of Poland, was spending a fortune on porcelain. He even traded a regiment of his army to Prussia for a collection of porcelain vases. As the country's wealth was being drained away to pay for porcelain imports, Tschirnhausen, one of Augustus's advisors and the man who started the porcelain project, said, "China is the bleeding bowl of Saxony."[5]

Johann Friedrich Bottger, an alchemist by trade, developed the European porcelain. He had been trying to turn base metals into gold for Augustus. When the experiments failed and expenses mounted, he was told to start on Tschirnhausen's project. His alternative was being put to death for his failure to make gold. Bottger did not, as is sometimes claimed, stumble on to the formula for porcelain while trying to create gold. He knew his goal, but resented being put to work on such a mundane project. He wrote on his lab door, "A goldmaker has been turned into a potmaker."[6]

In 1708, he succeeded in transforming humble clay into porcelain and wealth began to pour into Saxony. A factory was established in Meissen, just outside Dresden, which explains why fine porcelain is known as both Meissen and Dresden china.

To protect the secret of Dresden porcelain only a limited number of people knew all of its components. But where great wealth is to be won, there is always industrial espionage—and soon other centers lured away workmen or otherwise procured the necessary information. By 1713 an unsuccessful rival factory emerged in Prussia, and in 1719 a successful factory was set up in Vienna.[7]

The Saxons may have made great porcelain, but they did not have a sufficient army to protect themselves. In 1756 they destroyed the Meissen factory to keep it out of the hands of Frederick the Great's invading Prussian army. Ironically, Frederick loved porcelain and tried to keep the factory at Meissen going. He did this, in part, to obtain porcelain but also because an operating porcelain factory was equivalent to an operating gold mine.

Early on, the Saxon factory produced large porcelain table services for Saxon rulers and other rich and powerful people. One famous set, the Swan Service, had over two thousand pieces.[8]

As the secret leaked out and additional factories were built, more and more porcelain items were made. By the start of the nineteenth century, porcelain was within the reach of almost any well-to-do person.

By the beginning of Victoria's reign, fine china, as it is known today, was a standard part of each meal, but its use did not play as important a part in meals as it did later in the century. In service *à la Francaise*, the food literally took center stage, and the plate and silverware played a secondary role.

When service *à la Russe* became common in the 1870s, two

factors intertwined. First, flowers replaced the food at the center of the table. Second, and perhaps more importantly, the method of setting the table changed. More silverware was placed on the table. The extra silver that was set at each individual place drew more attention to the china. In time, people began using especially nice service plates as part of the first table setting that guests would see when they entered the dining room.

As the number of courses expanded, the need for china grew enormously. Eventually, serving course after course on the same type of plate became rather boring. Partly to alleviate boredom and partly because the Victorians simply loved specialization, they developed different style dishes for the different types of foods.

TYPES OF CHINA

Illustrated and described below are several different types of chinaware used by the Victorians and Edwardians. Not all were found in every home. The records of the White House show what plates were actually in use at a given point in the period 1857 to 1967. This is shown in the appendix at the end of this chapter. A quick glance will show that even the White House, which entertained extensively and formally, did not use every one of these plates.

Oyster Plate

Oysters were a common dinner food. The course used special plates with little oyster shells cast into them. Shown in Figure 5.1 are two of the major types—a six-shell model and a five-shell one.

Soup Plate and Soup Bowls

Soup containers were necessary for holding liquid, and different types developed. For a formal dinner a soup plate was used. As can be seen in Figure 5.2, it has a wide, flared, flat edge. Etiquette dictated that the diner, when finished, was to leave the spoon in it. With all other soup and bouillon bowls the diner left the spoon on the underplate, not in the bowl. The soup bowl, with or without handles was less formal. The handled variety, often referred to as a cream soup bowl, was considered the more formal bowl style. Figure 5.3 shows a cream soup bowl on the left and two different smaller bouillon cups.

Figure 5.1 Oyster plates.

Figure 5.2 Rimmed soup plate.

Figure 5.3 Left to right: cream soup bowl, bouillon cups (2).

Figure 5.4 Fish plates.

Bouillon Cup

Another type of soup container was the bouillon bowl or cup, which was developed for eating bouillon. It was about the same size as a teacup and seems to have been created, in many patterns, simply by adding another handle to a teacup. In formal etiquette, two handles on the bouillon or soup bowl meant that it could be picked up by both handles and the contents drunk.

Dinner Plate

The standard dinner plate was used with the joint and meat courses. It is about ten inches wide.

Fish Plate

The fish course came to have its own plates. Two examples are shown in Figure 5.4. These fish plates were normally six inches to nine inches across. Continental fish plates tended to be a bit smaller than English or American fish plates. What most had in common was a fish design to show their function. Often these were hand painted. Limoges was a very popular producer.

Some china patterns included a separate plate, with or without fish scenes, for the fish course. This is why one occasionally finds both large and small dinner plates in the same pattern. Later this size plate was known as a luncheon or entree plate.

Figure 5.5 Terrapin dish (1890s).

Figure 5.6 Terrapin pot (1890s).

Figure 5.7 Terrapin pots.

Figure 5.8   Escargot plate.

Terrapin Pot

The serving of terrapin led to the development of particular types of dishes. One, with a lid, was in the shape of a small turtle. Figure 5.5 shows an 1890s drawing of such a dish. Another variety took the shape of a small cooking pot. Figure 5.6 shows a drawing from a book published in 1893, and Figure 5.7 is a photo of existing examples. The cover is a key element as the terrapin was always served very hot.[9]

Escargot Plate

Occasionally, escargot was served at elegant meals. Snails call for their own special plates. The 1893 book, *The Epicurean*, gives several recipes for escargot and relates that they are often served in earthen or metal dishes expressly indented to receive the snail or the shell and the snail. It also notes a silver skewer or pick is used to remove the snail. The dishes must be earthen or metal as snails have to be cooked and served very hot to keep the butter from congealing. This type of dish could be placed in the oven and then carried directly to the dinner table. In Figure 5.8 an illustrated dish of modern material shows the classic shape of the escargot dish.

Asparagus Plate

Often asparagus was served as a separate course, with its own special plate. The plates shown in Figure 5.9 are typical. The plate

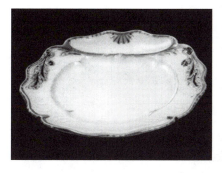

Figure 5.9 Asparagus plates.

on the right has three sections for the plant tip, the stalk, and the sauce.[10] The plate on the left has a large area for the stalk and a special area for the sauce.

Game Plate

The game course required its own china. Often these plates showed scenes of animals—usually some type of bird or game. These dishes ranged, like fish plates, from 6 to 9½ inches in diameter. Sometimes game plates were created by painting a game design on a regular dinner plate, as is shown in the blue flow plate in the upper-left-hand corner of Figure 5.10. The others are typical game plates and show the wide range of birds and animals that were pictured on these plates. Occasionally something different would be produced. Limoges is known to have produced a fine hand-painted set of square game plates.

Crescent Salad Plate

Salad plates are generally smaller versions of the dinner plate and may or may not be used at a formal dinner. They are almost certainly found at an informal dinner or luncheon. If the salad course is to be served with the game course, a practical problem arises—the game is hot, and the salad is cold. Anyone who has ever eaten a congealed salad with hot meat knows the salad will melt. In addition, the salad oils tend to mix with the game. To avoid these problems, the English started using a crescent salad plate. Figure 5.11 shows the combination of a dinner plate and the crescent plate.

Figure 5.10 Game plates.

Figure 5.11 Crescent salad plate next to a dinner plate.

Figure 5.12   Crescent bone plate next to a dinner plate.

Crescent Bone Plate

In the United States, such large crescent salad plates were not often produced; however, a smaller crescent bone plate was fairly common in American patterns. Figure 5.12 shows a dinner plate and a crescent bone plate. The crescent bone plate was used to hold the bones that were exposed when diners deboned their fish with their knives and forks. One can readily see the difference in size between a salad plate and a bone plate.

The use of the crescent plates presented some practical problems not associated with the regular salad or other side plates. The crescent plate normally sits off to the left of the main plate. But the crescent plate must be placed next to the main plate in space taken by silverware. Because of this problem the crescent plate was placed above the forks on the left or at times to the top of the main plate.

Artichoke Plate

Artichokes were a popular food with the Victorians. Period *haute cuisine* cookbooks offered many recipes, most of which called for the leaves to be coated with sauce or glaze, and served flat on a plate or a napkin. However, a simpler preparation, the steaming of the heart and the leaves, was also common. In the 1896 *Boston Cooking-School Cook Book*, and in Emily Post's *Etiquette*, this is the assumed method of preparing and eating artichokes, and it is

Figure 5.13 Artichoke plate.

this preparation that called for specialized plates. The artichoke dish pictured in Figure 5.13 is a turn-of-the-century French dish with separated spaces for the artichoke body, the used leaves, and the sauce.

Bread-and-Butter Plate

Bread-and-butter plates are normally about 6½ inches wide. They were not part of a classical formal dinner setting, since butter was not served at a formal meal. The meal was considered rich enough without it.

However, bread was served. It was simply put on the tablecloth. Without butter to stain the cloth and assuming the guest was careful to break off a piece for eating and did not put it back, the tablecloth was safe. The crumbs were removed when the table was cleared for dessert. Bread-and-butter plates could be used for less formal dinners and formal luncheons.

Pot-au-creme Pot

The sweet course led to the development of several different types of specialized dishes. Figure 5.14 shows a pot-au-creme pot and lid. It was used for a small, incredibly sweet pot of vanilla or chocolate custard. In the mid-Victorian period this pot was also called a custard cup.

Figure 5.14   Pot-au-creme/custard pot.

Custard Cups

Figure 5.15 shows custard cups. The example on the right was used at the turn of the century in American china patterns. The one on the left shows another type of custard cup, more common in England.

Figure 5.15   Left to right: custard bowl, custard cup.

Figure 5.16   Fruit plates.

Fruit Plate

Fruit, of course, deserved its own plate. These were about eight inches across and often depicted fruits, although one Victorian period etiquette book suggested having different French chateaux painted on them. This would stimulate a pleasant conversation about which chateaux one had visited and one's experiences at them. Figure 5.16 shows examples of fruit plates with fruit painted on them.

Ramekin

One of the treats served for the cheese course was a ramekin, and special dishes were developed for it. The ramekin is a mixture

Figure 5.17   Ramekin cups.

Figure 5.18   Finger bowls.

of cheese with bread crumbs, puff pastry, or eggs, baked in a mold or shell. It is held in a shallow, round cup about three inches across. Figure 5.17 shows examples. The decorative extended shoulders of the dish on the left are a bit unusual. The figure on the right shows the more typical shape.

Finger Bowl

Finger bowls, while often glass or occasionally silver, rather than china, are grouped here for ease of reference. Two examples are shown in Figure 5.18. Finger bowls are normally about four inches across and 2½ inches tall. They almost always come with their own underplates. Their appearance at a dinner table today normally loosens storms of uncertainty and furtive glances to see what the other diners are going to do. The classic faux pas is to pick it up and drink out of it. The bowl is for fingers only.

Trembleuse or Party Pack

A dish called a *trembleuse* was often used for teas. The origins of the *trembleuse* are hinted at in its name. It comes from the French word for tremble. Its construction allowed an elderly or ill person to take a beverage from a cup and saucer that would not spill as the drinker's hand trembled. The saucer on the left in Figure 5.19 shows a classic shape of the *trembleuse* with a small china cage built into the saucer to secure the cup. The cup on the right

Figure 5.19 *Trembleuse* set. Left to right: Saucer with cage and cup to go into cage.

would rest in the cage on the saucer. From this early shape, the *trembleuse* evolved into a plate with an indentation for the cup and an extended area to hold food. As time passed, this extended area grew larger and larger. Figure 5.20 illustrates a twentieth-century *trembleuse* plate. This type of cup and saucer are now often referred to as a party pack, as the term *trembleuse* was too

Figure 5.20 *Trembleuse*/modern party pack sets.

Figure 5.21   Egg cups, double and single.

cumbersome for the English-speaking public to use. Its shape is perfect for a tea party. The guest needs to handle only two pieces of china rather than three, as would be the case if a cup, saucer, and separate plate for food were used.

Egg Cups

Egg cups were designed to hold a single egg with one end up. The top of the eggshell was cut off using a knife or a special egg-cutting tool. The egg was then eaten out of the shell. Egg cups were commonly made of china, although some were made of silver. Often the egg cups would have two different-size openings, one on each end, as can be seen on the cup on the left in Figure 5.21. One would surmise that this was so a better fit could be achieved by matching the opening size to the egg. However, the size of one of the ends on this type of cup is often too large to hold an eggshell. Egg cups are perfect for serving a little sherbet in the middle of a formal meal to clear the palate.

SIZE OF PLATES

An etiquette book in 1928 supplied the following information.[11] The precise dimensions of plates cannot be given, since they vary somewhat with the make of china, but the following will act as a guide to average sizes:

Service or place plate	10½ inches
Dinner plate	10 inches
Entree plate	9 inches
Fish plate	9 inches
Luncheon plate	9 inches
Tea plate	8¾ inches
Breakfast plate	8¾ inches
Hors d'oeuvre plate	8½ inches
Oyster or deep dish plate	8½ inches
Salad plate	8½ inches
Soup plate	8½ inches
Dessert plate	7¾ inches
Bread-and-butter plate	6 inches

APPENDIX

Items of china ordered in different years for use in the White House.

China	1857	1861	1866	1879	1918	1934	1951	1967
Service plate					x	x	x	x
Dinner plate	x	x	x	x	x	x	x	x
Custard cup	x	x	x					
Soup plate	x	x	x	x	x	x	x	x
Dessert plate	x	x	x	x	x	x		x
Tea plate	x	x	x				x	
Breakfast coffee cup	x	x	x					
Teacup	x	x	x	x	x	x	x	

China	1857	1861	1866	1879	1918	1934	1951	1967
Demitasse cup	x	x	x	x	x	x	x	x
Preserve plate	x							
Egg cup		x	x					
Fish plate				x	x	x		x
Game plate				x				
Entree plate					x	x	x	
Salad plate					x	x	x	x
Bread-and-butter plate					x	x	x	
Oyster plate	x				x	x	x	x
Bouillon cup					x	x	x	
Ramekin bowl					x	x		
Oatmeal bowl					x	x		
Cocktail cup					x	x		
Cream soup					x	x	x	x
Butter pat				x				

NOTES

1. Jerry E. Patterson, *Porcelain* (Washington, DC: Smithsonian Institution, 1979), p. 17.

2. Ibid., p. 23.

3. Ibid.

4. See generally ibid.

5. William Bowyer Honey, *Dresden China* (New York: Pitman Publishing Corporation, circa 1954), p. 41.

6. Honey, *Dresden China*, p. 44. Patterson, *Porcelain*, p. 30. On the life and effort of Johann Friedrich Bottger, see Janet Gleeson, *The Arcanum* (New York: Warner Books, 1998).

7. Honey, *Dresden China*, pp. 49–50.

8. Patterson, *Porcelain*, p. 41. This set was still in existence as late as 1945. It disappeared when the Russians took over Dresden in 1945. As with so many other items that disappeared behind the Iron Curtain, such

as the gold of Troy, it may turn up in a Russian collection. Today only a few hundred pieces are still in Dresden and Meissen.

9. Charles Ranholfer, *The Epicurean* (1893; reprint, New York: Dover Publications, 1971), p. 424.

10. Julia M. Bradley [James Bethuel Smiley], *Modern Manners and Social Forms* (Chicago: James B. Smiley, Publishers, 1889), p. 171.

11. Helen Hathaway, *Manners: American Etiquette* (New York: E. P. Dutton & Company, 1928), p. 300.

Chapter 6

Crystal

Crystal and stemware were an important part of the elegant meals in the Victorian period, and have continued to be so today. The vision of wine glasses sparkling in the light is part of a diner's mental image of what makes for elegance in dining.

THE HISTORY OF GLASS

Glass working was originally a Mediterranean skill. The Chinese much preferred their porcelain and tended to treat glass as if it were a form of porcelain.[1]

The origins of making glass are lost in history. It is thought to have begun in the Middle East. The first records of glass are from the seventeenth century B.C. in Mesopotamia. The earliest examples of glass vessels have markings from the reign of Pharaoh Thutmose III (c. 1504–1450 B.C.). Early goblets and other vessels were formed by making a core of sand and then building up the glass around it either by dipping the core into a pot of glass or building up hot strands of glass around the core. When the glass cooled, the sand core was removed leaving a hollow vessel. This process involved a great deal of hand labor and thus vessels were very costly.[2]

Then about the time of Christ, someone in Syria or the Phoenician coast realized that glass was a unique material in that it could be blown into a bubble and shaped while hot. This allowed much faster creation of glass objects, and glass vessels became much more common.

However, with the fall of the Western Roman Empire to the barbarians, the art of glass making was largely lost in Europe, and almost everything had to be rediscovered. But, glass-making skills survived in the eastern part of the empire under Byzantine and Muslim rule.

Glass working was revived mainly in Venice. Perhaps this is natural as Venice had trading relations with the Byzantines and the Middle East. Also, after the Fourth Crusade of 1204, which resulted in the sack of Constantinople, Venice ruled Crete and other areas in what is today Turkey and Greece.

By 1224 a guild of glass workers existed in Venice. In 1291 all glass working was moved to the suburban island of Murano. This probably was done for two reasons: first, to protect the city from the threat of fire from the furnaces used in glass making; and second, to have better control over the glass makers. Glass making was a profitable industry to Venice, and the city tried to keep its skilled glass workers at home. This was done with a combination of concessions and threats. For example, the daughters of glass craftsmen could marry into the nobility, a very unusual privilege for the class-obsessed Middle Ages. On the other hand, if a glass maker tried to leave the Republic of Venice he could be killed.

In spite of these efforts the skill of glass working spread throughout Europe. But Venice remained a major force in the glass industry and a supplier to ultra-fashionable households throughout Europe. Part of the reason for this domination was the Venetian discovery of a way to make clear glass. Historically almost all glass had some color, which was caused by a trace amount of chemicals in the sand used in glass. Early glass makers did not have the scientific tools to measure these trace elements or to control them so color was a feature of the final product.

The Venetians discovered that if manganese was added to the glass mixture the result would be an almost colorless glass. At first this glass had some trace colors—pale yellow, smoky brown, and so on. But by the middle of the sixteenth century a clear, colorless glass was achieved. The Venetians called this clear glass *cristallo* because it was clear, just like quartz rock crystal. This is the source of our term "crystal," which even today is synonymous with fine glassware.

As the art of glass working spread across Europe, different types of glass were developed. The Venetians produced soda glass made from sand and the ashes of burnt seaweed; the soda acted as a flux to carry the heat to the sand.

Soda glass is lightweight. Its main characteristic is that when heated it remains plastic and flexible for a long time over a wide range of temperatures. This allows it to be stretched and formed into the fantastic shapes favored by the Venetians. It also made it easier to lay two of more strains of colored glass together in one vessel or piece. However, since it is light, it is not as easy to decorate by cutting or engraving.

In central Europe, far from the sea, the Germans and Bohemians made potash glass from sand and the ashes of plants such as ferns, used as flux. This style of glass is harder to form when plastic than soda glass, so it cannot be pulled and stretched into as many shapes. On the other hand, the glass itself is harder and as such takes cutting and engraving better. The Bohemians stressed the elements of cutting, and especially engraving, in their products.

In the 1670s an Englishman, George Ravencroft, developed a different formula. He substituted ground-up flint for sand and used lead oxide as the flux. This was called "lead glass." It is also known as flint glass or lead crystal. Leaded crystal from the first was distinguished by its distinctive bell-like ring when flicked by the finger. Of the three glass types it is the heaviest and hardest to manipulate into different shapes. But, it also has the most brilliance. For a time that was enough, and it was used to make vessels in the Venetian style. Then, gradually, the advantage its heaviness afforded when cutting was discovered. (The cutting style that worked best for lead glass was to make a thick-walled shape and then cut away glass to make the design.)

The Venetian styles started to lose favor in England. This was accelerated as northern European styles became popular when first a Dutchman and then Germans mounted the English throne in the seventeenth and eighteenth centuries. This period saw an ongoing improvement in the technology of making leaded glass that made it cheaper and less likely to break.[3]

Then economics trumped the trends set by technology. In 1745 the English passed the Glass Excise Act, which imposed a heavy tax on glass. The tax was on the weight of materials used in the making of glass. There is disagreement on the full effect of this tax. Some say it forced English glass makers to produce thinner and lighter glass. Others say the English tended to produce higher-value, elaborately cut glass. As it relates to table glass in America, the former seems to be the case. The wine glasses used during the colonial period are thin and decorated mainly by twisting the stems.

In Britain, the tax encouraged Irish glass making as the tax did not apply in Ireland. English glass makers set up glass houses in Ireland, mainly in Waterford and Cork. In 1780 the Irish Trade Treaty allowed Irish glass to be exported to England duty-free. Free of the tax, the Irish houses developed a style of thick, heavily cut lead glass.

The period 1745 to 1810 also saw a technological development that greatly increased the potential to produce cut and etched glass. Both are created by holding the glass against a revolving wheel that grinds away the glass. Historically this wheel was turned by a strap attached to a wheel that was hand-cranked by another person. The use of human power had two limitations. First, the person doing the hand cranking would get tired so the amount of cutting was limited. Second, the speed of the wheel would be uneven so full control of the cuts was limited. Both of these problems were eliminated by the advent of steam power during the Industrial Revolution. As untiring and even mechanical power became available, the cuts and engraving became deeper and more complex.

The British glass tax is of interest to Americans only to the extent that it had an effect on American glass. During colonial times Americans took social guidance from the old country and styles in England, as influenced by British tax policy, would be followed here. Thus much colonial glass is relatively thin and light with little cutting or engraving.

Once the United States became independent, its citizens were free to follow their own fashions, although it would take some time for their views of what was fashionable to change. By 1811, the White House was using cut-glass wine glasses and tumblers.

Whether or not the tax forced English glass houses away from heavy cut glass, its complexities seriously harmed the English glass industry. The tax rules grew steadily more complex and restrictive to avoid cheating. This tax regimen lasted until 1845 when the tax was repealed.

With the repeal of the glass tax in England, the way was clear for heavily cut glass to dominate the market. But then public taste changed.

By the time Victoria ascended the British throne (1837) the fashion in glassware had begun to change. Colored glassware was beginning to appear on the table in the form of green hock glasses and finger bowls.

An account of a four-hour dinner at the White House in 1845 describes the glasses forming a rainbow around each plate—with gold sherry, green hock, ruby port, and satuterine glasses.[4]

The rise in interest in colored glassware is usually attributed to developments made by the people of the Bohemian area in what is now the Czech Republic. First, they perfected cased glass. This is the art of laying colored glass over clear glass. By 1836 clear glass was being overlaid with several layers of colored glass. The colored glass could then be cut or engraved away, creating beautiful gem-like designs.

A cheaper and quicker way to create the cased-glass effect was to stain the glass by painting on the appropriate color. The stained glass would then be reheated to set the color and the glass engraved to reveal the clear glass below the stain. It took an expert to tell the two types of glass apart. The delineation between the colored and clear layers are somewhat sharper in stained glass, and the stained glass is a little thinner and lighter than cased glass.

In a reinforcing cycle the increase in interest in colored glass led to the development of new colors, which in turn excited the public. Improvements in the making of ruby glass and the development of a sealing-wax red shade led the way. In fact, red-tinted glass is almost synonymous with Bohemian glass. The rise in the importance of the red shade is traced to the development by the Bohemians in 1827 of a way to replace gold in producing a ruby shade.[5] Glassware as early as the 1840s and 1850s was often of a ruby shade.

Large amounts of Bohemian glass were imported into the United States in the 1840s as the fad of colored glass took hold. The American glass industry reacted by producing its own colored glassware.

The high Victorians liked the way color enhanced the table setting. A meal should also be a feast for the eyes, wrote Mrs. Sherwood, the Emily Post of the 1880s and 1890s. The importance of colored glass among the ultra-fashionable is seen in the type of glass bought for the White House during the middle years of the nineteenth century.

One of the best documented and most famous sets of glass used in the White House was the Lincoln service, ordered in 1861. The glasses contained a mixture of cutting and engraving. Some of the glasses were colorless. But, the hock glasses were green (the traditional color for hock glasses), and at least two other types of glasses were red. This glassware was used until it was replaced in 1885. The new glassware was the Russian pattern in the then-fashionable brilliant-cut colorless style.

The popularity of the brilliant-cut style can be traced to the Philadelphia Centennial Exhibition of 1876. The name "brilliant-cut" comes from the glittering effect produced by masses of miter cross-cuts in the glass. It is often compared to the shimmer of a diamond. This type of cutting needed a thick mass of glass to withstand the many cuts.

The cutting style was uniquely American. It featured curved cuttings as opposed to the straight cuts of Anglo-Irish style. This produced the heavy-looking object so typical of the high Victorian period.

A competing glass style that was also very popular during the same period was rock crystal. This was glass, normally lead glass in America, that was formed with thick massive large cuttings— thought to resemble cut quartz rock crystal. It also took a massive glass blank as a great deal of glass would be cut away to form the characteristic pillared decoration. The object was often engraved with flowers or other decorations.

Both the brilliant-cut and the rock crystal styles of glass cutting took a great deal of time by highly skilled craftsmen. In the United States this led to constant economic struggles over labor costs in the businesses creating these objects.

The original center of the glass-cutting industry was the New York City area, but the workmen there were felt by company owners to be too subject to unionizing influences. The answer for the companies was to move. Two alternate centers of glass manufacturing and cutting grew up. One was in White Mills, Pennsylvania, home of Derflingers, the makers of the Lincoln service. The other was Corning, New York, home of several glass-cutting firms. Corning was an industrial village that specialized in cut glass.

Corning remained a prominent glass-making center because of a constant infusion of skilled English and Bohemian cutters and engravers. The skills of the Bohemians were often the result of an organized apprentice system of training artisans—something that the haphazard American industry without a guild history could not match.

The industry was surprisingly small. At the height of the prosperity of Corning in the early 1900s there were only 490 cutters and forty-five engravers.[6] Engraving was just too expensive to support many craftsmen because of the high skill level of the workers.

In the period after 1900 the glass industry began to undergo a change in style. The heavy cut glassware of their parents and grandparents began to lose favor with the Edwardian generation. Lighter cutting and engraving became popular. But both of these styles, especially engraving, were hampered by the high cost of labor.

Two trends that would dominate glassware style in the United States for the next forty years began to appear during this period. The first was a return to colored glass. Following 1903, Hawkes, a leading glass producer, began to order more and more colored-glass blanks to cut and engrave.[7]

The other growing trend was etched glass. This was produced by allowing hydrofluoric acid to eat into a glass blank. Etched glass was made by placing a protective coating on the glass and then scratching a design through the cover to create a path for the acid. The glass was then dipped in a vat of the acid. The making of the design was the key restraint as it took a highly skilled craftsman to draw the design.

Etching became more commercially viable with the development of mechanical means of making the design in the wax coating. Early patents go back to the 1850s.

The other factor that made etching commercially lucrative for large-scale productions of table glassware was the perfection of industrial methods of producing large amounts of the acid, which occurred toward the end of the nineteenth century. This dropped the price of a key element of the process and meant a cheaper product without lowering profit margins.

The making of the etched design also underwent technological improvements. One was needle etching. Early patterns of etched glass tended to be needle etched. The design is drawn on the blank with a stylus that allows the operator to trace several lines at the same time. The resulting pattern is, of necessity, rather geometric.

The first needle-etched designs appeared in 1898 for Fostoria, which became one of the leading producers of etched glass in the United States following World War I.

The next technique used for making etched glass was plate etching, which appeared in the Fostoria line in 1904.[8] Here a master design was made on a metal plate and then a wax covering was placed on the plate to pick up the design. A sheet of paper was placed over the wax to hold it in place. The wax was then transferred to the blank, and the blank was given its acid bath. By using a master plate, produced just one time, it became economical to incorporate more detailed designs with flowing shapes, flowers, and leaves. This type of design became more common in the years just before World War I, and became very significant in the 1920s and 1930s.

EXAMPLES OF GLASSWARE

The Victorians and Edwardians stressed what glass was used to serve what wine and had a great variety of different glasses. Special glasses for hock (Rhine wine), claret, white wine, sherry, champagne, and many others all found their way onto the table. Using the correct glass was important. The philosopher Bertrand Russell, toward the end of his stormy life, which had included jail, divorces, and support for very unpopular causes, said that his most terrifying moment occurred when he, as a boy of seventeen, was left alone with William Gladstone, the famous liberal prime minister. After the ladies had left, Gladstone turned on poor young Russell and vented his indignation at being served port in a claret glass.[9]

Providing proper glass for a given wine was a complicated endeavor as fashions changed so frequently that it was difficult to formulate a general rule that would be good for several years, or for all patterns.[10]

An idea of the range of glasses used for serving a fine American Victorian meal may be garnered from looking at what Delmonicos', the well-known nineteenth-century restaurant, kept on hand for serving its fabulous meals for the Victorian upper class. The restaurant's collection consisted of glasses for water, chablis (white wine), bordeaux (claret), frontignan,[11] fine bordeaux, sherry, burgundy, liqueur, champagne, and punch or sherbet. Incidentally, Delmonicos' preferred Baccarat glasses.

The standard suite of glassware produced by American glass

Figure 6.1 Glass set of "Diamond Jim" Brady circa 1890s. Left to right: cordial, port, sherry, water, hock, champagne, red wine, punch. A finger bowl set is in the center. (Gift of M. H. Riviere. Courtesy of The Corning Museum of Glass, Corning, NY.)

manufacturers during the Victorian period consisted of a water goblet and hock, champagne, claret, wine (white wine), sherry, port, and cordial glasses. Because the difference in the shape of the glasses is often subtle, and there was a need for a set of glassware to have similar design elements, it is often hard to distinguish one glass from another without a catalog. (See Figures 6.1, 6.2, and 6.3.)

Water Goblet

This is a standard glass and is normally the largest glass in any glass set (Figure 6.1).

Figure 6.2 Glasses circa 1910. Left to right: high cocktail, low cocktail, sherry, sauterine (white wine), claret (red wine), champagne, cordial, whiskey.

Figure 6.3 Glasses circa 1910. Left to right: Water goblet, iced tea tumbler, water tumbler, champagne/apollinaris tumbler.

Claret

A claret or red wine glass was found in every Victorian and Edwardian pattern, as it is today. It holds about four ounces of wine and is the standard for comparing other wine glasses (Figure 6.1).

Wine, White Wine, or Sauterine

In the days of multicourse meals a special glass for white wine was more common than is our present practice. In Victorian and

Figure 6.4   Glasses designed circa 1910. Left to right: Water, burgundy/small water, claret, white, champagne coupe, champagne flute.

Edwardian catalogs this glass was normally referred to as a wine glass. It is slightly smaller than a claret glass (Figure 6.1).

Burgundy

The burgundy glass was not a common glass in American or English glassware sets. However, the French, with their emphasis on wines, normally used a special glass for burgundy. A burgundy glass was only ordered in a new set once by the White House (see the appendix at the end of the chapter) but was used up to 1914. The burgundy glass is normally larger than a claret glass, and has a wider bowl to allow the wine to "breathe" (Figure 6.4). However, some catalogs of the period show it as being smaller than a claret glass.

Hock

This shape, with its long stem, is traditional for the hock wines of Germany. The bowl holds about the same amount of liquid as a normal wine glass—so it is its long stem that defines a hock glass. Traditionally these glasses are colored, with green being the most common color (Figures 6.1 and 6.8).

Champagne

The champagne glass shape is one of the most mutable of all glass shapes. During the Victorian and Edwardian periods the standard shape was the coupe (also called a saucer) shape, shown in Figure 6.3. However, flutes, the tall narrow shape in use today were not unknown. In the saucer shape the stem could be long or short, and a hollow stem was common. Confusingly some catalogs in the Edwardian period show champagne glasses as being of the same shape as claret and white wine glasses, only larger.

Legend has it that the wide-mouth champagne "coupe" was modeled in the shape of Marie Antoinette's breast. No one knows how this story got started. One theory is that it is based on the activities of Marie Antoinette at her Dairy Temple, where she went to play at being a peasant. She is supposed to have had drinking bowls molded on her breast made by the Sevres China factory. One of these bowls still exists at the dairy near Versailles.[12] It seems to have been such a good story that it was applied to champagne glasses (Figures 6.1, 6.2, and 6.4).

Port

Port is a dessert wine that also has a high alcohol content so the glass is smaller than a regular wine glass. In the Victorian period there was not a standard shape for these glasses. The shape normally followed the design used for the white wine and claret glasses (Figures 6.1 and 6.7). Port glasses were also used for serving Madeira and some catalogs list these glasses as port or Madeira glasses.

Cordial

Cordials are sweet, high-alcohol drinks taken after dinner for a final touch of sweetness. The formula for these liqueurs often has herbs, so they also act as a digestive. Because of their intense taste and high alcohol content, only a small amount is drunk, hence the small size of cordial glasses (Figures 6.1 and 6.7).

Connoisseurs feel the glass should not flare out at the mouth or the aroma will be lost. They also prefer their liqueurs in small clear glasses so the bright gem-like colors can shine through. However, with clear liqueurs there is no reason not to use the elegant silver cordial glasses that are relatively easy to locate.

Figure 6.5 Other glasses. Left to right: Water, iced tea, iced tea, cocktail, whiskey sour, parfait.

Cocktail

The cocktail dates to the early 1800s. In the 1890s the cocktail was a fashionable drink and by about 1910 the White House was using cocktail glasses. Cocktail glasses typically had a wide-mouth bowl and held about two ounces of liquid (Figures 6.2 and 6.5).

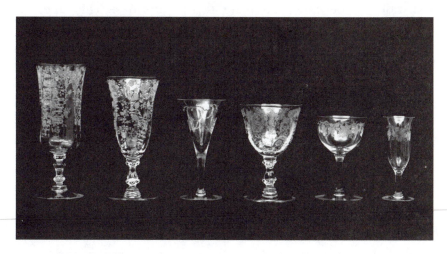

Figure 6.6 Other glasses. Left to right: Parfait, juice, sherry, oyster cocktail, creme de menthe, pousse-cafe.

Figure 6.7 Modern glasses. Left to right: Water, red wine, white wine, sherry, port, cordial.

Sherry

The traditional sherry glass was tapered and flared out from the stem, looking very much like a trumpet. It traditionally had a three-ounce capacity. It was not proper to it use for other drinks (Figure 6.6).

The alternate sherry glass, which is more common today, is taller and wider at the base than at the top (Figure 6.8). This tapering shape allows it to catch the fumes from the sherry. In some cases the sherry glass has the same shape as the other glasses in the pattern, but is just smaller (Figure 6.7).

Pousse-cafe

Pousse-cafe is another term for liqueur. The term literally means "push the coffee" and was drunk at the end of the meal as a digestive. The shape of this glass is typically that of a narrow thimble (Figure 6.6).

Iced Tea

With the popularity of iced tea in the early part of the twentieth century, iced tea glasses and tumblers became common. Iced tea

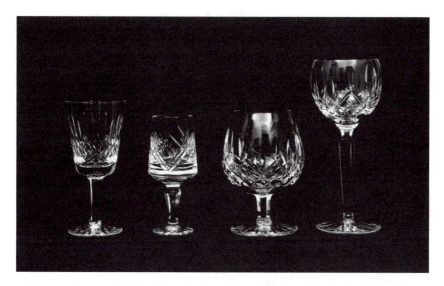

Figure 6.8 Modern glasses. Left to right: White wine, sherry, brandy, hock.

was not served at dinners but became a typical part of lunches. The iced tea glass holds more liquid than a water goblet. The shape could vary depending on the manufacturer, but it usually had a deep bowl (Figure 6.5).

Creme de Menthe

After 1890 it was common to drink two liqueurs at the end of an elegant dinner, creme de menthe and another cordial. Since creme de menthe is traditionally served with cracked ice, the creme de menthe glass needed to be slightly larger than a cordial glass in order to hold both the ice and the beverage (Figure 6.6).

Champagne Tumbler

Drinking champagne out of a tumbler is an alien idea today, but this was a common practice in the late Victorian period. The champagne tumbler was also referred to as a claret or an Apollinaris[13] tumbler. This tumbler was typically shorter and narrower than a water tumbler (Figure 6.3).

Parfait

The parfait[14] glass was used for eating dessert. The tall, narrow, footed shape is common in most patterns. Parfait glasses do not appear in sales catalogs until the Edwardian period, about the same time the parfait spoon was introduced (Figure 6.5).

Whiskey Sour

A whiskey sour glass is used for an American pousse-cafe—several layers of liquor of different colors. The layers do not mix, resulting in a rainbow effect in the glass (Figure 6.5).

Brandy

Brandy was an after-dinner drink. This glass comes in many different sizes, but all have the same basic shape. The small mouth allows it to trap the fumes from the drink (Figure 6.8).

APPENDIX

This chart shows how the types of glassware used in the White House has changed over the years.

	1849	1853	1865	1873	1885	1891	1897
Water	x	x	x	x	x	x	x
Champagne	x	x	x	x	x	x	x
Finger bowls	x	x		x	x	x	x
Wine	x						
Ice	x						
Claret	x	x	x	x	x	x	x
Jelly	x						
Hock		x	x	x			
Irving		x					
Lammertine		x					
Cordials		x	x	x			
Lemonades		x					
Burgundy			x				
Madeira			x	x	x		x

	1849	1853	1865	1873	1885	1891	1897
Sherry			x	x	x	x	x
Punch			x	x			x
Sauterine (white)			x	x	x	x
Apollinaris/ champagne tumbler						x	

NOTES

1. George Savage, *Glass and Glassware* (London: Octopus Books Limited, 1973), p. 53.

2. Paul Vickers Gardner, *Glass* (Washington, DC: Smithsonian Institute, 1979), p. 13.

3. G. Bernard Hughes, *English Glass for the Collector 1660–1860* (London: Lutterworth Press, 1958), pp. 27–28.

4. Jane Shadel Spillman, *White House Glassware* (Washington, DC: The White House Historical Association, 1989), p. 47.

5. Helen McKearin and George S. McKearin, *Two Hundred Years of American Blown Glass* (New York: Crown Publishers, 1949), p. 133.

6. Estelle Sinclair Farrar and Jane Shadel Spillman, *The Complete Cut & Engraved Glass of Corning* (New York: Crown Publishers, 1979), p. 139.

7. Ibid., p. 71.

8. Hazel Marie Weatherman, *Fostoria, Its First Fifty Years* (Springfield, MO: The Weatherman's, 1972), p. 4.

9. Bertrand Russell, *The Autobiography of Bertrand Russell 1872–1914* (Boston: Little Brown and Company, Atlantic Monthly Press Book, 1967), pp. 73–74. This was an easy mistake to make, as during this period the two glasses had about the same shape. The only difference was that the port glass was smaller than the claret glass.

10. Miss Leslie, *The Behavior Book: A Manual for Ladies* (Philadelphia: Willis P. Hazard, 1854), p. 61.

11. A liqueur made of grapes and usually fortified. Using a special glass for this wine was very unusual, even in Victorian times.

12. Hugh Johnson, *Hugh Johnson's Story of Wine* (London: Mitchell Beazely Publishers Limited, 1996), p. 346.

13. Apollinaris was a popular brand of sparkling water. It was commonly served after the end of the meal as a way to settle the stomach.

14. A parfait is a dessert food that has a different make-up in the American and French food systems. In the United States it consists of layers of ice cream and fruit. In France it is a frozen custard flavored with a fruit puree.

Chapter 7

Visiting Cards and Invitations

Before discussing invitations to meals, it may be useful to take a few moments to cover the use of visiting cards. The dropping of visiting cards was a key element of social control in Victorian times with its own set of rigid rules. Who you had to dinner, lunch, or tea depended on who stood where in introductions and in the leaving of cards.

The first key step was the introduction. In public, one took no notice of a person to whom one had not been properly introduced. For this reason, especially in England, if one was with one's friends and another friend was encountered, one did not automatically introduce the two people to each other unless both clearly indicated they wanted to take official notice of the other. One could chat amiably with a stranger at a dinner or a party and still not be considered introduced.

After a newcomer or social climber came to the notice of someone with whom she wanted to cultivate a friendship, she might follow up by paying a personal visit or call on the other. To stop a social climber from forcing herself on someone (these rules normally applied only to women, as women made almost all the social calls), there developed the custom of the established person taking the first step to deepen a relationship. It was up to the established person to make the first visit, or follow up with a return visit, if the social climber should call first.

The process went like this. If an established person called first, this indicated she wished to welcome the newcomer into an acquaintanceship and all was well. If the newcomer or a social climber called first, she often was told the subject of her visit was "not at home." "Not at home" was a social fiction meaning either the person was not in or did not wish to be visited at that time. It could be quite cutting to be told this when the visitor knew full well the person was, in fact, in the house.

Once a person had been visited, social etiquette called for a return visit. If the person called on did not return the visit, it was considered a social slight.

Since one's calling cards were sent around town for several different reasons, it was important to show one had called in person. A system grew up: bending the calling card in different ways to show why the card was at the house. Unfortunately the manner of bending differed, depending on the time and place.

The most common way to show a personal visit was to fold the upper right hand corner of the card down with the point toward the name.[1] But in other times and places the caller might turn down the whole end of the card, generally the right end, to show that she had called in person while the turning down of only one corner meant the card was left for more than one person.[2]

In some circles elaborate systems of folding corners were developed for all these different "calls." One etiquette book in 1887 stated specific folded corners sent the following messages:

Top left—a personal visit

Top right—congratulations

Bottom left—leave taking

Bottom right—sympathy.[3]

Note that three etiquette writers have given three different ways to show a personal visit, and two are directly contrary to each other.

To avoid confusion about what the folding meant, people usually wrote a set of letters in the lower left hand corner. "P.p.c." meant *pour prendre conge*—French for "to take leave." Other notations were "p.c." (*pour condola*), meaning "to condole; "p.f." (*pour feliciter*), meaning "to congratulate"; and "p.r." (*pour remercier*), meaning "to thank."

Once a woman was called upon, if she did not want to slight the person, she had to make a return call. How long she took to make this return call signaled how friendly she wanted to be. Then the person made a return call to repay the visit, with her own calibration of speed. Once this system got fully up to speed calling cards were everywhere. In order to avoid giving offense, a woman had to let people know if she could not return calls for a good reason, for example, if she were going out of town—in which case she sent or left a specific card, the P.p.c. card. Cards were also left to express sympathy for a tragedy—for example, the death of a loved one—or to express joy at a happy occurrence. These cards did not necessarily require a return visit right away or at all, although to do so when the woman was again ready to resume visiting was a nice touch.

One was expected to make a call within a week after being entertained at a dinner, lunch, or tea. The call normally was made between lunch and dinner, with between 4 and 6 P.M. being the ideal hours.

This card-leaving regime could lead to some fairly ridiculous results. In Newport, the summer social capital of the high Victorian social set, everyone in the smart set went out at 4 o'clock to call on their friends. The result was that the women spent an hour or two riding in their carriages from house to house, dropping off cards with doormen for people they knew full well were not at home. They were out making their own calls. This was so boring that the men absolutely refused to go on these missions, so the women either went alone or dragooned their daughters into going with them. The only consolation was that one could show off one's wealth by wearing a new dress and having a handsomely turned out carriage, horses, and coachmen in one's livery.[4]

About the time of World War I, women started to rebel against what had become a burdensome and largely meaningless duty. It started with the young, who now had more options of activities outside the home. When it was realized that a girl who neglected her calls did not suffer social ostracism, the visitation regime died away. By the 1920s the idea of visiting people every few days and keeping a record of one's visitors, and how often they came, was passe.

CALLING CARDS

There were strict rules on the type and shape of the calling card one left when one visited.

The card should be about 3⅝ inches in width and 2½ inches in depth for women. The married woman's name went in the center and her address was in the lower right hand corner.[5] A married woman's name was written "Mrs John Smith." A single woman's card read "Miss Sarah Jones." Single women began using cards when they were in their teens—some etiquette books said when a girl turned fourteen, others when she had been presented to society. Single women did not put their address on their cards.

Men's cards were narrower, 1½ inches in depth and three inches in width.[6] The word "Mr." went on a man's card only after he reached the age of twenty-one.[7] Men used "junior" only until their father died, at which time they dropped the term. If a man went by the name John Smith III, because he carried the name of both his father and his grandfather, he dropped the "III" on the death of his grandfather and started using "junior." Then when his father died he would drop the "junior." His wife's card would also change each time her husband moved from the III, to junior, and then to no addition at all.

Calling cards, to be proper, had to be engraved. The lettering could be either in script or in block letters, depending on the favored style of the time.

INVITATIONS AND ACCEPTANCES

Invitations to a formal Victorian dinner were engraved, or handwritten. Some hostesses who gave many dinners would have the bulk of the invitations engraved and would write in by hand the name of the invited party, and the date and time. The invitations were issued in the name of both the husband and the wife. The form was as follows:

Mr. and Mrs. John Smith, junior
request the pleasure of
Mr. and Mrs. John Doe's
company at dinner,
May twenty-seventh at eight o'clock

23 Beacon Street

Note how the date and time are written out in full. If junior is part of the name, it would be written out in full, and not capitalized. If the invitation is for the half-hour, the term "at half after six o'clock" would be used, and in the example above it would be written on the next line. Normally the quarter-hour was not used. If it was, the term would be "at one quarter after eight o'clock" or "at a quarter before eight o'clock."

The invitations were always in the third person. The term "R.S.V.P." or "R.s.v.p." often did not appear on the invitation as this implied the recipient did not have the social grace to know she must reply, and reply at once. R.s.v.p. was proper only for large parties or balls. R.s.v.p. did not appear on invitations to teas as a fixed head count was not considered necessary.

There is some disagreement as to how the R.s.v.p. was to be written when it was used. A common form in English-speaking languages was to capitalize the R. and have the s.v.p. in lower-case letters. However, it is said the French capitalized all four letters and this was sometimes picked up by Americans who looked to France for social guidance.

The invitations to dinner were sent out between ten and twenty-one days before the meal. The more formal the meal, the greater the notice of the dinner.

Even in Victorian times when having household staff was common, formal dinners were a major production for anyone, whether middle class or aristocracy. So a prompt reply was imperative. In the days when footmen were sent with the invitation, they often waited while the invited wrote her response. If there was any doubt about being able to attend, the proper step was to decline the invitation at once.[8] This is because once an invitation to dinner was accepted, only death, or perhaps a command to appear before the queen or president of the United States, could excuse the invitee. The deadliest social sin was to accept an invitation to a formal dinner and then later decline. In Victorian times it was unthinkable to accept a dinner invitation and then not show up. This was so far outside the social pale that most etiquette books did not even address it.

The proper form to decline an invitation was as follows:

Mr. and Mrs. John Doe
regret that they are unable to accept
the polite invitation of
Mr. and Mrs. John Smith
for Friday evening
May twenty-seventh.

The reply was in the same tense as the invitation. Note the use of the phrase "the polite invitation." Toward the turn of the twentieth century this changed to "the kind invitation." Which phrase was used depended on whether one followed the high Victorian form or that more common toward the end of her reign and into the Edwardian period, although both phrases can be found in either period. One might even wish to use the phrase "regret extremely that a previous engagement must deprive them of the pleasure of accepting the polite invitation of. . . ."[9]

There was disagreement over whether the French construction should be used in the reply, that is, if the reply should be worded "the polite invitation of Mr. and Mrs. X for dinner" (French) or "Mr. and Mrs. X's polite invitation" (English). Some thought the former an affectation as the invitation was written in English. Others thought the latter was too colloquial.

Some etiquette writers thought it was best to state a generally worded reason for declining the invitation, especially if it was a first invitation, or it might be supposed there was an intention to slight the hostess.[10] One might use the phrase "a previous engagement prevents accepting" or "absence from the city prevents accepting."

A solecism to be avoided in the acceptance was using the wrong tense. One should not use the terms "accepting," "will prevent acceptance," "will accept." One accepts or is unable to accept in the present tense, that is, when one writes the note. Therefore one should not use the future tense. Also one does not use the word "decline." Decline implies one does not want to come; "unable to accept" suggests something is preventing you from attending.

When one accepted an invitation the same rules applied. In addition, the acceptance should always state the date and time to avoid possible confusion. Basically the invitation was played back out. Often a card was used with the sender's address and date put on the lower left-hand side of the card. The acceptance went something like this:

Mr. and Mrs. John Doe
accept with great pleasure
the polite invitation of
Mr. and Mrs. John Smith, junior
for dinner on
May twenty-seventh at eight o'clock

123 Main Street
Monday.[11]

The idea was to create a great deal of formality, and to allow for fine shades of politeness. Thus one could accept with pleasure or with great pleasure. The layout of the acceptance or declination should be aesthetically pleasing. Others thought it was not good form to show these degrees of emotion; one accepted with pleasure to all dinner invitations, and did not differentiate by accepting with great pleasure some people's invitations.

NOTES

1. This was still being done as late as the 1940s. See Millicent Fenwick, *Vogue's Book of Etiquette* (New York: Simon & Schuster, 1948), p. 598.

2. Florence Howe Hall, *Social Customs* (Boston: Estes and Lauriat, 1887), p. 41.

3. DeB Randolph Keim, *Hand-Book of Official and Social Etiquette and Public Ceremonials at Washington* (Washington, DC: DeB Randolph Keim, 1889), p. 163.

4. Newport was an exception. At Newport there was a six to ten week social season packed with dinners and dances. Consequently there was a need to always be paying thank you calls. This is why everyone went out every afternoon. Away from Newport a more leisurely social schedule was followed, and the system of a woman having an "at home" one day a week or month could be followed.

5. A Member of the Aristocracy, *Manners and Rules of Good Society or Solecisms to be Avoided* (London: Frederic Warne and Co., 1911), p. 20.

6. Ibid., p. 27.

7. Fenwick, *Vogue Book of Etiquette*, p. 602.

8. Mary Henderson, *Practical Cooking and Dinner Giving* (New York: Harper & Brothers Publishers, 1877), p. 28.

9. Hall, *Social Customs*, p. 28.

10. Ibid., p. 60.

11. Ibid., p. 59.

III

Status and Etiquette

Chapter 8

Seating Etiquette

To the Victorians (and diplomats today), where one sat at the table was very important. Feelings would be hurt, and tempers would flare, if these rules were violated.

In England, the order of precedence was set by one's rank in the tables of nobility. Dukes ranked above counts, and so forth. If two people held the same rank, then the order in which the titles were granted was the deciding factor. The holders of the title were men, and women took the precedence of their husbands. For example, when nineteen-year-old Consuelo Vanderbilt, as the wife of the duke of Marlborough, went to dinner she took precedence over women in their fifties and sixties who had not married as well. In British colonial society this was carried further, and the order of precedence depended on the husband's job. Books of official order of precedence were published to set out the relationship between different jobs and time in those jobs. If one wanted to know the order of precedence of an assistant inspector general of forests, a district judge in Lower Burma, a lieutenant with seven years of service, and a sanitary commissioner, one merely looked in the official warrant of precedence.

In the United States, the question of precedence was mostly confined to Washington, D.C., where the order among diplomats and politicians' ranks was important. Many hostesses did not use precedence in seating their guests—they placed people to ensure good conversation.

It was a common fiction that the order of precedence mattered more to the women than the men. The idea was that the men were too busy getting on with the work that needed to be done to worry about unintended slights. One suspects this fiction was no more true than the idea that men do not gossip.

In most of the United States there was little order of precedence, there being no nobility, or diplomatic or bureaucratic ranking to go by. What order there was took the form of the oldest woman being first or perhaps an out-of-town woman being first. If a new bride was present she often took precedence.

The lady of honor, the one with the highest precedence sits on the host's right. The lady with the next highest rank sits on his left. The lady of the third highest rank sits on the right of the man of the highest rank. The fourth-ranked lady sits to the *left* of the man with the second-highest rank, and so on down the table.

The man of the highest rank sits to the right of the hostess. The diagram in Figure 8.1 makes this easier to follow.

At most tables the host and hostess sit at either end of the table. This means that the lower-ranking guests sit in the middle of the table. (This is exactly the opposite of the medieval custom and renders meaningless the term "below the salt.") In dinners where the number of guests is divisible by four (i.e., eight, twelve, sixteen, and so on), the man-woman seating will be thrown off if the hostess sits at the end of the table. In such a case the hostess sits to the left of the man opposite the host. This puts the host and the highest-ranking male guest at the heads of the table.

There was some dispute in etiquette circles about who should be served first. In the United States it was common that the hostess would be served first. Others thought this very discourteous (Emily Post grew almost apoplectic at the idea) and insisted that the lady of honor (the woman to the right of the host) be served first. Other etiquette writers thought it was a good idea to serve the hostess first. This allowed the hostess to correct any errors the footmen might make in serving, and allowed her to be the first to break a complicated item such as an aspic. Most people could not afford a staff of servants who were very familiar with serving a complicated formal dinner. Most had to make do with inexperienced recent immigrants or hired waiters. The hostess-first method of

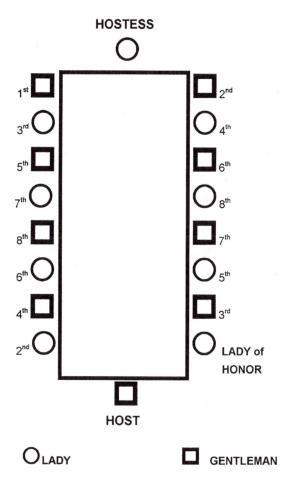

HOSTESS

HOST

O LADY   □ GENTLEMAN

Figure 8.1 Seating chart showing order of precedence. The number shows the person's order of precedence.

service is a good idea today when most of the people serving the meal will need a little help.

After the first person is served, then the order of service is clockwise, that is, service goes next to whomever is on the left of the person just served.

Normally when going into dinner a man escorted the woman who would be seated on his right. This presented the practical problem of knowing whom to escort into dinner as a man did not know ahead of time whom he would be seated next to. This difficulty was overcome by having the hostess tell each man whom to take in, or writing a card to the man telling him whom he would be escorting. These cards were handed out by the hostess, or more properly left in envelopes with the man's name on it on the front table. Another method was to have a seating chart on display with each person's place at the table noted. Everyone had the duty of looking at the chart prior to going into dinner. Special leather-bound charts were made with slots where the hostess could insert slips of paper with each person's name. Place cards will be discussed in more detail in chapter 11.

The host and the lady of honor would go into the dining room first and the hostess last. In the United States there was no order in which the others went in. In England the people want in by order of the lady's rank (which she derived from the rank of her husband or father).

In England if a person spent a long period at a country home, this strict seating by rank could make for a number of very dull dinners. He or she would always be seated next to the same person, and if the twosome did not have any common interests to talk about, or if one was a bore, they were in for a dull evening.

Partly to avoid this the custom of "turning the table" developed. The convention was that for the first half or so of the meal the woman talked to the man on her left. At some point about halfway through the meal the hostess "turned the table" by turning and talking to the man on her right. The other women would be watching and waiting for this maneuver, and they would also turn and talk to the man on their right. Old conversations would end and new ones begin. Hostesses were expected to be quite ruthless in turning the table. If a woman did not or could not end her conversation with the man on her left, the hostess would send a note or say something to the woman to remind her of her duty to start talking to the man on her right.

In England there was a strict order of table procedure noting who sat where and who was served first. In the United States this was not followed as strictly. Hostesses were often more interested in the dynamics of conversation during the dinner, wanting to create a pleasant and stimulating meal. They would mix and match guests based on who was talkative and vivacious and who was shy and taciturn. The secret, of course, was to not put all the talkers at one end of the table and all the quiet people together at the other end. Things went far better if a talkative person could be seated next to a quiet one.

However, some American hostesses placed stress on seating by order of rank. This was the norm in Washington, D.C. In Washington there was an official order of procedure that could be followed. In other parts of the country a rough order of procedure was adopted. Victorian writers did not spell this out; they only alluded to it. It was left to a later generation to give the details. A 1948 etiquette book gave the following order:

1. A person with an official position
2. A person from another country
3. A guest brought by a friend
4. A person who in the past held an office
5. The person who has been a guest a few times in the past
6. Frequent guests
7. Relatives and house guests
8. Children.[1]

The above list assumed the people's ages were roughly the same. Differences in age affected and modified this list. If a guest had a great age, he or she would probably take precedence over a younger foreigner. Closer differences in age could also affect the order. Being ten or fifteen years older than someone on the list just above one might bump the person up. A person might also be bumped higher if he had a record of achievement that the hostess wished to recognize. Normally this was a record of achievement as a scholar or in a learned profession. Merely having made a lot of money did not help a person move up the order of procedure.

The above ranking was for men. Women took their husband's ranking. This could cause the young wife of an official or foreigner to rank higher than an older woman whose husband held a lower rank on the order of procedure. This was often very galling to an accomplished, mature woman who saw a vacuous young woman given a seat at dinner with higher status. There was one great exception to this general rule—a young bride at her first dinner after the honeymoon was often given precedence.

In Victorian times there was no question of a woman being in a learned profession or holding office so the smooth flow of precedence went strictly by what a husband had done.

If a woman's husband was not present at the dinner, she lost his status ranking. This was normally an unlikely event since married couples were almost always invited as a couple. It was slightly risky to invite a married person without his or her spouse, and perhaps even more risky to accept such an invitation.

A woman whose husband was not present did not fall to the bottom of the list of precedence—only down a few rankings. Since opinions could differ on what was a proper reduction in precedence, and hard feelings could result if someone thought the hostess's judgment was wrong, it was far easier to just not have a woman guest without her husband.

Among women without a spouse whose ages were about equal, the widow took precedence over a divorced woman who in turn took precedence over an unmarried woman. During the Victorian period there were almost no divorces, so seating of a divorced woman was not an issue. By the start of the twentieth century one found a few divorcees, so rules had to be developed on how to rank divorced women. The above general ranking of unmarried women was also subject to the rule that a marked difference in age gave the older woman precedence.

NOTES

1. Millicent Fenwick, *Vogue's Book of Etiquette* (New York: Simon & Schuster, 1948), p. 449.

Chapter 9

Table Etiquette

The Victorians placed great importance on one's ability to show good manners and follow the rules of etiquette. One etiquette writer in the 1860s put it as follows:

Nothing indicates the good breeding of a gentleman so much as his manners at table. There are a thousand little points to be observed, which, although not absolutely necessary, distinctly stamp the refined and well-bred man. A man may pass muster by *dressing well*, and may sustain himself tolerably in conversation; but if he be not perfectly *"au fait"* dinner will betray him. (emphasis in the original)[1]

What then are rules the Victorians, and people today, live by?

The word "etiquette" comes from a French word that carries a connotation of stickers, labels, or pieces of paper stuck or nailed up to tell one where to go and what to do. It is said to have originated in the court of the Sun King, Louis XIV. The nobles living at court had apparently not yet developed the refined manners that they later were famous for. They were in fact a bit crude and walked over the flowers the king's gardener had worked so hard to grow and present. Finally, the head gardener, traditionally a Scotsman, put up a "keep off the flowers, grass, and so forth." sign. This did not work until the king was prevailed upon to tell his nobles to mind the *etiquettes* (the posted signs). This word gradually flowed over into the manners that were being taught at court to tell people where to go for each ceremony, and how to behave while there.

The goal of this section is not to teach today's table manners. If a person is unsure, he or she can easily check any number of current books. Rather this section will revisit some of the shifts in manners in the past.

Drinking from the saucer

Eating off the knife

Using a napkin versus the tablecloth

Gargling with water

Three forks on the table

Fidgeting

Breaking bread

Knife with salad

Drinking from cups with handles

Carving

Finger bowl

Doily

Use of salt

Most people today know the general rules of etiquette at the table—don't pour coffee or tea in the saucer, don't eat off one's knife, don't drink out of the finger bowl, don't wipe one's hands on the tablecloth, no more than three forks on the table, and so forth.

The reason many of these rules are so well known is at one time all of these activities were common and socially proper. When the norms that sanctioned these activities changed, the writers of etiquette books had to reinforce the idea that these things were no longer to be done.

DRINKING FROM THE SAUCER

Up to about 1750 the design of teacups followed the Chinese custom of being handleless bowls. This design is still used in China, and can be found in Chinese restaurants in America. The hot beverage, in thin porcelain cups, often was uncomfortable to

Figure 9.1 *A Family of 3 at Tea* by Richard Collins showing three ways teacups were held circa 1740 when teacups did not have handles. (Courtesy of V&A Picture Library. © The Board of Trustees of the Victoria & Albert Museum, London.)

hold. Figure 9.1 shows a painting, circa 1740, that shows three different methods of holding the handleless teacup. It is thought the need to hold the cup by the rim and base gave rise to the archetypical raising of the little finger while drinking tea.

In Europe the cup was placed on a saucer that had more of a bowl shape than today's relatively flat saucers. The reason for this shape was to make it possible for the tea to be poured into it to cool down. Pouring the hot tea into the saucer avoided the need to handle the hot cup when the tea was first poured, and the saucer, with its wider shape, gave the tea more exposure to the air and allowed it to cool off faster. While waiting for the tea in the cup to cool, the tea in the saucer could be drunk. This gave the tea drinker faster access to the tea.

When handles were added to the cups in the mid 1700s, it was easier to handle the hot teacup and pouring tea into the saucers to cool was no longer necessary. The design of the saucer and the rules changed. Some people held onto the old ways after the *haute mode* changed. Even with handles on the teacup, the tea was still hot and hard to drink when it was first poured. The custom of pouring a little tea or coffee into the saucer and drinking from it lingered on. Etiquette books had to stress over and over again that this practice was no longer acceptable. Small plates, about 3 to 4 inches across, called "cup plates," which were used to hold the teacup when the saucer had tea in it, were produced up to the 1860s. They were used in the White House as late as the Tyler administration (1841–1845).

EATING OFF THE KNIFE

The same pattern occurred in the area of eating off the knife. For many years the fork had narrow prongs, usually two, placed far apart. Its purpose was to spear meat and carry it to the mouth. The wide gap between the prongs rendered it unsuitable for eating vegetables. The knife, on the other hand, with its wide spatula-type blade, worked well for this purpose.

Then in the middle of the nineteenth century this changed. Because of the switch to steam-driven tools in the production of silver, forks began to be manufactured with four or more tines placed close together. A curve to the tines was added to make the fork operate more like a spoon.

With the fork now used to carry loose food, the rules changed and putting the knife in the mouth became improper. However, this new custom was not implemented everywhere at the same time. For years there was a "knife line" across Europe with the French, English, and those who took their social cues from these countries eating off the fork. In Italy, Germany, and the Austrian Empire people continued to use the knife. In Russia, where both France and Germany gave social guidance, some people used one method and some the other. There were also generational deviances, and the etiquette books pointed out that grandma was still a lady even though she put a knife to her lips. This change in custom worked its way through society from the top down. The less sophisticated, or those who did not care, continued for a long time to use their knives in eating vegetables. A famous gathering of very rich Texas self-made oilmen in the 1920s was derogatorily labeled "The night Texas ate off a knife."

USING A NAPKIN VERSUS THE TABLECLOTH

In the Dark Ages, people wiped the grease of a meal off on their pants or their skirts. Then the sophisticated introduced the social refinement of the napkin, as a handy place to wipe the hands. However, the napkin fell out of favor in the early 1700s, and it became common for people to wipe their hands on the tablecloth. There was no reason they should not. After all several tablecloths were placed on the table, and one was removed after each course was over. (A table setting normally consisted of two or more tablecloths laid on top of each other.) With so many tablecloths in use, a napkin was a bit of a social affectation for most of the dinner. During the late eighteenth and early nineteenth centuries, napkins were in vogue intermittently. One generation would supply them, the next would not. People could not decide whether it made more sense to wipe their hands on a large cloth that soon would be removed or on a small cloth that would have to be held on their lap for the duration of the meal.

Napkins were furnished with the dessert course, which was served after the table was cleared, that is, after the last of the tablecloths were removed. In fact, doilies started out as loosely woven napkins that were given out with the fruit for the dessert course. It was not until the 1830s that the use of napkins at meals became *de rigueur*, and doilies assumed their purely decorative function.

When service *à la Russe* became popular, table decorations were more important. These elaborate table decorations were left on the table throughout the entire meal, and the tablecloth was not removed. Since no one wanted to see a tablecloth soiled by one's neighbors wiping their greasy hands on it, napkins became a real necessity. They were required and etiquette writers had to remind diners to remember to use their napkins rather than the tablecloth.

Since no one wanted their good dinner cloths heavily soiled, there grew up the present convention of not using the napkin much during the course of the meal. It lay in a person's lap only to catch anything that may drop onto it.

GARGLING WITH WATER

In the Middle Ages diners ceremoniously were given water to wash their hands before and at the end of a meal. The latter was a real necessity since the fingers were used in eating. When forks came into common use the washing of one's hands at the end of a meal became largely ceremonial. With no real purpose served the washing of the hands became a symbolic rinsing of the fingers. There was confusion over how the finger washing should be performed and the water presented. Use of the finger bowl, or finger glass, also underwent a period of uncertainty and how it was used changed with fashion. For a time an individual finger bowl would be provided to each diner, and then in the next generation a large bowl of water would be carried around the table by the servants and each diner would dip his or her napkin in it. The wet napkin was then used to clean off one's hands and mouth. As late as 1828 authors recommended the use of a common glass of water for cleaning the diner's hands.[2]

When individual finger bowls were provided, there was disagreement on how they were to be used. In the 1840s it was customary to dip one's fingers in and then drink the water in them and use the water to gargle. The used water was then spit back into the glass or bowl. As may be expected not everyone found this custom edifying. One dismayed etiquette writer said of it, "Custom sanctions in vain what is of itself disgusting."[3]

For much of the Victorian period tobacco was chewed rather than smoked. A mass of tobacco juice in one's mouth made the presence of spittoons a necessity. Its use, even after being spit out, rendered the taste buds incapable of distinguishing the fine gradations of flavors that French chefs worked so hard to create. This problem was solved by having the diner wash out his mouth before eating. This was done by supplying a "finger" bowl of water as part of the original table setting.

THREE FORKS ON THE TABLE

As was noted in chapter 1, the changeover to service *à la Russe* caused the established ways of serving and eating meals to undergo a major modification.

In the colonial period the only silver on the table was a knife, a fork, and perhaps a spoon. Part of the reason for this was that the tablecloth was removed after every course. To have a lot of silver and many glasses on the table would have made the removal of the tablecloth too hard.

When the change to service *à la Russe* took place in the 1860s and 1870s, the tablecloth stayed in place throughout the entire meal. In addition, the servants were busy carving and serving food. It now made sense to put out all the silver the diner would need and leave it there throughout the entire meal. The footmen had other things to do and less time to hand out silverware. In addition, the mechanization of the production of silverware, together with a drop in the price of silver, meant that the host now acquired more silverware.

There were some practical limits. Clearly if the hostess put out the eight or ten forks one would use at a formal meal, the diners would be too spread out to comfortably talk to each other. Convention quickly settled on three or four forks as the maximum number the hostess could put out so guests could still talk easily to their neighbors. For some twenty years after the Civil War there was disagreement about whether three or four folks were proper. In the end three forks won out—perhaps because the game course became less common. But, because this was a change and an arbitrary number, it was necessary to keep reminding people that they should never put out more than three forks at a table setting. We personally like the look of four forks and knives. It creates an exotic and opulent look, and visually sends the cue that this meal will be something a little different.

FIDGETING

The thrust of the etiquette books in the Victorian period was somewhat different from today. Modern etiquette writers tend to stress that the goal of refined manners is to put others at ease, not to cause mental pain, and how to handle interpersonal conflicts.

Older etiquette writers concentrated on the individual. At a meal a diner was to show he or she was in control. Readers were advised to eat slowly and deliberately to show they had mastered their animal drive of hunger. A hostess was careful not to show dismay when a servant did something wrong in cooking or serving dinner, a common occurrence when one depended on inexperienced people from a foreign culture. (Most servants were immigrants who had come off farms and had no more idea about how to act at a high Victorian formal dinner than in a Japanese tea ceremony.) A guest did not apologize when he or she broke a glass or dish, and the hostess should not show the least concern either, no matter how valuable the item. A diner did not fiddle with the food or silverware as this showed he or she was not perfectly at ease.

BREAKING BREAD

It has always been considered good manners to break one's bread into small pieces, often just bite-size ones. This left the uneaten portion untouched by the mouth or whatever was spread on the bread. This custom arose because in ancient times it was a common act of charity to give the uneaten bread to the poor after a meal. This is probably why the baskets of bread were collected after Jesus' miracle of the bread and fish feeding the multitudes. Today we throw away the uneaten bread, but continue the old custom of breaking our bread.

KNIFE WITH SALAD

There is some confusion over whether it is proper to use a knife when eating salad. The traditional rule was that knives were not put on the table or used for the salad course. The reason was that in the days before stainless steel there was a good possibility of a slight chemical reaction between the knife blade and the salad oil, which could discolor the knife blade and cause an off-taste in the salad. Sometimes an exception to the rule was made so knives with silver blades could be used with salad. The silver in the blade did not react as readily with the salad oil. When stainless steel for blades was developed, knives, which are very useful in eating salad, started to be put out with the salad course.

Today some hostesses still remember the rule barring the knife from the salad course and pass up this very useful instrument in serving a salad. Of course, when using a very old set of silverware, made before the twentieth century, it might be prudent to pass up the knife when serving salad. In this case, care should be taken to cut the salad into bite-size portions.

The same problem of chemical reaction with the old knife blades existed when serving fish or fruit. The answer was to use silver for the blades of fish knives. This was possible because a sharp cutting edge was not necessary with fish—the knife being used only to separate the flesh from the bone, not to really cut the flesh.

With fruit it was necessary to have a sharp cutting-edged surface, which silver could not form. There the answer was to make a silver-plated fruit knife. Since the silver plating would wear away with time, it was common not to invest in fruit knives that matched one's other silver. This made the fruit knife easier to replace when the silver plating wore off. Once stainless steel became available for blades it was common to produce fish knives with stainless steel blades. The same was true with fruit knives, and it became more common for the fruit knife to match the other silver.

DRINKING FROM CUPS WITH HANDLES

The cups that are used to serve cream soup and bouillon have handles on both sides of them. It has always been acceptable to pick up these items by both handles, using both hands, and sip out of them. This is an exception to the usual strong rule of drinking out of the soup dish. In fact, the rule against drinking out of a soup bowl or a flat-rimmed soup plate is so strong that one is not even supposed to tilt the bowl or plate to get the last bit of soup out.

CARVING

The ancient art of carving is now largely lost in today's world of grazing and prepackaged meals. But, for the early Victorians it was a very necessary part of every gentleman's and gentlewoman's education.

During the Renaissance carving was done by professional carvers whose activities formed a part of the entertainment of the meal. They carved by holding the meat or foul out in front of them with a large fork in one hand, and cut the meat with a knife held in the other hand. Ideally, the slices that they cut fell to the plates in such a way as to form a flower or other artistic design.[4]

As time went on and the meals became more intimate affairs, the carving duties were taken over by the diners. The ability to carve was the mark of a well-bred person. Lord Chesterfield, in one of his famous letters to his godson, on the art of being a gentleman, said: "To do the honors of the table gracefully is one of the outlines of a well bred man; and to carve well, little as it may seem, is useful twice every day, and the doing of which ill is not only troublesome to ourselves, but renders us disagreeable and ridiculous to others." Carving also allowed the carver to distinguish between guests, show his knowledge of which portions of a joint or piece of a bird were the noble portions and which were not, honor select guests with the choicest portions. There is a story about Talleyrand (1754–1838), the well-known French statesman, that shows the fine nuances that could be made when carving.

First he turned to the highest ranking diner picking out an honorable piece of meat and said with an air of deference "Monsieur le duc, may I have the honour of presenting you with a little beef?"

Then with a graceful smile, "Monsieur le marquis, may I have the pleasure of offering you some beef?"

To his third guest, with a familiar, affable gesture: "My dear Count, shall I offer you some beef?"

To the fourth, with a benevolent air: "Baron, will you accept some beef?"

To an untitled though upper-class fifth: "Sir, would you like some beef?"

And finally, to a man at the end of the table (table ends are "low" in France), he raised his eyebrows slightly, smiled, and said: "Beef?"[5]

In Victorian meals prior to the introduction of service *à la Russe*, this old tradition of carving was kept alive. The fish, joint, or bird was placed whole on the table and the host and hostess, one at each end, carved the animal. They then apportioned out the meat to each diner's dish. The carving was done while seated, and one would have been considered ridiculous if he or she had stood while carving as is done today at Thanksgiving dinners.

When service *à la Russe* became the norm, carving moved from the dinner table to the sideboard. There, at the sideboard, it was done by the butler or one of the footmen. This made life far easier for the host and hostess as they were not forced to perform a difficult art in front of the guests. And, the art of carving was thence never acquired by many in the upper classes.

FINGER BOWL

During most of the Victorian period the finger bowl was treated as if it were a separate course, that is, the bowl and underplate were brought out together. The diner used the bowl to wet his or her fingers, and the bowl and underplate were then taken away. As can be seen in Figure 6.1 the underplate was not designed to be eaten off of in the Victorian period.

By the Edwardian period there were two proper ways to place finger bowls on the table: the private home and the hotel methods.

The normal or private home method presented the diner with a stack of plates, bowls, and silverware and relied on the diner to know how to untangle them. A finger bowl and a glass plate were put on a china fruit plate with a doily between the finger bowl and the glass plate. A dessert fork and spoon were put on the glass plate. The fork was on the left side and the spoon on the right. When this stack was put down, the diner removed the silverware and put fork and spoon on either side of the plates. The finger bowl and the doily were then lifted and placed on the left side of the plate at about the 10 o'clock spot. Ice cream was then eaten off the glass plate. The glass plate was then removed and fruit was eaten off the china plate.

The main disadvantage to this method, even in Edwardian times, and it is especially true today, is that it relied too much on the diner knowing what to do. It was not uncommon for the diner to forget to remove the silverware or the finger bowl. Or the diner would place both the finger bowl and the glass plate on the left, a natural mistake since they were a set. Its main advantage was that it put less work on the servers and thus allowed dinners to be served with a slightly smaller wait staff. But this savings was largely illusionary as the footmen still had to bring the silverware for the fruit course, and, of course, remove the glass plate after the ice cream had been eaten.

The most common way of presenting the finger bowl and the last courses was the "hotel method," which in spite of its name was often used in private homes. The "hotel method" had the plate for ice cream, together with its silverware, put on the table when this course was served. Then a plate for the dessert (i.e., fruit) would be put out with the finger bowl and the silver. The classical way to place the silver was on the plate, fork to the left and knife to the right with a doily in between the finger bowl and the glass plate.

The diner would then place the silver on either side of the plate and lift both the doily and the finger bowl up and put them to the left of the plate at the 10 o'clock position. The fruit was eaten off the main plate.

The main objection to this method, other than extra work for the footmen, arose out of the convention that the ice cream was to be eaten off a glass plate. This meant that a glass finger bowl would rest on a china fruit plate, and the glass plate, which matched the finger bowl, was put out in a course when the finger bowl was not present.

Today both sets of problems can be overcome by simply ignoring them. Follow the Victorian custom of serving the finger bowl and underplate as one unit after the ice cream and fruit courses. This means one will not eat off the glass plate. An advantage of this method is that it allows for the serving of a sweet course between the ice cream and the fruit.

In Edwardian times once the fruit had been eaten and the plate and silver were removed, the diner then lifted both the doily and the finger bowl up and put it in front of him or her and dipped his or her fingers in the water. The doily was not used in any way. Originally the doily was a napkin for drying ones fingers off after washing them and a way to be sure that fruit stems did not get on the white dinner napkin. During the Victorian period, the doily napkin was a bit larger and draped over the finger bowl. But by the end of the nineteenth century the doily was merely a decorative element. Often these were round and made of fine lace.

DOILY

This change in function has led to our modern confusion over the term "doily." Today the doily is a piece of lace or crochet work that goes under a plate or on the back of an easy chair. Originally it referred to rough, loosely woven cloth. The derivation of the word comes from Monsieur Doyly or D'Oyley, a Frenchman living in London in the seventeenth century whose shop became fashionable for selling this type of cloth. Since it was often used to wipe off one's hands after eating the fruit course of a meal, his name stuck to the cloth used for this purpose.

USE OF SALT

If no salt spoon was provided with the individual salt dish, then the diner used his or her knife to take a little salt from the dish.[6] This could even be done from a master salt cellar if a salt spoon was not provided with it. It was important to wipe the knife off on the plate or on a bit of bread before putting it in the common salt cellar. It was, however, not proper to use the handle of one's fork or spoon.[7] If a master salt cellar was used, one could put the salt on the side of one's plate or even on the tablecloth. If this was done then the diner picked up a pinch of salt and sprinkled it over the food with his or her fingers.

NOTES

1. *Civil War Etiquette: Martine's Handbook & Vulgarisms in Conversation* (reprint; Mendocino, CA: R. L. Shep, 1988), p. 67.

2. Louise Conway Belden, *The Festive Tradition* (New York: W. W. Norton & Company, 1983), p. 211.

3. *The Ladies Hand-Book of Etiquette and Manual of Politeness* (New York: James Miller, n.d.), p. 54.

4. Margaret Visser, *The Rituals of Dinner* (New York: Penguin Books USA, 1991), p. 235.

5. Ibid., p. 242.

6. Florence Howe Hall, *Social Customs* (Boston: Estes and Lauriat, 1887), p. 98.

7. Theodore Child, *Delicate Feasting* (New York: Harper & Brothers, 1890), p. 190.

IV

The Dinner Stage and the Props

Chapter 10

Dress

Victorian dress and costume is complicated, and is the subject of many books.[1] Therefore, this chapter will provide only a short primer on women and men's dinner dress for those wanting to replicate a Victorian dinner.

WOMEN'S DINNER DRESS

Women's clothing experienced more changes in the eighty years between 1840 and the 1920s than did men's clothing. Because of the many changes of style, the intricacies of trim, color, and fabric, only a general review of the major changes in the dress silhouette of women will be included. This review will limit itself to evening wear for dinner and dresses for teas.

During the period from 1840 to 1865 skirts and dresses grew steadily wider. At first, this was accomplished by merely wearing more petticoats under the dress. The waist and bodice were tight fitting (Figure 10.1).

As the 1850s wore on the petticoats were expanded further by the use of "crinolines." These were made of horsehair or stiffened cotton incorporated into the outermost petticoat. The early 1860s saw the introduction of "artificial crinolines." These were concentric whale bone or metal hoops hung on strips of material from

1835   1840   1845   1850

1870   1875   1880

Figure 10.1 Outline of women's clothing 1835 to 1900. (Courtesy of V&A Picture Library.)

the waist. These artificial hoops allowed for skirts larger than those that could be obtained with mere petticoats. This is the hoop skirt so reminiscent of the Civil War and the antebellum South.

By the end of the Civil War the silhouette had changed. The skirt grew fairly flat in front. This was compensated for by a shaped metal frame that extended behind the wearer. The silhouette changed from being basically round to protruding fore and aft.

The early 1870s saw the extended train-type skirt replaced by the bustle. At this period it was a framework, often cane, held by strips of cloth around the waist. The framework created a small bulge in the back of the wearer and the skirt then flowed back and down at a slope, creating the effect of a train.

In the late 1870s, the bustle disappeared and the silhouette was shaped by the so-called *cuirasse* bodice. The bodice came down over the hips and made the dress look much like a corset with a skirt falling from it. It is often thought that the Victorian dress showed nothing of the body. This is not true. The upper body was

1855   1860   1865

1885   1890   1895   1900

often clearly delineated, which is why corsets were so necessary. What often was obscured were the hips and the legs. And even the hips could be tightly outlined as is shown by the *cuirasse* style shown here.

In the mid-1880s, the bustle came back into style. Now the bustle took the form of arching up and away from the back and then falling straight down. The whole effect was rather like the woman wearing a small barrel behind her, under her skirt.

The coming of the 1890s saw a new outline. The bustle disappeared and the skirt, while full, fell more naturally. The bodice took on a mono-bosom look with a tight, low-cut waist. The shoulders were often delineated with puffs of cloth. By the mid-1890s the puffs of cloth had grown into the "leg-o'-mutton" sleeves, which were so typical of the gay nineties. At the turn of the century the full sleeves disappeared. The skirts were often tight over the hips and fell away to a large base at the floor.

As the new century progressed women began wearing "hobble

skirts," skirts that were cut tight all the way to the floor. The other major change during this period was the abandonment of the corset, first in France and then in the United States.[2]

Hats and gloves completed the costume and their wearing followed rather complex rules.

Headdress

A hat was never worn at dinner. However, during the Edwardian period women often wore feathered plumes in their hair. Throughout the Victorian and Edwardian periods jewels were often worn in the hair for dinners.

When a woman went out of her home during the day she wore a hat. Consequently guests wore hats at teas and luncheons. A woman did not wear a hat in her own home or in a home where she was an overnight guest. For this reason she did not wear a hat in the lobby and other common rooms of a resort where she was staying. However, if she were a day visitor she would wear her hat. Etiquette books warned hostesses not to wear hats when they gave luncheons or teas; but pourers at teas were to wear hats.

Sometimes hostesses would wear hats at formal luncheons, but they could not have veils on them. Guests' hats could have veils, which were turned up to eat.

Gloves

Women wore long over-the-elbow gloves for dinners. These were taken off at the dinner table and kept in one's lap while one ate. It was not easy taking off a tight-fitting set of gloves and keeping them on one's lap when wearing a slick silk dress. Etiquette books warn against leaving the gloves on and just folding back the portion that covered the hand. So this must have been a common expediency. A common sight at the end of the dinner when the women were ready to withdraw was men down on their hands and knees picking up the gloves and fans that had fallen to the floor during the dinner.

When one took tea one wore gloves, but one took off gloves to eat at that same tea. Women put on gloves to shake hands while men would remove their right glove to perform this honor. A hostess would never wear gloves.

MEN'S DINNER DRESS

Men's dinner dress on the other hand saw little change in the eighty years under review. In the 1840s dinner coats were very similar to the cut of ordinary dress of the Regency and King William periods, so familiar to moviegoers today from productions of the works of Jane Austin. The coat was tight fitting, cut off at the waist, and had tails. A vest (in England called a waistcoat) was worn under the coat. The coat was worn open, showing the vest. The general shape remained constant up until World War II, with slight variations in the cut of the collar, the fullness of the pants, and so forth. The vests for tails or a tuxedo were slightly different. The tuxedo vest came together in a V-shape, which is common today. The full dress vest worn with tails was in a U-shape (Figure 10.2). The waistcoat in one year might be double breasted, in another year single breasted. Collars on the waistcoat came and went and the depth of the waistcoat moved up and down, showing more or less shirt. Just before World War I, it was fashionable to have the bottom of the waistcoat show beneath the front of the coat. The coat and pants were always black and the shirt was always white (Figure 10.2).

The color of the bow tie and the waistcoat varied over the years. In 1914 both were white. In 1922 Emily Post, with her usual confidence, stated that a white bow tie and a black waistcoat were worn only by butlers. This combination is repeated as dress for a butler in a book of etiquette written after World War II. However, drawings made in the 1880s show the normal formal dinner dress for men was a white bow tie and a black waistcoat. So no firm rule can be set for the entire period. One etiquette book probably came closest to the mark when it said in general the dress for butlers was that worn by diners a generation or so earlier. The wearing of white tie with tails largely ended after World War II and tuxedos took their place, as a new generation rejected the conventions of their elders.

The tuxedo (or dinner jacket as it is called in England, or the Monte Carlo as it is called on the Continent) is not formal dinner wear. It is said to have gotten its American name from the fact that it was introduced in 1886 by Griswold Lorillard, at an autumn dance held at Tuxedo Park, New York—fashionable in the spring and fall for the rich. This story may not be true. See Appendix 1 at the end of the chapter for an extended discussion on how the

Figure 10.2 Evening wear circa 1910. Left to right: tails, woman's evening gown, tuxedo.

tuxedo came to be. The word "tuxedo" is thought to come from an Algonquian Indian word, *P'tauk-seet-tougb*, meaning "home of the bears."

It is often said Edward, the prince of Wales, developed a tuxedo by cutting off the tails of a formal dinner jacket on a trip to India in 1875. This was done to make a cooler garment to be worn in the Indian heat. This is not quite true, but the short coat without tails was the ancestor of the military formal, mess jacket, which is covered below.[3] The tuxedo was introduced for dances, informal dinners, and evenings out. That is why all those playboys in the 1930s movies wore tuxedos in their nightclubs and all the old people wore stiff shirts and tails at their dinners.

The cummerbund, now worn with the tuxedo, was originally not limited to tuxedos. In the mid-1880s, when the cummerbund made its appearance, it was worn with any item of dress. Cummerbunds were a fad and never caught on with anything except the new tuxedo-style jacket. The origins of the cummerbund were the shawls the soldiers of the British Indian Army wore around their waists to add a bit of color to their uniforms. They would fasten a ten-foot shawl to their shirt and then slowly pivot while a servant walked toward them holding the other end level. In this way they were wrapped in the shawl—in layers of cloth around their waist. This is why the fake cummerbunds commonly worn today have little overlapping folds in front. (The cummerbund is traditionally worn with the overlapping up so a man can tuck theater tickets in the fold.)

The Victorians often wore vests with their tuxedos rather than the cummerbund that is common today. As noted above the tuxedo vest had a V-shape.

To be truly correct, the pants that are worn with tails should have two satin stripes and those worn with a tuxedo should only have one. A butler's pants would not have any satin trim.

The Top Hat

One accessory to men's formal dress merits special mention. The top hat was an integral part of the evening wear of men. The top hat was developed by John Heatherington, a London haberdasher and milliner. When first worn in 1797, in a world where men wore tricornered hats, it is said to have caused a riot. Heatherington was charged with a breach of the peace and ordered to pay a fine. The tall silk hat had a shiny luster, supposedly calculated to frighten timid people. In spite of this rocky beginning the hat caught on, and by the Regency period was the normal hat worn by gentlemen. It was worn with tails and later the tuxedo. It is still worn today at the Ascot races in England and certain grand weddings, funerals, and diplomatic occasions.

One of the main attractions of the top hat is that it adds the illusion of height to a man and makes him look commanding. It is said one short man ordered two-foot-tall top hats.

The top hats of the Victorian and Edwardian periods were made of silk with a slightly curved side to the cylinder of the hat. The brim curved up a little bit.

The top hat came in two colors. Black silk was worn with evening wear—tails and tuxedos. A gray hat was worn with a morning coat.

The hat was made by creating the requisite shape in gossamer calico and then painting it with shellac to stiffen it. Up to the 1960s silk plush was sewn onto the creation. Unfortunately, the method of making silk plush has been lost, and it is now impossible to obtain a new silk hat. Today the top hat is covered in polished rabbit fur. This has led to a strong market in used silk hats. However, there is a problem with head sizes. Today head sizes are larger than those of the Victorians and therefore many men cannot find an antique silk hat.[4]

MESS DRESS

During the Victorian period the military developed its own version of formal dinner dress, which was called the "mess dress." Mess dress is still being worn in the United States Army and Marines today as their dress for formal occasions.

As noted above, it seems to have developed from the action of the prince of Wales in his state visit to India in 1875. He cut off the tails from a formal tail coat, and this is the basic shape that served as military dress. The resulting shell was smartened up by the addition of brass buttons and braids in various shapes.

The shell jacket has two basic shapes: a shell with a collar and brass buttons and one with a high collar that was closed up the front. The latter normally had braid, brass buttons, or horn toggles

Figure 10.3   Examples of Army mess jacket.

up the front. In some cases there would be loops of braid across the front of the jacket. (See Figure 10.3.)

The waistcoat, worn under the jacket, would be either closed to the neck or cut in a "V" showing some of the white shirt. The vests that closed to the neck often had trim on the front of the vest and where the side pocket would be. The cut-away vest often had trim in the same places or was closed with gold buttons.

In England the jacket was normally the color of the regiment's uniform with cuffs and collars the color of the regimental facing trim. In the United States, the jacket was black. It normally had a gold braid shoulder strap that carried the badge of rank. In England the vests would be red, the regiments' facing color, or, in Scottish regiments, the regimental tartan. In the United States they were black or white.

In England the pants were the normal full dress officer's pants. For Scottish regiments the pants, called "trews," were in the regimental tartan. In the United States they were black.

FOOTMEN'S DRESS

Formal dinners were served by footmen. Prior to the Civil War footmen often wore their own everyday dress while acting as servants. This was in keeping with America's democratic tradition. After the Civil War, with the increase in wealth and number of servants because of immigration, the equality between employer and servant began to crumble and footmen were given special dress. The most common was a black tail coat and black pants. The tail coat was easily distinguished from that of the butler and the diners by the fact that it had large brass buttons (Figure 10.4). The waistcoats often were in special family colors, another distinguishing mark of a footman.

Some employers in deference to the U.S. democratic tradition did not use special family colors for the waistcoat but issued either plain black or white waistcoats. However, many families went further than colored waistcoats and used a special color for not only the waistcoat, but also the coat itself. For example, the coats of the Astors's footmen were blue, and the Vanderbilt footmen wore maroon.

A few grand families went even further and for special events dressed their footmen in "court dress"—cut-away coats, knee breeches, stockings, and pumps (some with silver buckles). Sometimes the hair was powdered white (Figure 10.5). Court dress was also worn by waiters in upscale restaurants.

Today a server wearing white gloves while serving a meal is the height of elegance. The Victorians looked with scorn on footmen wearing white gloves while serving dinner. White gloves were for waiters and should not be worn in private homes. There the footmen were to wrap a napkin around their hands when serving plates and foods. They were instructed to be careful that a fold of the napkin came between their thumb and the plate.

GIVING A FULL-DRESS DINNER

When giving a Victorian dinner guests may wish to consider dressing in proper period clothing. This adds a little fillip to the meal as everyone admires each other's costumes or clothing. Most formal shops have both tuxedos and tails.

The women's costumes do not need to all conform to one period—one gets the same feeling from dressing up in a hoop skirt

Figure 10.4 Footman's dress.

Figure 10.5 Footmen in court dress circa 1895. (Note the white powdered hair and the knee breeches.) The man in the middle is a butler.

of the 1850s as in a hobble dress from the 1910s. It is all in fun and few can tell the dress of one period from another (Figure 10.6).

Good places to find period dresses are costume shops and the local community theaters. Many of the latter rent their costumes as a way to earn a little extra income to support their programs. There are also stores that will sell second-hand Victorian clothes, and, if truly ambitious, a woman can sew her own clothes, using a dress pattern designed by one of the companies that specialize in Victorian patterns.

APPENDIX 1

Griswold Lorillard is the man often credited with having invented the tuxedo by cutting off the tails of a tail coat and wearing the short coat to an autumn dance held at Tuxedo Park in 1886. Lorillard was an heir to a tobacco fortune and the son of the man who developed Tuxedo Park along with several friends. He died at age twenty-five, three years after the famous ball. The library at Tuxedo Park, however, has several references that cast doubt on the idea that Lorillard introduced the style. According to these accounts the style was brought to Tuxedo Park by

Figure 10.6 A couple dressed for a recreated Victorian dinner. He is in mess dress and she in a hooped skirt (circa 1860).

James Brown Potter, one of the founders of Tuxedo Park. He and his wife had spent a weekend in England with the prince of Wales where he saw the prince and his friends wear it for informal meals. See manuscripts by J. Earle Stevens, Tuxedo Park Library, 1979 and 1988. Mr. Stevens claims to have received this story in 1929 from Grenville Kane, one of the founders of Tuxedo Park.

Edwin Post, the son of Emily Post, in his book on his mother's life states that Tuxedo Park followed the lead of the prince of Wales in using the tuxedo dinner jacket. He should know. His grandfather, Bruce Price, the noted architect, had planned Tuxedo Park and for years lived there.

Emily Post grew up there. She wrote her book on etiquette in her Tuxedo Park home. Edwin Post also grew up at Tuxedo Park.[5]

The story of the tuxedo coming from the prince of Wales is more logical than the idea that a group of sophisticated, rich, and powerful older men would adopt a blazer-like coat for informal dinners and evening wear because a twenty-two-year-old cut the tails off his dinner jacket to shock people at a dance. In addition, the buttons and cut of the two coats are very different. It is hard to see how cutting the tails off one would lead to the other.

NOTES

1. See, for example, Alison Gernsheim, *Victorian and Edwardian Fashion* (New York: Dover Publications, 1963); Anne Buck, *Victorian Costume and Costume Accessories* (London: Herbert Jenkins, 1961); Charles Gibbs-Smith, *The Fashionable Lady in the 19th Century* (London: Her Majesty's Stationery Office, 1960).

2. Peter N. Stearns, *Fat History: Bodies and Beauty in the Modern West* (New York: New York University Press, 1997), p. 159.

3. It also became the ancestor of the little red coats worn by organ grinder monkeys for so many years. The pillbox cap the monkeys wore was another item of military dress at the turn of the century.

4. John Morgan, *The Financial Times*, reprinted in *Winston-Salem Journal*, July 6, 1997.

5. Edwin Post, *Truly Emily Post* (New York: Funk & Wagnalls Company, 1961), p. 24.

Chapter 11

Setting the Victorian Table

CENTER DECORATIONS

It is difficult to clearly describe how tables were decorated in the 1800s as individual choice played such a large part. However, a general outline of trends can be attempted.

When the serving style was "everything on the table," as was common in the colonial period, there was little room for decorations (Figure 11.1). One or two of the main dishes could be emphasized by raising them, that is, placing them on rings or holders so that they stood higher than the other foods. When society switched to service *à la Russe* and banished the foods to the sideboard, it left a vast expanse of space on the table that was open for decoration. Table setting in the 1800s blended four elements of design:

Central Decorations

Flowers

Color

Mirrors.

Central Decorations

Toward the end of the 1700s, about the time of the American Revolution, hostesses started placing central decorations—

Figure 11.1 Table setting for dinner *à la Francaise* (circa 1870).

Figure 11.2   Table setting circa 1900 for dinner *à la Russe*.

epergnes or plateaus—on the table. The plateau was a raised mirror, often with silver or gilt decorations on the raised sides.
Epergnes were tall stands with hanging arms that held baskets of
sweets, or platforms that held glasses containing sweets.

George Washington, for example, had a plateau that sat grandly
in the middle of the table, reflecting the figurines put upon it.[1]
Epergnes were the ancestors of the family cruet-stands of Victorian
years.[2]

The plateau would often have figures placed on it. These were
made of porcelain if one could afford it, otherwise of sugar. Surviving correspondence states that George Washington had in addition to figures, vases for flowers.[3]

Flowers

In the early part of the 1800s the custom of placing flowers on
the dining table at formal meals began to take hold in the United
States.[4] By the end of the century there began what would become
a common theme in the twentieth century, the use of a tall and
heavy candelabrum and elevated dishes alternating with low
dishes.[5] Large masses of flowers often so covered the table that the
individual place settings were almost crowded off the table (Figure
11.2). Often the individual place settings were delineated by
strands of ivy or other flowers strung between place settings (Fig-

Figure 11.3 Table setting circa 1910 for dinner *à la Russe*. Small round tables at formal dinners were very popular at the turn of the century.

ure 11.3). During the Victorian period masses of flowers were commonly placed on the table even if an epergne or plateau was used.

Color

Color was an important item in Victorian table decoration. Hostesses would place colored runners down the center of the table, or cover the white cloth with a lace cloth of a color that matched the dishes or the wallpaper. Colored glasses were an important element. The diner would see green hock glasses and one or more of the ruby red wine glasses that had been popular since the 1840s.

By the end of the nineteenth century color on the dinner table was falling out of favor, first in England and then in the United States. One English writer stated that colored cloths or ribbons on the dinner table were a very "Yankee thing to do."

Mirrors

Another popular decoration was to have a mirror placed on the table if a mirrored plateau with figures on it was not used. The mirror might depict a lake with swans, boats, and overhanging trees, or perhaps a meadow or other peaceful scene.

Figure 11.4 The Edwardian style of table setting lasted well into the 20th century. This is a photograph from the 1940s.

Edwardian Period

The Victorians were not given to dainty understatement. The modern style of sparse elegance was not theirs. They tended to favor clutter and overstatement in clothes, furniture, and home and table decorations.

However, by the 1890s a more geometrical and sparse table was coming into favor. It consisted of candelabra, bowls of fruit, and flower arrangements set one after the other along the length of the table (Figure 11.4): In the middle there might be a centerpiece or a large container of flowers or an epergne. Then in line off to the left would be a bowl of flowers; a candelabrum with colored satin, paper, or flower shades; a bowl or compote of cakes, petit fours, or fruit; another bowl of flowers; and perhaps another candelabrum. Just how many depended on the length of the table. Off to the right would be a line of candelabra, flowers, fruit, and so on that was a mirror image of the decorations on the left. The exact order of candelabra, flowers, and fruit did not matter as much as the fact that the two halves of the table should be identical.[6]

LAMP SHADES

In the early nineteenth century a large number of candles were placed on the table. They made a brave show but put off a great deal of heat and an unpleasant glare. The tide of opinion turned against this custom and fewer candles became the norm in the period after the Civil War. Each candle was often covered with an individual shade to keep down the glare, which people now found objectionable. The shades also put more light on the table service. The candle shades were normally made of paper. One etiquette book carried a section on what to do if a paper shade caught fire: One should not blow on the fire to put it out for that might scatter the flame. A better course of action was to wait and let the paper burn itself out. For those who wish to use candle shades but are a bit uneasy at the idea of using paper, a good idea is to use a shade of beads strung together.

SALT CELLARS

Over the course of the Victorian period the use of individual salt dishes came and went. In some periods each guest was given a small individual container for salt and a small salt spoon. The container could be a small round bowl or a more whimsical container such as a small wheelbarrow. In other years the individual container fell out of favor and a larger salt bowl, called a salt cellar, was set out. The salt cellars were normally set out one per every two guests. A larger salt spoon was normally provided with the cellar. If one was not on the table it was permissible to use a clean knife to pick up a little salt and transfer it to one's plate.

TABLECLOTHS

The tablecloth for formal dinners in Victorian times was a white "damask" cloth. This name is said to come from the original source of this type of weave—Damascus, Syria. The damask cloth is patterned with designs—quite often lozenges. In the United States eagles were popular.

These damask cloths were expensive as they were normally hand woven. They had to be spotless, which involved a great deal of work in the days before washing machines.

Up to the mid-eighteenth century, tablecloths, when not being used, were screwed into linen presses to keep a sharp fold in them. The presses made the creases run both ways and formed a criss-cross pattern.

In the colonial period, and up to the 1870s, the fashion was to have no crease at all in the tablecloth. Tablecloths were kept rolled on tubes to make sure there were no creases when the cloth was placed on the table.[7] After the Civil War there developed the custom of having one central crease—which must go down the exact geometric center of the table.[8] This is still the custom today.

When dinner was served in two or more courses *à la Francaise* there were several tablecloths laid on the table—one for each course, except the dessert course. As a course ended, the top tablecloth was removed. For the dessert course the table was left bare. This allowed the beauty of the table's wood to be shown. The forerunners of today's placemats, squares of cloth, were placed under each plate. They were large enough to allow room for the dishes and drinking glasses, and protected the wood of the table.

Undercloths

Under the damask tablecloth was placed a flannel cloth to deaden the noise, protect the wooden table from heat, and give the tablecloth a pleasing lie.

These undercloths have a curious history. In the seventeenth century the undercloths were the center of attention. They were heavy woven cloths much like today's carpets. The table carpets could be of plain, one-color wool, or what we call today Oriental carpet. (These were known as Turkish carpets in the seventeenth century.[9]) In time another cloth was laid over the carpet to protect the carpet. At first the top-covering cloth did not hang too far off the table so as to show off the main table covering, the carpet. Over time the protective cloth got bigger and more ornate and became the main tablecloth. The Oriental tablemat, or carpet, was put on the floor as a decorative rug and a simple heavy flannel cloth took its place.

MENUS

A feature found at many Victorian and Edwardian dinners was menu cards. Some etiquette writers did not approve of menu cards in private homes, feeling they were more suitable for public banquets. However, menus were so obviously useful in allowing diners to gauge how much of each course to eat that they were very common.

In high-fashion dinners the menu was always written in French. This was not always done at middle-class formal dinners as many could not read French. As one etiquette writer put it, "If the diner did not read French, the menu might as well be written in Choctaw." She encouraged her readers to write the menus in English. Yet even for her the pull of fashion for "proper" menus was so strong that she provided French menu terms for the use of hostesses who did not know French. See the glossary for her list of French terms.

Surviving examples of menu cards are surprisingly small—about four inches to five inches tall by three inches wide. Between being small, in French, and in the hostess's often bad handwriting, many times they must not have been much help to the guest.

The menu items were written one to a line, centered on the page. If a vegetable or potato was served with the main dish, this item was listed on its own line, also centered. This makes it hard to tell if one's peas were being served with another food, or as a separate course. To avoid this problem the menu would sometimes have a small centered dash between each course. Occasionally hostesses would use menu cards that listed the course—soup, roast, and so on—as a major division between the list of the foods to be served. But, this was not common in private homes as the small size of the menu left little room for this information.

The paper the menus were written on was about the stiffness of ordinary writing paper, which makes it doubtful that menu holders were used. The Victorians did have specially made menu holders, and these tend to hold the menu about six inches off the table. This was necessary to see the small menu cards. The main disadvantage of these menu holders is that the metal clamps that hold the menu in place cover up part of the writing, thus defeating the purpose of the menu.

A more common system of presenting the menu was to simply put the menu on top of the napkin, if the napkin was laid flat on the plate, or next to the plate. Some hostesses used small porcelain sheets on which the menu could be written and then erased. These sheets could then be used over and over again.

In recreating menus for modern Victorian dinners, use stiff note cards that can be found at local stationery stores. These cards are typically 5½ inches by 7½ inches and often have a design around the border. Most stationery stores today have a machine that will write out a message in script. These are designed for party invitations, but they work well with menus. Having a machine write the menu is far easier than having the hostess try to write out the menus by hand and ensures that the menu will be legible. Being stiff, these menu cards can be held up by the metal place card holders that can be purchased at department stores or gift shops.

An example of such a menu is shown in the table settings that follow in chapter 12. Victorian menus normally had the date of the dinner as the first line, but this was not universally followed.

PLACE CARDS

Place cards are still relatively easy to find today in card or stationery stores. They typically measure 1⅞ inches by 2⅞ inches to 2⅜ inches by four inches on the writing face. Some come folded and some are a single sheet. The Victorians often used this type of card for their formal meals. They would often be laid on a napkin folded flat on the plate.

They also used place card holders, which would sit above the plate. Figure 11.5 shows examples of place card holders.

When writing the name on a place card at a formal meal the proper form is the title and the last name—for example, Mr. Jones or Miss Smith. The exception one most likely ran into was the case of an English knight whose title would be "Sir" and the first name—for example, Sir John.

Figure 11.5 Place card holders and place cards.

THE INDIVIDUAL SETTING

The individual setting was referred to as a cover. In the eighteenth century the cover was rather minimal. Glasses for the beverages were not a major part of the table setting. Often there were no glasses on the table, or at most one for the wine the diner was drinking. Servants replaced glasses as the diner needed them. The extra glasses were kept on the sideboard, often in bowls of water to keep them cool and clean.

During the Revolutionary period, glasses became a more normal part of the table setting; but, their number was still limited. There was little point in putting out several glasses for the entire meal when the tablecloth was going to be removed before the next course was served. Removal of the tablecloth meant that everything on the table would have to be picked up and then replaced. The number of glasses and silverware put on the table was kept to a minimum to limit the amount of work the footmen had to do.

When service *à la Russe* became the norm, the tablecloth was not removed, and now it made sense to put all the glasses on the table at one time. During the period 1860 to 1900 there were often six or more wine glasses facing the diner as he or she came to the table (Figure 11.6).[10] One writer referred to this array as a forest of glasses.

The glasses were normally placed above the knives and spoons. If there were more than three or four glasses on the table they were likely to be placed in two rows. The first row would have the glasses one would use first, sherry, white, and claret. The back row would have the burgundy and champagne glasses. The water glass would be placed at the top of the row just above the tip of the

Figure 11.6 A forest of glasses—formal dinner circa 1899. (State Dining Room, President McKinley's State dinner for Admiral Dewey in 1899. White House Collection, courtesy White House Historical Association.)

meat knife in a position where it could be reached at any point in the meal.

On the continent of Europe, the custom was to line the glasses in a straight line across the top of the plate. This setting was sometimes adopted by American hostesses.

The silverware was placed around the plate—forks on the left and knives and spoons on the right. Sometimes the dessert fork and spoon were placed crosswise above the dinner plate. Up to about 1750 to 1770 in England and America, the forks and spoons were placed face down as is still done today in France. This presented the back of the instrument to the diner as he or she sat down. For this reason the back side on French silverware is the side with the pattern, and is where monograms are placed.

Then around the middle of the 1700s in English-speaking countries, the style of the handle changed for spoons and forks. Eating utensils at this period had a rather pronounced central tip. Prior to the middle of the century the tip had turned down, but now the tip of the handle turned up. This meant that the instruments would need to be placed on the table face up, rather than face down, or they would be resting on the point of the handle and would be unstable.[11]

Number of Forks

The 1880s were a period of transition from the old French service, where basically everything was on the table to the new service *à la Russe* where food was served from the sideboard or directly from the kitchen. There was apparently a period of uncertainty about exactly how these meals *à la Russe* should be served and how the table should be set for them. The rule in this time period seems to have been to place three forks and a fish fork—for a total of four forks—on the left with corresponding knives to the right.[12] The forks would have been the fish fork, a fork for the removes, a fork for the game course, and a salad fork. As the number of courses was reduced by dropping the game course, the rule controlling the number of forks on the table became the modern norm of three forks. The right hand side of the plate would have three or four knives, depending on whether one was set for the salad course, a soup spoon, and a oyster fork. (The oyster fork does not count as a fork.)

When the fourth fork was banished from the proper dinner table, this affected the spacing of the table setting. It became common to have tighter place settings so more people could be placed at the table. The usual rule was twenty to twenty-five inches between the center of the plates. This usually gave ample elbow room. The silver would be laid out in the space between the plates. The silver was normally placed one inch from the edge and totally straight.

NAPKINS

Writers in etiquette books of the Victorian period are full of warnings against elaborate napkin foldings. As often happens, etiquette writers issue jeremiads or ukases against a practice because it is quite common. But, in spite of these decrees there is room for napkin folding at a Victorian dinner.

The problem lies in what is an elaborate napkin folding. If a napkin is very heavily starched and folded while still wet, it can be bent into almost any shape. Napkin folding had been quite an art in earlier times. The French kings had special napkin folders on their staff who created fantastic shapes for the royal table. It was considered a breach of propriety to actually use one of these creations to wipe one's hands. The idea of napkins as purely ornamental objects had dropped away during the the late seventeenth century, when placing a napkin on the table had gone out of fashion. By the mid-nineteenth century some hostesses and restaurants were again bending their napkins in the shape of birds or other similar fantastic shapes. Several things seemed to have bothered people of the Victorian era about trying to use a heavily starched napkin at a meal: the possibility that the napkin might still be damp, and the idea that a servant's possibly dirty hands had been all over the napkin. Advising aspiring hostesses not to use overly elaborate napkin foldings was a way of telling them to avoid these problems.

However, that does not mean that all napkin folding was untoward. This is fortunate because a simply folded, standing napkin lends an undeniably festive air to a table setting.

Whether or not this type of fold was used depended on the year. In some periods the napkin would be folded into a standing shape, and at other times it would be folded flat and laid across the plate or even on the forks.

Napkin Rings

Napkin rings had no place on elegant formal dinner or lunch tables. The purpose of the napkin ring is to identify a napkin used at a previous meal so the same person can reuse it. This was done in a family context where it really did not matter if a person had used the same napkin two or three meals running. A guest was something else. He or she would have been horrified at the appearance of napkin rings on the table as it carried the connotation of a napkin saved and not washed from a prior meal.

Refolding Napkins

After a formal meal the diner did not refold the napkin upon leaving the table. The refolding of napkins was sometimes done in family settings when it was intended that the napkin be reused at the next meal. To suggest this would happen after a formal meal was anathema, and guests laid the napkin loosely to the side of the last plate on the table at the end of the meal.

Types of Napkins

For dinner a special large napkin was used. It was white and often had the family's cipher (that is, interlocked initials) embroidered on it. This embroidery was done in white thread, and was rather small, as it was considered vulgar to have a large or colorful cipher, which would call attention to the family.

The napkins the Victorians used were much larger than those in use today. Mrs. Beeton, a noted writer on household management in the mid-nineteenth century, stated dinner napkins should be thirty-inch squares.[13] Because of their size it was considered proper to leave the napkin folded in half when placing it on one's lap.

Luncheon napkins in the late Victorian period, 1860–1900, were the same size as dinner napkins.

During the Edwardian period a special smaller napkin for lunch became common. In this period napkins came in three sizes. Breakfast napkins were seventeen to twenty-two inches square, luncheon napkins twenty-three to twenty-seven inches, and dinner napkins twenty-nine to thirty-one inches. By the 1920s these had shrunk to thirteen to seventeen inches square for luncheon napkins and twenty-four to twenty-eight inches square for dinner napkins.[14]

The breakfast-sized napkin was often used for tea, although some preferred a special fringed napkin.[15]

TEA TOWELS

One occasionally hears the term "tea towel" in connection with household linens and this causes some confusion. A tea towel was not used as part of the tea service. Rather it was a dainty linen towel put out for the women who came to teas to dry their hands after washing them in the water closet. Tea towels were often part of a bride's trousseau and many times had the bride's maiden initials embroidered on them.

NOTES

1. Georgiana Reynolds Smith, *Table Decorations: Yesterday, Today and Tomorrow* (Rutland, VT: Charles E. Tuttle Company, 1968), p. 143.

2. Margaret Visser, The *Rituals of Dinner* (New York: Penguin Books USA, 1991), p. 162.

3. Smith, *Table Decorations*, p. 145.

4. Visser, *Rituals of Dinner*, p. 163; Louise Conway Belden, *The Festive Tradition*, (New York: W. W. Norton & Company, 1983), p. 85.

5. Foster Coates, "How Delmonico Sets a Table," *Ladies Home Journal* 8 (November 1891): 10.

6. Ibid.

7. Belden, *The Festive Tradition*, p. 14.

8. Visser, *Rituals of Dinner*, p. 165.

9. Belden, *The Festive Tradition*, p. 6.

10. Sometimes there were as many as thirteen different glasses used. One manual on fine dining, *The Epicurean*, gave the following directions. When first setting the table, place in front of the plate or on the right the following: (1) water, (2) white wine, (3) sherry, (4) hock, (5) champagne, and (6) bordeaux glasses. Then before serving the entrees, remove the white wine, sherry, and hock wine glasses and replace them with the following: bordeaux and burgundy glasses.

With dessert put out glasses for dessert wines. This in itself could mean another two or three glasses. After that could come another two glasses for the cordials. Charles Ranholfer, *The Epicurean* (1893; reprint, New York: Dover Publications, 1971), p. 5.

11. Belden, *The Festive Tradition*, p. 24.

12. Florence Howe Hall, *Social Customs* (Boston: Estes and Lauriat, 1887), p. 76; Julia M. Bradley [James Bethuel Smiley], *Modern Manners and Social Forms* (Chicago: James B. Smiley Publishers, 1889), p. 166.

13. Linda Hetzer, *The Simple Art of Napkin Folding* (New York: Hearst Books, 1980), p. 6.

14. Ibid., p. 32.

15. Hall, *Social Customs*, p. 96.

V

The Formal Meal as a Performance

Chapter 12

The Progression of the Meal

SERVICE OF THE FOOD

The period when the service *à la Russe* was coming into wide use was a time of transition and there was uncertainty on how the meal should be served. It was the French custom to eat each element of the meal separately. This practice was followed until the Prussians beat the French in 1870. The French lost status, and Americans were less likely to follow French customs. When the French custom was followed, peas or cucumber would not be served with the fish or meat but rather would be served separately as its own course. Some people thought it was unhealthy for the digestive system to mix food on one plate and then eat them together. (The idea was that the stomach had an easier job if it was digesting only one food at a time.) This custom was occasionally carried so far as to not eat mixed salads. It could explain why the Grant administration had such a reputation for gluttony.

It was fairly easy to reach twenty courses if the potatoes, cucumbers and peas were eaten as separate courses. This also placed a strain on the footmen as they would need to serve prepared plates to the guests, rather than allowing the guests to choose their own portion, if the meal was not to be too long. It also meant that the staff was preparing the next course while the first course was eaten, and there was strong pressure on slow eaters to finish their dish as one person could create a bottleneck that would make the meal last interminably long. This also explains the French custom of having knife rests on the table and keeping forks and knives from one course to another. If the vegetables were being served as different courses, it would take an incredible number of knives and forks to serve a table if new silver was issued for each course. This expense could be reduced if guests would but hold on to their knives and forks and use them at the next course.

There was another way around the large number of knives and forks on the table when service *à la Russe* was beginning. That was to have the knife and fork brought in at the side of the plate, normally an empty plate, when it was carried out from the kitchen. Then the guest would simply take the knife and fork from the plate and put one on either side of his or her individual place setting. The etiquette books of this period strongly stressed the necessity to the guest to be alert and to take the knife and fork off the plate. If forgotten, it interfered with the smooth flow of service. In time placing the silver on the plate fell out of use as it forced the guest to take an affirmative step.

The everything-on-the-table French or English method had been used for several hundred years, and it did not easily fall out of favor. There were numerous attempts to introduce what was called a combined service. People could see the advantage of service *à la Russe*, but they thought that the homey touches of one person helping another was something worth keeping; therefore what they would do is serve the early courses—soup and fish—from the sideboard and then set the joint or the game in front of the host, who would cut the pieces off individually. This had the advantage of allowing hosts and hostesses to continue to exhibit their hard-earned carving skills and also made it a little friendlier as there was more interaction between the guests and the hosts, as they would ask which portion each would like.

SERVICE PLATES AND CHARGERS

The terms "service plate," "place plate," and "chargers," and how to use them, produce a great deal of confusion as today these terms are often used interchangeably. The Victorians and Edwardians did not use chargers.

Service Plates

Victorian etiquette books are silent on the subject of service plates. It was assumed that the first plate on the table would be the oyster plate, which was set on the table before the guest entered the dining room.[1] The books then blandly state the soup is served next. The first service plates show up on White House inventories in 1918. However, service plates predate World War I. Lenox China got into the china business in 1902 by making service plates as a sideline to its normal product line of vases and other art china. The service plates were for show and were not meant to be eaten off of or to rest under another plate. These plates were very elaborate, heavily banded with gold, and often had a gold coat of arms or initials on them. A dozen service plates in 1905 cost between $200 and $500. This was in comparison to regular dinner plates that cost between $12 and $17 per dozen. Some people used service plates of sterling silver.

Use of Service and Place Plates

The service plate as an expensive show item was on the table when diners first entered the room. It would normally then be removed when the next course was served. Sometimes the service plate would act as an underplate for the soup or oysters.

For the middle class, often the service plate was the dinner plate so there was no need to remove the service plate. A wide-rimmed soup plate would simply be placed on the dinner plate. When the soup was finished, the soup plate would be removed. The dinner plate would then just be left in front of the diner for the fish course.

If the service plate was left under the oyster and soup plates, it would be replaced by a plate for the fish.

If an hors d'oeuvre course was to be served between the soup and the fish courses, the dinner or service plate would be replaced by a plate for the hors d'oeuvre, and a plate for the fish course would replace it when it came time for the fish course.

By 1922 Emily Post, who favored the Edwardian practice, gave two hard and fast rules on dinner service. One, there must always be a plate in front of the diner. Two, a plate with food on it could never be substituted for one that had been eaten off of. For most of the meal this did not cause a problem as an empty plate was placed on the table, and the food, meat, fish, and so on were carried around by the servers for the guests to help themselves. It would then be replaced by a new empty plate and the process repeated.

Problems could arise in following these rules if a course was served already on the plate. An empty exchange plate would have to be placed on the table before the plate with the food could be laid out.

Sometimes a hostess did not put out empty plates and have the footmen serve from the side. Rather footmen put out plates with the food already on it. This was done to speed up the meal as it was far more efficient and easier on footmen. This is the type of service used in restaurants.

Today the use of a charger offers a nice approximation of the old rules of always having a plate in front of a diner, and always replacing a plate with food on it for an empty plate.

Chargers

In contrast to the use of service or place plates is today's use of chargers, which go under the plate with the food and stay on the table. This was not a Victorian practice. The use of permanent underplates seems to have developed for informal meals in the 1960s. At this point they were still being referred to as service plates, but they were not being used as the Edwardians had used service plates.[2] This was perhaps seen as a way to dress up the one-course meals that had taken hold in the 1950s and 1960s.

The term "charger" began showing up in newspaper articles, but not in etiquette books, in the 1980s. Chargers were described as large plates—about 11½ to 13 inches in diameter. They had designs on the outside edges that would show when another plate was put on them.[3] Several designers brought out lines of these underplates, often made of metal. During the 1980s the function and use of these new items was perfectly captured in an article where they were considered analogous to place mats. Their use was contrasted to traditional service plates, which were removed after the first course.[4] Having a plate on top of a charger fit in with the layer-on-layer look then being developed by designers.

One article stated that people began adopting them at home because they were used to seeing them in restaurants. By the 1990s the White House was using chargers in its state dinners.

There are one or two practical problems with using a charger throughout the entire meal if several courses are served. First, the charger may become soiled from drips and this is unsightly. Second, some of the courses, terrapin, Roman Punch, sherbert, salad, and so on, may require smaller plates. It looks silly having a large charger under these small plates. One answer is to use several chargers during the course of the meal. By removing the charger when a small plate is brought in one avoids the silly sight of a small plate on a huge charger. Then another charger can be put on the table for later courses that use larger plates. This has the added advantage of keeping the charger fresh and clean. Another option is to place a larger plate between the charger and the small plate. This fits in well with today's layered look in table service.

HOW THE INDIVIDUAL SETTING LOOKS AT EACH STAGE OF A DINNER *À LA RUSSE*

Figures 12.1 through 12.16 show a table setting at each stage of a typical *à la Russe* multicourse meal.

Figure 12.1 Individual place setting as diner first sees it. Six glasses and nine items of flatware. (Menu in background.)

Figure 12.2 Oyster course. Napkin has been removed and oyster plate brought in. Note oyster fork on right resting in the bowl of the soup spoon.

Figure 12.3 Soup course.

Figure 12.4 Fish course. Sherry glass has been removed.

Figure 12.5 Joint course (Remove course). White wine glass has been removed.

Figure 12.6 First entree (terrapin) course. Terrapin pot and fork together with a butter pat to hold the terrapin pot lid have been brought in.

Figure 12.7 Second entree (ramekin) course. A ramekin fork and plate have been brought in.

Figure 12.8 Sherbet course. A sherbet spoon has been brought in and red wine glass removed.

Figure 12.9 Game course.

Figure 12.10   Salad (asparagus) course. Burgundy glass has been removed. Note new flatware has been brought in.

Figure 12.11   Cheese course. New flatware has been brought in and a new wine glass put out. This is a good time to drink the wine left over from earlier in the meal.

Figure 12.12 Sweet (mousse) course. Table is cleared and crumbed (crumbs swept away). This sweet is served in a bouillon cup. A dessert spoon has been brought in.

Figure 12.13 Ice cream course. New flatware has been brought in.

Figure 12.14 Dessert (fruit) course. Fruit knife and fork have been brought in and champagne glass removed.

Figure 12.15 Finger bowl.

Figure 12.16 Demitasse (after dinner coffee) and cordial. Demitasse cup and spoon, and cordial glass have been brought in.

NOTES

1. Florence Howe Hall, *Social Customs* (Boston: Estes and Lauriat, 1887), p. 76. Mrs. John Sherwood, *Manners & Social Usage* (New York: Harper & Brothers, 1887), p. 241.

2. Arlene Hirst, *Every Woman's Guide to China, Glass and Silver* (New York: Arco, 1970), p. 51.

3. The use of the term "charger" for a plate goes back to the Middle Ages. During that period, a charger was a large plate put on the table with food for several diners on it. The normal ration was one charger for every four to six diners. They would then transfer food from the common plate to their individual plates.

4. Home Section, *Los Angeles Times*, October 30, 1986.

VI

Giving an Elegant Dinner

Chapter 13

Giving a Victorian or Edwardian Dinner

This is the chance to put it all together, the china, silver, glasses, food, and wine. Think of it as a play, where you and your friends will be playing the part of the grand dames and gentlemen of one hundred years or more ago. There are several different players: those who are putting on the dinner, the guests, and the people helping.

Almost everyone will be a little nervous and unsure of themselves. The important thing is to not let errors bother you. The Victorians had the same problem. For most of them large formal dinners were an unusual event and there was always the chance the people helping, or the guests, would make a mistake or break something. Every Victorian etiquette book reminds readers that they should never show that anything bothered them—not plates breaking, footmen spilling soup, or anything else.

You can help ensure that things go smoothly. First, do not in any way try to give people the idea that this is how you live normally. You do not, and to act otherwise will only make you seem pretentious. Second, remember that as little as you may know, it is likely your guests will know less. We have found our guests feel more at ease if we take a minute to tell them what the silver is and what to use at different points in the meal. This has the added advantage that if they know what to use they will know when to place it on their plate, and it will be easier for the waiters to take it away.

The dinners are complex operations, so diners should not ask for seconds or to keep drinking one particular wine for several courses. Leaving a wine glass on the table when that glass is being removed around the rest of the table will create problems for servers.

On the other hand, the meal should be fun. Do your best to follow the Victorian and Edwardian table rules, but do not worry if you make a false step.

The people serving the meal are also uneasy. Almost everyone wants to do a good job, and when they see all the food, wines, silver, and so on, they are almost always nervous. This is why good, detailed directions are so important. The Victorians would hire a head butler or housekeeper who knew what to do, and he or she would teach everyone else, often including the lady whose newly rich husband made it all possible. She was, in theory, the mistress of the house, but often the butler, fresh from a great house in England, called the social shots. You do not have this resource. Give the servers written directions, and time to read them. Everyone we have ever worked with has said that when they saw the table, the silver, and the food they were scared, but once they had read the directions it was not hard.

We always take a little time to talk after the meal is over. Actors always like to talk about a missed cue or how an error was avoided. It is fun to talk with the people who ate the meal and those who served it. Both normally have funny stories about how they, at some point, did not know what to do, and how they finessed their way past the problem.

SERVANTS

Before we present the directions for the performance, we should consider assembling the cast. What about the servers, cooks and other personnel needed to operate a Victorian household?

The Victorians did not have the labor-saving devices we take for granted today—no washing machines, vacuum cleaners, and so on. What they did have were servants—or at least the upper and middle classes had them. It took a large number of servants to run a household or serve a formal meal. England had a tradition of people working as servants, and up to World War I a large percentage

Figure 13.1 The dress
of a household domestic
circa 1900.

of the population was in service. In 1851, in England 13.3 percent
of the employed population, men and women, were servants. This
had risen to almost 16 percent by 1881.[1]

Servants were much more likely to be women than men (Figure
13.1). In England in the 1890s, one-third of all women between
fifteen and twenty years of age were servants.

In the United States 50 percent of all female wage earners were
in domestic service in 1870. This fell to about 33 percent in 1890,
and 17 percent in 1920.[2]

In the United States where opportunities were greater because
of a lack of a strong class system, the frontier, and a rapidly expanding economy, fewer people were willing to go into service.
Households that needed servants depended on immigrants, who
had trouble finding work when they came to the New World. In
the years when there was heavy immigration it was easier to obtain
servants. The Victorian period saw heavy waves of immigration so
even middle-class households could obtain servants to help the
woman of the house with the heavy, constant, back-breaking job
of running a home. Later it was harder to find servants. In New
York City the number of servants per 1,000 families in 1880 was
188. This had dropped to 141 in 1900 and 66 in 1920.[3]

Most servants were first-generation immigrants. In 1900 60.5

percent of Irish-born wage-earning women in the United States were servants. But among the second generation only 18.9 percent were.[4] Domestic service was unpopular, which is why only new immigrants with few options followed this profession. In 1897 it was reported that former domestics rated waitressing, fruit picking, and factory work above household service.[5] This was in marked contrast to England where household service was an honored occupation and children followed their parents generation after generation into this field.

Cost of Servants

How much money did a household spend on servants? There are two references that give a rough idea. The wages and income numbers have been converted into today's value. This computation is by necessity a rough one as it is hard to achieve exact equivalent numbers. And it should be remembered that these numbers do not directly correlate to comparative living standards.

The following are typical annual wages for help in 1907.[6] The second column shows an approximation of this pay in today's dollars.

WAGES PER YEAR

	1907	Today
Chef from Paris	$5,000	$84,350
Maid	$ 240	$ 4,050
Butler	$ 900	$15,200
Footman	$ 625	$10,500

In reviewing these wages it should be remembered that normally servants lived in their employer's house so they received room and board. Their work clothes (uniform) were also usually provided by the employer. In many cases servants were as young as thirteen so they were in effect apprentices.

The average annual income in the United States during this period was about $7,000 in today's money, while $1 million during this period was worth about $17–18 million in today's money. If a millionaire's money was just invested in bonds he would be paid interest each year of about $500,000 in today's money. This amount should be doubled because there was no income tax.[7] So a millionaire could easily afford extensive household help.

In 1861, Mrs. Beeton, a writer on household management, set out approximate wages for servants and household help in England. The numbers below are rough. The normal exchange rate of $5.00 equals one pound sterling is used. She gave a range, and the chart below takes the mid-point of that range.

WAGES PER YEAR[8]

	British	American	Today
Cook	£30	$150	$2,700
Butler	£38	$190	$3,400
Footman	£30	$150	$2,700
Under-footman	£16	$ 80	$1,432
Maid	£14	$ 70	$1,300

These are but a few examples of the many different servants employed. Mrs. Beeton described a wide range of household help: cook, kitchen and scullery maid, butler, footman, page, coachman, stable boy, valet, lady's maid, parlor maid, housemaid, dairy maid, and laundry maid.

When one compares the wages in England and the United States one can see why people immigrated to the New World. The difference in wages between the two was not necessarily caused by inflation. The value of the dollar was exactly the same in 1860 and 1899. There had been inflation in the United States during the American Civil War. In 1865, it took $1.96 to equal an 1860 dollar. But, the monetary history of the rest of the nineteenth century was one of deflation from the high reached in 1865. Rather, at least in the United States, it was a case of rising standards of living. A bricklayer earned $1.53 per day in 1860 and worked sixty hours per week. By 1899 he earned $3.60 per day and worked forty-eight hours per week.[9]

Mrs. Beeton also provided a helpful list of how many servants one should have in England when one earned a certain income. In 1888 if one had an income of £500 a year ($43,000 in today's money), one would have a cook (not Paris trained, of course), housemaid, and a footboy or nursemaid. An annual income of £1,000 ($86,000 in today's income) called for a cook, upper- and under-housemaids, and a man-servant. Again it should be stressed that income went much further in Victorian and Edwardian times as there was not any income tax in England. The upper middle class, physicians, country squires, barristers, and business owners had an income of £1,000 to £2,000 per year. The middle of the middle class, doctors, solicitors, civil servants, and senior clerks had an income of £300 to £500 per year.[10] Thus even in England it took a great deal of household income to be able to afford a butler and several footmen.

It was much harder in the United States where servants' wages were higher. The answer for most people who wished to give a formal dinner in the United States was to hire the servers from an agency. This option offered several advantages in that the people were used to waiting on tables and so would know just what to do at the dinner. The negative part of this system was that a visitor was likely to see the same people serving at dinner after dinner. One Englishman visiting the United States during the Victorian period was said to have joked about how American servants all looked the same. With the servants costing less in England, a household was likely to have less need to hire outside servers.

The Work of Servants

Mrs. Sherwood, writing in the 1880s, stated that servants nowadays expect every other Sunday afternoon and evening off, and hard as that is on the mistress they must be given it. But, she went on, the least the servants could do was to get up at 5:00 A.M. to get in two hours of good work before it was time to prepare the breakfast and lay the table at 7:00 (the normal time to get up and start work was 6:00 A.M., or an hour or so before the family woke up). After cleaning up the breakfast and doing more work, and serving and cleaning up lunch, she could have her half-day off.

A maid with an indulgent mistress might be free in the evenings after eight o'clock. But most worked until after the family went to sleep.

SERVERS TODAY

The availability of servers, or rather lack of them, is part of what doomed the Victorian lifestyle. It will be one of the difficulties encountered in giving a Victorian dinner today. An excellent source of servers is students at the local college. Other sources are high school students, and if all else fails one can network, for example, try the children of your friends. All of the people who helped us said it was fun to see how this type of meal was put on.

We do not put the burden on our helpers to do any cooking. They need only to warm precooked food, put it on the plates and carry it into the dining room. That is quite enough work for anyone. Food can be prepared ahead of time or bought from a store that sells precooked meals and dishes. Since the served portions in the dinner will be small, one dish can be divided among several people. The store may even package the food in small portions.

SERVICE À *LA FRANCAISE*

In the United States prior to the Civil War the normal method of service was *à la Francaise* where the food was placed on the table family style and then passed by the diners among themselves or passed by the servants. Thus this was the method of service used in the antebellum plantation South (Figure 13.2). What follows is a description of how to serve a dinner *à la Francaise*,[11] which works well with a *Gone with the Wind* theme dinner party.

Dinner *à la Francaise*—Waitstaff Directions

Helping at a dinner *à la Francaise* is very different from serving a meal today. All the food is on the table and all the servers will really need to do is take fresh plates and glasses off the side table and carry loaded plates from one place on the table to another. Mostly the servers will be standing in back of the diners waiting for a signal that someone needs help. In a way, this is tiring for the servers, who will not have a chance to sit down while the diners are eating.

The servers will do the following:

- The hostess will ladle soup into the bowls that are stacked near her and the server will carry the soup bowls to each diner.
- When the soup is eaten, the hostess will ask the server to bring in the fish. The server will clear away the soup and the underplates.
- While one person is placing the fish in front of the host, another will put a stack of plates by his side. The host will put the fish and other food on the plates, and the server will carry them to the different diners.

Figure 13.2 Before the Civil War dinners *à la Francaise* were served at Southern plantations.

When people are done eating, carry away each diner's plate.

One server then removes the master fish plate and one removes the soup tureen.

- The hot meats are then brought in and one is put in front of the host and another in front of the hostess. One server will stand by each person and hand a plate to the host or hostess as he or she carves the meat, and puts the meat and vegetables on the plate. The server then carries the plate to the diner the host or hostess indicates and that diner will say what other foods he or she wants off the table. The server goes to that food and either loads it on the plate or has one of the other diners assist him or her.

- After that, the server stands by behind the diners ready to help if called upon. A diner may ask for another type of food off the table or want a new wine glass and another type of wine. The server may do very little as the diners will often help each other, even pouring more wine for one another.

    If a diner wants a new plate before trying a new food, supply one from those stacked up on the side table.

- Eventually, the diners will eat their fill of what is on the table. The hostess or host will signal the server to remove the food and the top tablecloth. To do this takes teamwork. First, remove all the food—leaving only the decorations, the flowers, and so forth. Then, two of the servers position themselves, one at either end of the table, and start to roll up the tablecloth. The rest of the servers stand by to pick up any table decorations that are on the table as the rolled-up tablecloth gets to them. The decorations are then put back on the cloth remaining on the table. (The table has two tablecloths on it—one on top of another.)

    A server takes the rolled-up tablecloth out to the kitchen and drops the crumbs into the sink, and then folds up the cloth.

- Servers put another round of food on the table, using the chart the hostess provided before the dinner started. One server places a stack of plates next to the meat the host and/or the hostess will carve.

- Servers will then stand at either end of the table—one by the host and the other by the hostess.

- A server takes the food the host or hostess hands him or her to the person the host or hostess indicates. Then the server will help fill that person's plate as requested with additional foods from those set out on the table. The balance of the meal the server stands waiting to help—as was done with the first course.

- When the diners are finished eating, the servers remove everything from the table, roll up the tablecloth, take it to the kitchen, shake out the crumbs, and fold it as before.

- Then they take out the finger bowls and the underplates and place them in front of each diner. They next bring out the fruit and place one piece of fruit on each plate and put it in front of each diner.
- When the guests are finished eating, the server takes away the used plates, silver, and finger bowls.
- The women will move to another room at this point. One of the servers will take tea to them in the drawing room together with cups and other serving needs.
- Another server will put a glass in front of each male diner along with a small plate (Figure 13.3).
- A port decanter and a bowl of walnuts will be put in front of the host. The servers leave the room and do not come back until specifically asked to do so by one of the men.
- Servers should, however, stand by to help the ladies with tea by bringing more hot water, cookies, and so on.

SERVICE À *LA RUSSE*

The method of service normally used after the American Civil War was service *à la Russe*. This is what most Americans think of when they think about a Victorian or Edwardian meal. It has come to be regarded as the ideal elegant meal.

There were two types of service followed in service *à la Russe*. The most common was to place an empty plate in front of the diner for each course of the meal. A footman would then offer a platter with the food for that course—meat, vegetables, sauce, and so on, and the diner would serve him- or herself. The problems with this method were twofold. First, it slowed down the meal as everyone waited their turn to serve themselves. Second, it lent itself to accidents. Sauce could be tipped over and spilled down the front of a dress or meat knocked to the floor. These accidents were a traditional method of revenge that footmen used against overbearing people. These types of accidents occurred naturally often enough that it was never clear whether or not the servant had done something on purpose. In the service *à la Russe*, as soon as the diner was through eating, his or her soiled plate was removed and a fresh one for the next course put out. This was necessary as one of the rules of formal service *à la Russe* was that there was always a plate in front of the diner until the table was cleared for dessert.

Another method was to have the food put on the plate by the kitchen staff, or the butler, and then served to the diner. This was

Figure 13.3 The table cloth was removed for the dessert course, and for drinking port after the dinner. (*The Dinner Party* by Henry Sargent. Courtesy, Museum of Fine Arts, Boston. Reproduced with permission. © 2000 Museum of Fine Arts, Boston. All Rights Reserved.)

far less common, but not unknown. The big advantage to this was that it made the meal go faster. This was a prime goal at a time when a meal could run four to five hours if not expeditiously served. This method was faster, but it had its own problems. In order to always have a plate in front of the diner, the soiled plate would have to remain on the table until the next course was served. Many Victorians followed a cult of purity and sanitation, so the sight of a soiled plate was very distasteful to them. They carried this fetish to the extreme of having a soiled plate taken away the second the diner stopped eating or even put his or her eating utensils down to converse. Some hostesses made such a point of serving a meal rapidly that the diners were constantly uneasy lest their half-eaten plates of food be snatched away from them.[12]

Today, the method of having the food placed on the plate ahead of time is probably best. Americans are used to this style from restaurants, and the sight of a companion's used plate does not bother them as much as it bothered the Victorians. In addition, Americans are not used to serving themselves from a platter held on their side even if the waiter tries to hold it low. Accidents are very likely to happen. There is also a danger of accidents from untrained wait staff who try to hold the platter flat as the diner takes his or her portion. If, however, a host and hostess have access to wait staff who are used to serving meals this way, it enhances the ambiance of the meal.

Also, keep in mind that this method of having the diners serve themselves greatly slows down the meal. This can be a problem as diners today do not have the endurance of their ancestors. Sitting too long at the table, no matter how delicious the meal, becomes fatiguing. In addition, people today, unused to so many courses, are likely to take too much food from the serving platter in the early courses and become uncomfortably full before the meal is half over.

What follows is a description of how a Victorian *à la Russe*–style dinner was served in modern times to a small group of guests. Because of the need to adjust for the garlic flavor of the escargot, the order of the courses was slightly different from the typical order of a Victorian meal set out in chapter 12 and elsewhere in the book. This shows how the order of the entrees, the side dishs, can be moved about. Note the usage of chargers to give the dinner a layered look for today's guests. Just for fun, food pushers were put on the plates to be used with the peas to help get them on the forks.

Dinner *à la Russe*—Wait Staff Directions

Service *à la Russe* is very complicated. Following are a sample menu; directions for serving the food; directions to be followed in the kitchen; general guidelines; directions for serving the wine; and directions on how to place food on the plates.

SAMPLE MENU

March 6, 1999

Consomme

Salmon with Dill Sauce
Cucumbers

Terrapin[13]

Lamb Chops
English Peas

Escargot

Calvados

Chicken Timbales

Sherbet

Duck with Orange Sauce
Petite Potatoes

Asparagus

Cheese

Tokay

Chocolate Mousse

Vanilla Ice Cream

Fruit   Coffee   Bonbons, and so forth

DINING ROOM CHART

SERVE FOOD FROM LEFT—REMOVE FROM RIGHT
SERVE DRINKS FROM RIGHT—REMOVE FROM RIGHT

	SERVE	**REMOVE**
A. (in living room)	• Pour: champagne	
	• Serve: strawberries	glass
		strawberry forks and
		so forth

	SERVE	**REMOVE**
1. SOUP		
	• Pour: sherry	
	• Serve: filled soup plates	
		soup plate
		soup spoon
		sherry glass
2. FISH		
	• Pour: white wine	
	• Serve: fish plate	
		white wine glass
		fish plate
		fish fork and knife
		charging plate
3. CELERY	• Put out: terrapin under-plates	
	• Pass: celery boat	
4. TERRAPIN	• Serve: terrapin cup and lid	
	• butter pat plate (for lid of terrapin pot)	
	• terrapin fork	
		terrapin cup
		lid
		butter pat plate
		terrapin fork
		white wine glass
5. LAMB		
	• Pour: red wine (red wine glass)	
	• Put: charging plate on table	
	• Serve: meat plate on charger plate	
		meat plate
		meat knife and fork

6. ESCARGOT

• Serve: escargot plate
and underplate
escargot fork

escargot plate and
underplate
escargot fork
small red wine glass
charging plate

7. CALVADOS

• Serve: Calvados glass
and underplate
• Pour: Calvados

Calvados glass
underplate

8. MEAT PASTRY

• Serve: pastry plate
pastry fork

pastry plate
pastry fork

9. SHERBET

• Serve: sherbet cup and
underplate
sherbet spoon

sherbet cup and
underplate
sherbet spoon

10. GAME

• Put: small charger on
table
• Pour: red wine
• Serve: small meat plate
on small charger

red wine glass
meat plate
meat knife and fork
flat sauce spoon

11. SALAD

• Serve: asparagus

Salad plate
Salad knife and fork

Small charger
salt and pepper

12. CHEESE

- Put: fork and knife on table
- Place: cheese plate in front of each person
- Place: big cheese plate on left of man to left of hostess
- Place: nut plate on left of hostess
- Put out: wine goblet (goblet to the right of person)
- Ask: which type of wine a person would like and pour it—pour from the right
- Put: open wine on table on right of host

cheese plate
cheese knife
cheese fork
wine goblet
wine bottles

13. TOKAY

- Put out: underplate
- Serve: fill Tokay glass

Tokay glass
underplate

14. SAVORY

- Put out: underplate and put spoon on table on the right
- Serve: mousse cup
- Pour: champagne (tall glass)

mousse cup and
  saucer
underplate
small spoon

15. ICE CREAM

    Put: rounded ice cream
       fork on table on the left
    Serve: ice cream glass and
       underplate with cookie

                    ice cream glass
                    under plate
                    ice cream fork

16. FRUIT

- Put: fruit on the plate
- Serve: fruit plate with fruit fork and knife on the plate (fork on left and knife on the right of fruit)

                    fruit plate
                    fruit knife
                    fruit fork
                    champagne glass
                    nut cup

17. FINGER BOWL

- Place: finger bowl and underplate in front of each person

                    finger bowl
                    underplate

18. LIQUEUR

- Place: underplate in front of each person
Put: filled liqueur glass on underplate

                    Ask if person wants more liqueur with coffee. If yes, move glass and underplate to glass area. If no, take away glass and underplate.

19. COFFEE

- Place: coffee cups, saucer, and spoon (spoon on right of person— serve from the right)

— 229 —

- Place: cream and sugar
  on left of woman to
  right of host (serve
  from the left)
- Pour: coffee (pour from
  the right)
- Put: chocolates on left
  of hostess and stand by
  to pass them around

coffee cup and spoon

B. After dinner:
   (in living room)

Set out: liqueur glasses
          liqueur bottles
          ice bucket

KITCHEN LIST

Directions for three servers, numbered 1, 2, and 3. The number by each direction shows which person does what.

A. AFTER EVERYONE IS HERE AND JUST PRIOR TO DINNER
- (2)   Put in ice and pour water (up to 1 inch below top)
- (1)   Light candles
- (1)   Make sure lights are turned down to dim
- (2)   Make sure nuts are in nut cups (at top of plates)
- (1)   Give nod to hostess to let her know table is ready

---

1. SOUP
- (3)   Dish out soup
- (1)   Open sherry
- (1)   Pour a little sherry in soup
- (2 & 3)   Serve
- (1)   Start warming terrapin at 325 degrees

2. FISH
- (1)   Open white wine
- (1)   Cucumbers on plate (from refrigerator)
- (2)   Pour white wine at table
- (3)   Fish on plate (from refrigerator)
- (3)   Sauce on plate (a lot), on the fish

(2 & 3)   Serve

(3)   Start warming meat and peas at 325 degrees

3. CELERY

    (1)   Put out terrapin underplates

    (2)   Pass celery

4. TERRAPIN

    (2)   Put terrapin fork and small pat dish on table

    (3)   Put seafood mixture into terrapin dish

    (1)   Put terrapin dish on underplate

    (2)   Serve (point handle to the *left* and put forks on *right* of plate on table)

5. LAMB

    (3)   Put chargers in front of each person

    (1)   Open red wine

    (1)   Pour red wine at table

    (2)   Put lamb and English peas on plates

    (2)   Put food pusher on plate at 9 o'clock spot

    (2 & 3)   Serve

    (1)   Put 5 escargot shells in holes in each escargot plate

    (1)   Start warming escargot at 350 degrees—warm for about 15 to 20 minutes

6. ESCARGOT

    (3)   Put escargot fork on right of each underplate

    (1 & 2)   Put escargot plates on underplates

    (1, 2, 3)   Serve

7. CALVADOS

    (1)   Open Calvados

    (1)   Put Calvados glass on underplate

    (1)   Take underplate and Calvados to table

    (2)   Pour Calvados into Calvados glass at table

    (3)   Start warming pastry at 325 degrees

8. MEAT PASTRY

    (1)   Put warmed pastry on plates

    (1)   Put pastry forks on *left* of plate (do in kitchen)

    (2 & 3)   Serve

9. SHERBET

    (1)   Spoon sherbet into cups and put cups on silver plates

    (1)   Put spoon on *right* of plate

    (2 & 3)   Serve

    (1)   Start warming duck and potatoes at 325 degrees

10. DUCK
   - (2)   Put *small charging plate* on table
   - (1)   Open red wine
   - (1)   Put duck and potatoes on china plates
   - (1)   Put sauce on duck
   - (1)   Pour red wine
   - (2 & 3) Serve (put china plates on charging plates)

11. SALAD
   - (1)   Put asparagus on plates
   - (1)   Add dressing
   - (2 & 3) Serve

12. CHEESE
   - (1)   Uncover cheese on serving plate
   - (3)   Place wine glasses on table (on person's right)
   - (2)   Put fork and knife on table
   - (1)   Put individual cheese plates (empty) on table
   - (2)   Take big cheese plate with cheese to dining room
   - (1 & 3) Take out wine (white and red wines) to table and ask what person wants—pour what person wants ½ full (put bottles on empty spots on table near host)

13. TOKAY
   - (2)   Put underplates in front of each person
   - (1)   Open Tokay
   - (1)   Pour Tokay into Tokay glass in kitchen, about ⅔ full
   - (2 & 3) Put Tokay glass in front of each person

14. SAVORY
   - (2)   Put underplates in front of each person
   - (3)   Put spoon on right of person
   - (1)   Open champagne
   - (1)   Take mousse out of refrigerator and uncover
   - (1)   Pour champagne
   - (2 & 3) Serve one per person

15. ICE CREAM
   - (2)   Put rounded fork to left of place
   - (3)   Spoon ice cream into silver and glass sherbet dishes and put on underplate
   - (1)   Add cookie to right of plate
   - (2 & 3) Serve
   - (1)   Pour more champagne if needed: ask if wanted

16. FRUIT
   - (1)   Put fork on *left* and knife on *right* of fruit plates
   - (3)   Put fruit on plates
   - (2 & 3) Take out loaded fruit plates

17. FINGER BOWL
     (2)   Put lukewarm water in finger bowl; put cloth doily on un-
              derplate; put finger bowl on cloth
     (1)   Add 3 rose pedals to water
     (2 & 3) Take finger bowls to dining room and put in front of each
              person

18. LIQUEUR
     (2)   Take liqueur underplates to dining room and put in front
              of each person
     (3)   Pour liqueur in small silver glasses
     (1 & 2) Take liqueur glasses to dining room and put on underplate
              in front of each person

19. COFFEE
     (2)   Take coffee cups and spoons to dining room (spoons on
              person's right)
     (3)   Pour coffee
     (1)   Take cream and sugar to dining room (on left of woman to
              right of host)

B.   AFTER DINNER
     (3)   Set out in living room (while people are having coffee in
              dining room):
              liqueur glasses
              liqueur bottles
              ice bucket

ODDS AND ENDS

1. There is a lot of time and few dishes, so there is no rush.

2. Carry one plate or glass per hand, if the course has 2 plates PLATE
   AND UNDERPLATE)—for example, sherbet, ice cream, and so on—
   carry just those two each trip.
   When carrying soup, pastry, sherbet, ice cream, and fruit plates use
   both hands, hold level with both hands.
   When there is a plate with a spoon or a knife and fork, carry one
   plate per trip—hold level with both hands.

3. Leave swinging door between kitchen and dining room open when
   taking things into dining room or cleaning off a course.
   Leave swinging door closed while people are eating. Be careful when
   opening door! Pull it open into the kitchen.

4. When cleaning off a course do not stack up dishes when taking them back to kitchen.

5. Pick one person to be the wine person. That person will open and pour the wine throughout the meal.

6. Wrap wine and water bottles in a cloth when pouring.
   Pour water up to 1 inch from top.
   Pour wine glasses ⅔ full.

7. Serve food from the LEFT and remove from the RIGHT.

8. Pour and serve drinks from the RIGHT and remove from the RIGHT.

9. Check periodically to see if people need more wine or water.

10. In serving food, be careful not to hit people in the head with an elbow. Try to use outside hand if possible.

11. In clearing the table, after taking the glasses to the kitchen just pour out the drink, and set glass on counter. Don't rinse out. With plates just put scraps in waste and stack dishes in their old place on the counter. Don't rinse them off either. Silver should be wiped clean and put flat on counter, but not stacked up.

12. The big silver plates are the charging plates; one is taken off after the fish, the lamb, and other courses.
    There is also a small charging plate; it is brought out with the duck course.
    First dinner plate comes off with soup plate.

13. When the hostess buzzes for the next course, don't panic.[14]

14. When removing plates and pouring wine, start with hostess—she can give advice.
    Give host just a little bit of wine, host will taste it. When he says okay, fill up everyone else's glass and then fill up host's glass.
    There are two rows of glasses. Place the water glass above the knives and then lay glasses out in this order:
    Top (back) row (left to right):
    Water
    Champagne
    Red (burgundy) wine (big/tall)
    Bottom (front) row (left to right):
    Red wine
    White wine
    Sherry
    Fill glasses 1 to 6 in this order:

1. Water

2. Sherry

3. White wine (white wine glass)

4. Red wine

5. Red wine (big/tall glass)

6. Champagne (tall)

Remove glasses in this order:

1. Sherry

2. White wine

3. Red wine

4. Red wine (big/tall)

5. Champagne (tall)

6. Water

DIRECTIONS FOR LOADING THE PLATES IN THE KITCHEN

A. Strawberries
   • 6 to 8 per bowl so they look nice

1. Soup
   • Fill bowl ⅔ full
   • Take to table—put on dinner plate
2. Salmon
   • Put 1 piece fish on plate with cucumbers
3. Celery
   • Put celery in celery dish
4. Terrapin
   • Fill in each terrapin pot and put on lid
5. Lamb Chops
   • 1 lamb chop
   • 1 ½ tablespoons peas
   • Put food pusher on plate at 9 o'clock point
6. Escargot
   • Put 5 escargot shells in each escargot plate
   • Heat escargot in oven at 350 degrees for about 15 to 20 minutes or until butter starts to bubble
   • Put escargot plate on dinner plate
7. Calvados
   • Fill glass ⅔ full
   • Carry glass and bread-and-butter plate to the table

8. Chicken pastry
   - Chicken salad heated in pastry shells—fork on left side of plate
   - Take to the table

9. Sherbet
   - Fill egg cups full
   - Silver egg cups on silver bread-and-butter plates, which go on table
   - Spoon on right

10. Game
    - Put 3 to 4 strips of duck on plate
    - Pour sauce over duck
    - Put 5 to 6 small potatoes to side of duck

11. Salad
    - 4 asparagus spears, all turned same direction with vinaigrette sauce spread on top

12. Cheese
    - Cheese on glass plate
    - Biscuits on round plate
    - Fork on left of round plate
    - Knife on right
      Wine (left over from earlier courses)
    - Bring to table with cheese

13. Tokay
    - Take Tokay in green glasses to table
    - Silver plate under glass

14. Savory
    - Chocolate mousse in refrigerator
    - Put in silver/china 2-part dishes
    - Bread-and-butter plate goes on table first

15. Vanilla Ice Cream
    - Put in silver sherbet dishes
    - Bread-and-butter plate under sherbet dishes
    - Fill ⅔ full
    - Serve with 1 pirouette on bread-and-butter plate

16. Pears
    - Serve pear on plate
    - Knife on right of pear
    - Fork on left
      Nuts
    - Nut Refill nut cups on table

17. Finger bowls
    - Fill ⅔ full with lukewarm water
    - Put in 3 rose petals

18. Liqueur
    - Fill silver glass

19. Coffee
    - Serve with chocolate candy or petit fours

---

20. Liqueur
    - Served in living room after dinner
    - Take out ice

NOTES

1. Sally Mitchell, *Daily Life in Victorian England* (Westport, CT: Greenwood Press, 1996), p. 50.

2. Thomas J. Schlereth, *Victorian America* (New York: Harper Perennial, 1992), p. 71.

3. Ibid., pp. 71–72.

4. Ibid., pp. 73–74.

5. Ibid.

6. A dollar in 1907 is worth about $13.00 today. *This Fabulous Century, Volume 1, 1900–1910* (New York: Time-Life Books, 1988), p. 220; Ed Scott Derks, *The Value of a Dollar* (Lakeville, CT: Grey House Publishing, 1999); U.S. Department of Labor, Bureau of Labor Statistics, Consumer Price Index—All Urban Consumers 1982–1984.

7. The income tax was introduced in the United States in 1913.

8. Isabella Beeton. *The Book of Household Management*, rev. ed. (London: Ward, Lock & Co., 1861), p. 6.

9. A dollar in 1899 is worth about $17.90 today, the same as in 1860. See Derks, *The Value of a Dollar*, 1860–1999; U.S. Department of Labor, Bureau of Labor Statistics, Consumer Price Index—All Urban Consumers 1982–1984.

10. Mitchell, *Daily Life in Victorian England*, pp. 33–34.

11. Also called *à l'Anglais* because the English kept on using this style of service into the 1880s—long after the French (and the Americans) changed to *à la Russe*.

12. On speed in removing plates, see generally Mary Henderson, *Practical Cooking and Dinner Giving* (New York: Harper & Brothers, Publishers, 1887), p. 20; Florence Howe Hall, *Social Customs* (Boston: Estes and Laurait, 1887), p. 81.

13. This is not really a terrapin, but rather a seafood medley with some turtle.

14. Rather than use a bell, a battery-operated, wireless doorbell set can be used. The buzzer is put in the kitchen, wrapped to deaden the sound. The hostess can keep the ringer in her lap and use it as needed. This is far less intrusive than using a bell.

VII

Other Elegant
Entertaining

Chapter 14

Tea, Coffee, and Chocolate

HISTORY

We normally think of tea and a tea party as a British institution steeped in centuries of tradition. The truth is more interesting than this.

Tea, as a beverage, was first developed as were so many other items—paper, gunpowder, porcelain, and silk—in China. For centuries China was the only source of the product. The Europeans had little or no acquaintance with the drink until after the Portuguese, under Vasco da Gama, sailed around Africa and reached the Indies in 1497.

The Portuguese, and then the Dutch, shipped tea back to Europe as a medicine for sale in apothecary shops. Gradually, people began drinking the beverage for its refreshment and stimulant value. The first sale of tea took place in England in 1657.

Tea was introduced into England as a "social" beverage when the Portuguese princess Catherine of Braganza wed King Charles II in 1662. The ladies of the court began sipping tea in imitation of this royal fashion.

At about the same time, coffee was introduced into England from the Middle East, where Arabs had drunk it for centuries. It is said that Nathaniel Conopios, a student at Oxford who was a native of Cyprus, introduced coffee to his fellow students in 1637. London's first coffeehouse opened in 1652. At first coffee was much more popular than tea and coffeehouses became the rage; cliques developed around different coffeehouses. One would be the home to writers, another to newspaper men, and still another to merchants. Lloyds of London, the insurer of ships, Rolls Royces, and a movie star's legs, got its start in a coffeehouse that catered to merchants in the shipping business.

Then the tide turned, and tea replaced coffee as the beverage of choice in England. No one is really sure why this happened. One theory is that tea was imported from the Far East by the East India Company, a large business with ties to the nobility, who still were the powers in England. Coffee, on the other hand, was imported from the Middle East by a host of small companies, run by middle-class merchants. Then, as now, large companies with close ties to those in political power dominated trade. And, of course, it probably did not hurt that tea was the drink of the nobility and coffee the drink of artists and the middle class. Whatever the reason, England changed from a nation of coffee drinkers in 1700, to a nation of tea drinkers by 1750.

This had a dramatic effect on world history because of the simple fact that for years the only source of tea was China. In the days before the Industrial Revolution, Europe produced little that was of interest to China, or indeed the Far East. Early products shipped east by the East India Company consisted of woolens, saltpeter, and tin. (Saltpeter was used for making gunpowder and tin for making bronze, mostly for cannons. They carried woolens because the government had passed a law that a certain percentage of each ship's load must be woolens. This was done to protect the woolen producers, a key English industry.) There was not much profit to be made in these products, as woolens were not in high demand in warmer countries that had access to silk from China and cotton from India. Saltpeter and tin were commodity items.

Thus, to buy tea and other eastern products so much in demand in England, the East India Company had to ship silver to the East. The problem was particularly acute when it came to tea. China did not want anything from the West except silver, so silver drained out of England. The efforts of the East India Company to solve this profit-limiting state of affairs had two major effects on world history. First, the company used its political ties to maximize the price for tea, and limited its transport to company ships. This was the cause of the Boston Tea Party and sparked the American Revolution. The other untoward effect came from the English trying to find a product the Chinese did want. This turned out to be opium, which could be grown in the parts of India that they controlled. It was grown in India, shipped to China on British ships, and then sold to the Chinese—either through normal legitimate trade routes or by smuggling. In time, China became a nation of drug addicts. China, of course, tried to stop the flood of drugs coming into the country—with many of the same methods being used in the United States today. However, it did not succeed because the British government supported the drug merchants, and China did not have the military power to overcome the British. From then on, the silver flowed one way—out of China to pay for opium. England was not the only country engaged in the drug trade—only the most successful as it controlled a nearby source of supply. For years, the Americans had to go to Turkey to get their opium to trade to the Chinese for tea and other products.

In time, the English were able to break the Chinese monopoly on tea. In 1823, they found wild tea plants growing in the mountains of Assam, in northeast India, and a British agent in China, Charles Bruce, was able to recruit and smuggle out some Chinese who could show the British how to grow and prepare the tea. Then, in 1842 and 1848, the aptly named Robert Fortune, a plant collector for the Royal Horticulture Society in London, was able to disguise himself as a Chinese man and travel into the tea-growing areas of China. On his second trip he smuggled out seedlings for shipment to India. The English now could grow both Indian- and Chinese-style teas.

All this industrial espionage and its repercussions were safely removed from England, and unknown to the British people as they enjoyed their tea.

In the early 1800s, tea was drunk morning, noon, and night by all classes of society. It, with its caffeine and lacing of sugar, was a stimulant almost unique in a simpler time largely devoid of non-alcoholic stimulants.

The concept of tea as an afternoon social ritual did not come to the forefront until the 1840s. During this period, the main meal of the day was dinner, eaten at about seven or eight o'clock. This left a long void between lunch at noon and dinner.

One noble lady, Anna, Duchess of Bedford (1783–1857), found this just too long a period to go without nourishment. She began secretly drinking tea and nibbling on bread, butter, and sweets in her boudoir at about four o'clock in the afternoon. This secret imbibing is traditionally dated to 1840. Her indulgence was found out, and her friends began joining her. With a duchess and her social set doing it, afternoon tea soon became fashionable.

Later, the time for the tea and snack break was moved back to five o'clock. Teatime for children stayed at four o'clock. And since these people lived in style, the simple act of eating and drinking tea became an elegant occasion.

TYPES OF TEA PARTIES

A tea covers many types of activities. These range from an intimate "cuppa" with one or two friends, to rather formal gatherings with three separate courses of food, and on into large open houses where a buffet is spread out.

There are a confusing number of terms for teas, and remarkably little uniformity to their names. One generation will refer to "kettledrums," another to "at homes" or receptions. There are afternoon teas, high teas, and clotted teas. There are teas held at four o'clock, five o'clock, and six o'clock.

For the sake of clarity, in discussions of how tea was taken in the United States, the terms will be used as follows: A five o'clock tea is the most informal. The kettledrum comes next and then the reception or "at home." These denote the degree of formality in the dress and the service, not in what was served.

Afternoon teas, kettledrums, and receptions merge into each other by almost imperceptible gradations, and often the dividing line depended on local usage or even the views of the hostess. Clearly at some point the duties of leading conversation, waiting on guests, and pouring tea became too much for the hostess. First, servants or family members would help, and then it became necessary to have other ladies pour at a large table, most commonly the dining room table. Emily Post arbitrarily set the dividing line for the large table at twenty guests. In the same way, up to a point, a larger number of guests allowed for more elaborate foods to be offered (i.e., more courses), and then the number grew so large that a simple buffet-style layout was necessary.

A tea, at its most intimate, would consist of a few friends, and one to three items of food. The food would be cakes, cookies, toast, or sandwiches.

Occasionally, a hostess would have a really large at-home "open house" or reception. The term varied over the years and from town to town. Today, the term "open house" carries the connotation of alcoholic drinks and finger food. In the Victorian period, alcohol was more frowned upon and the serving of tea and food was more common. In the 1870s and 1880s there was an institution called "kettledrums." It is not clear where this term came from—some say from the custom of army wives using regimental drums as tea tables for their feminine gatherings. Others say the term comes from the incessant racket of many merry people talking at once.

In the United States today, the very formal afternoon tea, with several courses of food, is normally referred to incorrectly as "high tea." In Britain, a high tea is a supper where hot or cold meats are served. It is traditionally thought of as the activity of working-class families who eat their main meal at midday and now are closing the day with a light meal. The tradition also appears in country houses as a light meal to be taken in the late afternoon following tennis, boating, riding, and so forth. As such, it is a form of buffet with friends picking up the tea and food as they came back to the house and eating and drinking together in a congenial manner.

In the past, in the United States, the term "high tea" originally referred to a somewhat more hardy form of tea, often taking place at six o'clock. In some towns it was an entertainment given on Sundays when the servants were not available.

More meat was the main addition in an American high tea. These might be little grilled sausages on toothpicks, grilled sardines on toast, fish balls, chicken livers wrapped in bacon, or anything else that might be served today as heavy hors d'oeuvres.

Teas have always been the domain of women. Men seldom infringe on this activity, at least in the United States. A tea evokes images of delicate teacups, dainty food, silver, and elegant, composed ladies in subdued but gay conversation.

FOOD AT A TEA

The classic formal tea has three courses. There are two different standard menus. One consists of sandwiches, scones, and a last course of sweets. This is the standard in England. The American version is a hot course (toast or biscuits with a hot filling, cheese toast, and so on). The next course is sandwiches, and finally sweets. The idea in the American system is to have a contrast in taste—hot and spicy, then light and bland, and last very sweet.

Tea sandwiches at a tea are, by tradition, very light finger food—very thin slices of bread, with the crust removed, that are cut into finger, triangle, or even heart shapes, with a cookie cutter. The traditional sandwich is dainty and exotic—with cucumber, walnut, cream cheese and olive, and asparagus sandwiches being common.

Scones are the heart of an English tea. The scones can be eaten plain, but are normally taken with jam and clotted cream.[2] The English mini-meal closes with sweets. Rather bland sweets are taken with the scones' menu. Pound cake and shortbread cookies are a perennial favorite, but in reality, any pleasing cookie or cake can be served. If the American non-scone menu is followed, the "desert" is very rich—chocolate cake or tortes.

The food at a tea was to be dainty, no more than a bite or two. Most of the time, it was to be finger food, cookies, small cakes, sandwiches, and so forth. Of course, if something larger or gooey was served, a fork would be offered. Knives were needed for spreading jellies and jams. Butter was normally not served, any butter being placed on the toast in the kitchen.

SETTING

Tradition dictates a "setting" for a formal tea as surely as it dictates a setting for dinner.

The tea table is covered with cloth of nice linen and with a tea tray on it. If no tea tray is available just put the teapot, dishes, and food directly on the tablecloth.

Figure 14.1 shows a rather formal afternoon tea laid out for a small group of friends. The idea is to bring all the equipment out on one tray, but of course, today, in houses that no longer have strong footmen or butlers, this is not possible. In that case, the tray is brought in with as much as can be conveniently and safely carried, and extra trips are made as needed. As can be seen, the tray is in the center with the kettle in the back. The teapot sits directly in front of it. The cream and sugar containers are set to the right of the kettle. The lemon is on the left.

The lemon can be cut in conventional wedges or very thin slices. Each has its advocates and detractors as neither method is without flaw. The wedge, when squeezed, leaves a residue of juice on the hand and shoots out droplets of lemon acid that can land in unfortunate places. The slice of lemon is not squeezed, but put in the cup. It looks nice, but gets in the way when sipping. A special

Figure 14.1 Tea table set for a formal afternoon tea.

utensil was developed to solve the problem of the lemon wedge coming into contact with the hand—the silver lemon squeezer. This was more refined than touching the lemon, but did not solve the problem of shooting out drops of lemon juice.

The tea caddy sits toward the back after its contents have been placed in the teapot. (The term "caddy" comes from the Malay word *Kati* or *Catty*, which was a standard unit of measure of about 1⅓ pounds. Tea was packaged in units of one *Kati* when sold to the Europeans. Each *Kati* also had a small seashell packed with it, which is why tea scoops often have a seashell motif.) A dreg or slop bowl and the strainer are set out on the right.

There are no rigid requirements about the ordering of this layout. It is merely convenient for a right-handed person to have the cream and sugar on her right. A left-handed hostess can reverse the layout without the type of social violation that would come from placing forks on the right of the dinner plate.

The teacups, plates, and silverware are set out around the tray. The layout of the cups and plates depends on what type of plates are used. If a tea saucer and a separate plate for food are used, the combination is stacked one way. If the very convenient *trem-*

bleuse or party pack (see chapter 4 for an explanation of these terms) is used, another system would be followed. The Victorians used special tea plates, but today people simply use their salad plates as plates for tea, failing that a bread-and-butter plate can be pressed into service.

If separate saucers and food plates are used, the saucer rests on a small napkin, about twelve inches square, and this all sits on a slightly larger plate for food.

If a *trembleuse* is used, the plate for the food and the cup for the tea are in one unit. These can be stacked one on top of another with a small napkin on top of each plate. The use of a *trembleuse* means fewer plates for the guest to balance and, thus, removes one of the banes of a tea party—too much chinaware and no place to put it. They are particularly convenient if the plates must be balanced on one's knees. The tea spoon, either a standard tea spoon or the slightly smaller five o'clock tea spoon, is placed on the edge of the tea saucer. A knife rests on the plate. A flat butter knife is very useful here as it does not throw the structure out of kilter, as would a tea knife or a full round butter knife. (See chapter 4 for pictures and an idea of the size of the different types of silver.) There is nothing wrong with having the forks and knives in separate stacks on the tea tray or table if there is room.

As the tea is served, the cup is filled with tea, and sugar, cream, or lemon are added, as requested. The ritual of pouring tea is well known. The stereotyped "milk, sugar, or lemon" question is asked. Then, this is followed by "one lump or two?" How far one can go in offering the perfect cup of tea is shown by the classic account attributed to service at the home of Baron Alfred de Rothschild, although this is sometimes attributed to other English great country homes.

When being offered tea, the guest was first asked, "China, India, or Ceylon?" Upon picking one he or she was then asked, "with lemon, cream, or milk?" If he or she choose milk he or she was then asked what breed of cow was preferred, "Jersey or Hereford?"

Whether or not the milk (or cream) goes in the cup before the tea is a matter of personal preference. While normally referred to as cream, milk is usually put in tea as cream overpowers the tea. It is thought the custom of putting the cream in the cup first arose from a fear the hot tea would break the thin delicate teacup. The cream would dilute the shock of the boiling water hitting the cold porcelain. To put cream into tea first is thought to be a bit gauche.

Some doyennes, older women, harbor quite strong prejudices against the type of people who put their cream in their teacup first. However, some tea connoisseurs prefer to put their cream in first as the hot tea slightly cooks the cream and this is felt to give the drink a better flavor.

The making of hot tea for a proper Victorian tea party did not involve the use of tea bags. They only came into common use in 1904.

Tea, when made from grounds, is poured into the cup through a strainer, as even the most careful packing could not prevent the odd bit of stem from being mixed in with the tea leaves. Those bits the strainer caught were placed in the dregs bowl.

The cup and saucer was handed to the guest together with the napkin. Then, the plate was served with whatever the first course happened to be—either sandwiches, or hot items, or a piece of cake. It was considered more friendly and intimate to have the hostess pour the tea and serve the guests herself. But, one or both of these jobs could be done by a servant, although this was a slight breach of etiquette as the ambiance of a tea was one of intimacy and normally servants and waiters were not in the room. One compromise that was often followed, for slightly larger gatherings, was to have the hostess pour the tea and gentlemen guests or a servant carry the food to the recipient. If gentlemen guests and servants were not present, the guests would come get it themselves.

It was completely at the discretion of the hostess as to whether or not the subsequent "courses" were served on the same plate or a new round of plates were brought out for each "course." Some preferred the more friendly and casual hominess of using the same plate; others disliked the idea of different foods being placed on the same plate. As at a dinner, no one was obligated to eat all three courses.

These rather formal teas were normally no more a common part of a week than were formal dinners. They were special occasions that called for elaborate preparations. Much more common were more casual social gatherings where the hostess might offer a few sandwiches or toast and a cake or cookies.

At a kettledrum or a large reception, the tea and food were set out on a large table, often the dinner table (Figure 14.2). There were typically two women pouring: one for the tea and another for coffee, hot chocolate, or, in the summer, cold punch or lemonade. What the other beverage was varied over the years, but hot

Figure 14.2   Reception tea table.

chocolate was considered more formal and correct, especially in the late Victorian and Edwardian periods. While it meant work, it was an honor to be invited to pour, rather like being invited to be a bridesmaid.

The job of pouring tea was the higher status job. In the military, young wives were always warned to have the person pouring tea be the wife of the highest-ranked officer.

Normally when the table for a reception or kettledrum was set up, the tea would be on the left end as one faced the table and the chocolate or coffee on the right. The other guideline was to place the tea furthest away from the door. But, these were not hard-and-fast rules, and much depended on the layout of the room.

The job of pouring the chocolate or coffee was not quite as high a status job as being a tea pourer. For this reason a person with a little less status was chosen to pour this beverage. The person pouring seated herself at one end of the table, with the cups, saucers, and teaspoons, and so forth in the middle. The food, cakes, cookies, and sandwiches were organized symmetrically in the middle of the table.

Figure 14.2 shows a reception table set up with the tea equipment on the right side, furthest from the door; the cups, plates, and food in the center; and the coffee on the left. At a reception, especially in winter, the blinds were closed and the room was lit by artificial light. In summer the hostess more often chose the sunlight to illuminate the room.

Because of logistical difficulties, it would be less likely that a full three courses would be served at a kettledrum or a reception. The press of people meant that a self-serve buffet type of service would be required.

INVITATIONS

Invitations for a five o'clock tea were often written on the lady's calling card in keeping with the intimate and rather informal nature of the gathering.

On the other hand, an "at home" or reception called for a more formal card.

Mrs. Albert Smith
At Home
on Tuesday, the tenth of May
from four to six o'clock
123 Beacon Street

The term "RSVP" might or might not appear, depending on the social convention at the time and in the city. The British and some Americans did not like the RSVP as it implied the recipient did not have the social grace to know that a response was necessary. Or, it may be that a response was not really necessary. One person more or less at an open house was not all that important. Then, as now, the RSVP was more for the hostess's peace of mind rather than very detailed party planning.

DRESS

The dress of the women depended on the formality of the event. For receptions a rather formal afternoon dress was called for. For the more intimate teas a more comfortable, less corseted dress could be worn. The women wore their "walking-out" dresses and a hat. Everyone, including those pouring, wore a hat. The hostess, since she was in her own home, did not wear a hat. Beginning in the 1880s special tea dresses were often worn. This was more common in England than in the United States. These were cut loose, and made of lighter, more free-flowing material. It does not appear that corsets were worn with them. In style, the tea gown occupied a middle ground between a peignoir and a normal afternoon dress.

Because of their informal nature, the wearing of a tea gown was more common among hostesses and house guests. They did not have to go outside. Because they were casual wear, worn only in the house, a hat was normally not worn when a woman had on a tea dress.

When going out into the street in a day dress, gloves were always worn. Their absence showed a complete lack of breeding. Tea was taken with gloves on if you were a guest, but the hostess did not wear them. The ladies pouring wore gloves as they were in the final analysis guests, albeit honored ones.

If a short-sleeved dress was worn, gloves often reached the elbow. But, it was more common to find shorter gloves with about four buttons. The most typical style was white kid gloves.

Gentlemen, when they attended, often wore "morning dress" in spite of teas being an afternoon affair. This consisted of a black or dark coat, often cut back below the waist, with a high vest to match. They wore dark or gray trousers and a scarf or necktie. Or, a man could wear the frock coat—the long coat so common in Victorian times. If a butler was helping, he wore a normal suit, or, in more formal establishments, he wore a morning coat, as butlers did not wear tails until after six.

When gentlemen attended a tea, they brought their hat and walking stick into the room with them and laid them on the floor next to them. It is not really clear how this custom started. It may have been a way for a male guest to signal to the household he was not making himself too much at home, and did not plan to linger long.

The formal rules on the wearing of hats and gloves at teas were often not followed at small, very casual get-togethers. It is very common to see photographs of intimate teas where the women are without hats or gloves.

ICED OR ICE TEA

Surprisingly, the United States is one of the leading tea-drinking nations in the world. Americans do not drink much hot tea, but consume an incredible amount of tea in the form of tea with ice. This is driven primarily by the South's love of chilled tea. It is interesting to note the different terms used for chilled tea in different parts of the United States. In the North the term is "iced tea." In the South one does not say "iced tea"; to say iced tea implies there is another way to drink tea other than with ice. In this section the term "iced tea" is used unless specifically referring to tea drinking in the South. In the latter case the term "ice tea" will be used.

It is often said that iced tea was invented at the 1904 World's Fair in St. Louis (along with the hamburger, and the ice cream cone). But, iced tea is referred to in an 1887 book on entertaining by Florence Hall, and there is a passing reference to drinking tea with ice in an 1860 book entitled *How to Live*, by Solon Robinson, a New York newspaperman.

As the temperance movement gained force in the Victorian period[3] and in the years leading up to 1920, iced tea became a common drink at ladies' lunches. This increase was aided by the fact that by 1900 almost every town in the United States had a local ice-making plant. As was noted in chapter 4, the widespread drinking of iced tea led to the introduction of the iced tea spoon during this period.

The true southerner drinks ice tea pre-sweetened. The sugar is added to the tea water while it is still hot. This creates a deep, sweet richness to the tea that cannot be replicated by adding the sugar later when the tea is served cold. This is a matter of cultural taste and not everyone loves pre-sweetened ice tea.

PUTTING ON A TEA

Today, teas are enjoying a modest comeback, and entrepreneurs have set up businesses to put on a tea for a busy hostess. They are enjoyed by both young girls and mature women as a chance to dress up, enjoy a novel experience, and recall a more languid and elegant time.

When planning a tea party, the first consideration is the tea. This can, of course, be made using tea bags, which is not a bad idea for beginners. However, it is possible to do as the Victorians did and brew tea right at the tea table.

The perfect tea is brewed as follows: Start with cold fresh water and bring it to a boil. Many people feel cold water is important because it has a higher oxygen content, and this makes the tea taste better. Others feel this is an old wives' tale and regular tap water is fine. Pour the hot water into the teapot to warm the pot. Let it sit a bit and then pour this water out into the sink. The warmed teapot is then carried into the drawing room. Put in one rounded teaspoon of tea leaves for each person, and one more for the pot. Pour in boiling water from a kettle to cover the tea leaves. Always bring the pot to the kettle to ensure the water is as hot as possible. Let it steep for about three to five minutes. Then pour it into the individual teacups through a strainer and add the amount of hot water necessary to dilute the tea as the guest desires.

Numerous hostesses have written that far more important than having high-priced tea leaves, or expensive cream, is taking the care to brew a fresh pot of tea every ten to fifteen minutes. It is hard to follow this regime with meticulous care. It is so much easier to relax, chat, and pour the old, already brewed tea when a guest wants a refill, but it is worth the effort. It is also a good idea to replace the water in the kettle periodically so that fresh water is always being boiled.

Be careful not to let the tea stand in the teapot too long as it can lose its good taste rapidly. Because of this, it is not a good idea to try to make too much tea at one time.

If one wants to make iced tea, the same routine is followed. The only difference is that the tea is stronger when put in the pitcher or glass to make up for the dilution of the ice.

Southern Ice Tea

The method of making southern ice tea is different. The water is brought to a boil and poured into a container. Then tea bags and sugar are added to the *very* hot water and the whole mixture is allowed to steep and cool down. Others swear the best method is to bring water to a boil, then remove the pot from the stove and add tea bags. Let the tea bags steep in the hot water for about five minutes then remove the tea bags and pour the hot tea into a large container; add sugar to the hot tea so it will dissolve; and then add enough cold water to make the desired strength of tea.

Be sure the tea is cool before adding it to an ice tea glass with ice in it, otherwise, the shock of the temperature change may shatter the glass.

The making of ice tea was greatly eased by the invention of the tea bag in 1909. Tea bags were developed by accident by Thomas Sullivan, a tea and coffee merchant in New York City. He wanted to promote his mixtures of tea by sending out samples for people to try. To save money he sent out his samples packed in muslin (or silk) bags instead of the small metal cans usually used for samples. To his surprise he was flooded with orders for more of the little bags of samples. People learned they could make tea rapidly by dunking the tea bag in hot water. Because of the popularity of this method of making tea, the tea bags soon were packaged by a machine specifically designed for this purpose.

Thus by 1909 there was everything in place to make ice tea— the widespread idea of chilling tea, the ice, and the tea bag. Ice tea ruled supreme, especially in the South, until air conditioning became common.

Coffee

For the great majority of Americans during the Victorian and Edwardian periods coffee was their everyday drink. As mentioned above, in the elegant kettledrums and receptions tea was the main beverage. But, coffee and chocolate had their place at these events, too.

Victorian etiquette books are careful to tell the hostess how to make proper tea, but typically do not give directions on preparing coffee. Perhaps this was because coffee was a more common drink, and it was assumed that everyone knew how to make a good cup of coffee.

In contrast to tea, which was normally brewed at the table, coffee was prepared in the kitchen and put in the coffeepot. The coffeepot with the already prepared coffee was then put on the table.

In addition to being served at normal meals and receptions, coffee appeared at two other types of formal occasions.

At a formal breakfast coffee was typically offered. The cup used for breakfast coffee was traditionally larger than the everyday tea or coffee cup. (See Figure 14.5 for a comparison of sizes.)

The other time coffee would appear in elegant entertaining was at a formal dinner. A coffee served in a demitasse cup was the traditional end to a formal dinner. When served at such a dinner, the coffee was very strong. The cook would put half the water normally used in preparing coffee. By tradition neither sugar nor cream was added to dinner coffee served in demitasse cups. This rule was often not followed as most after-dinner coffee sets (demi-tasse sets) had matching cream and sugar bowls. This very strong coffee had a stimulating effect on the diner, who was perhaps groggy from the rich food offered at a formal dinner.

Chocolate

Another alternate drink to tea at receptions was chocolate. The hostess could choose whether she wanted to offer coffee or choc-olate in addition to tea at her reception. Many chose coffee, but chocolate was the more formal option.

If chocolate was to be served, the table setup was the same as shown in Figure 14.2. Only a chocolate pot, described in the next section, would be used in place of the coffeepot.

The chocolate served at receptions was quite different from the instant chocolate used today. It was a rich, thick drink.

Chocolate was also normally drunk by the Victorians at formal luncheons. A cup of chocolate with whipped cream was one of the traditional courses for a Victorian luncheon.

Surprisingly, chocolate reached Europe earlier than tea. The co-coa bean is a New World plant and the Aztec nobles drank choc-olate. The Spanish brought the custom of drinking chocolate back home in the sixteenth century and from there it spread to Portugal, France, and Austria. There are several reasons why the drinking of chocolate did not become widely popular in England and hence in the United States.

Perhaps the most important was that for several centuries choc-olate was not sweetened. This made it a bitter drink that was very much an acquired taste. Another factor is that chocolate, when drunk in Spain and France, was taken in the morning. Noble ladies would drink it as they had servants comb their hair, prepare their wigs, put on their make-up, and dress them. There are examples of matching sets of mirrors, brushes, chocolate cups, and pots. Because most people could not afford the luxury of having servants dress them while they drank chocolate and talked with their friends, the drink never caught on. There never developed in England the institution of the chocolate house, unlike the prevalence of coffee or tea houses.

Also Spain, a traditional enemy of England, controlled the source of chocolate. It was easier, and perhaps more patriotic, to drink tea or coffee, which could be obtained from other sources. The last possible element is religion. Chocolate was the drink of Catholic countries and after England became Protestant in the sixteenth century there may have been an unwillingness to drink this "popish" beverage.

Pot Shapes

By tradition there are different shapes of pots used for tea, coffee, and chocolate.

The teapot is short and often more rounded. It is said the teapots used in China took their shape from a melon, and this idea of a lower pot has been carried forward. The exact shape of the teapot in a tea and coffee set will depend on the design element. But, normally a teapot is shorter than a coffee pot.

The coffeepot is taller and less rounded, copying the shape used by the Arabs. By the Victorian period the coffeepot often did not look Arabic, but it was almost always taller than the teapot.

Sometimes the Victorians used a special pot for the strong coffee served after dinner. These demitasse coffeepots were smaller than the regular coffeepot and often retained a marked Arabic look. They normally had a rather tall, slender body with a long pouring spout.

The chocolate pot, by tradition, had a tall columnar shape. Figures 14.3 and 14.4 show these three shapes, as well as that of a claret jug. The jug was used to serve a type of punch made with claret, a light red wine.

Cups

The Victorians naturally had specially shaped cups for the serving of different hot beverages.

The serving of after-dinner coffee called for its own special cup. The demitasse cup was quite small as the after-dinner coffee was so strong that not much was drunk at one time.

During Victorian times, a trace of the special shape, found in the 1700s, for a normal everyday coffee cup was still in evidence. During the eighteenth century there was a difference in the shape of

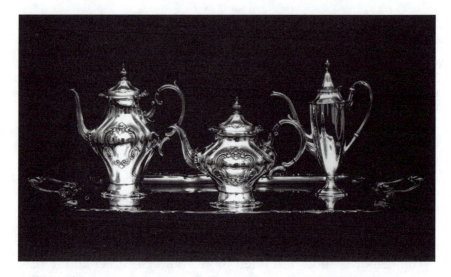

Figure 14.3 Left to right: Coffee pot, tea pot, demitasse pot.

Figure 14.4 Left to right: claret pitcher/jug, tea pot, chocolate pot.

Figure 14.5 Cups. Left to right: chocolate, breakfast, coffee, tea, demitasse, chocolate.

tea and coffee cups. These two shapes are shown in Figure 14.5. As can be seen, the coffee cup is a bit taller than the teacup. However, by Victorian and Edwardian times the custom of using different-shaped cups for coffee and tea had largely disappeared. People simply chose one shape or the other based on personal taste and then used that shape for both coffee and tea.

A separate coffee cup was used for breakfast. The breakfast cup was larger and normally had the special coffee cup shape.

There were two shapes for chocolate cups. One, the more common, was a tall narrower cup that echoed the shape of the chocolate pot. The other shape was smaller than a regular teacup, but with about the same shape. Its size was about midway between a teacup and a demitasse cup. The two shapes can be seen in Figure 14.5.

NOTES

1. Tea was originally referred to as "chu" or "cha," the common name used in most of China. The term "chu" (or "cha") was used by the English until the center of the English tea trade changed from Canton to Amoy where the word was pronounced "T'e." From there it was an easy step to "tea."

2. Clotted cream is a specialty of England and most typically comes from Devonshire. To obtain it, one heats unpasteurized milk until cream forms on the surface of the milk. This layer of cream is removed and when cooled is clotted cream.

3. The first state to pass a law prohibiting alcohol was Maine in 1851.

Chapter 15

Breakfast and Lunch

BREAKFAST

In societies where there are two main meals a day, breakfast is a large meal. This was still true in the United States in early Victorian times in spite of the fact that it was common to have three meals a day.

In 1843, Charles Dickens reported that American breakfast tables had tea and coffee, bread and butter, salmon and shad, liver and steak, and potatoes and pickles.[1]

In 1877, the following bills of fare were given for a breakfast party, which would be held at about nine or ten o'clock. It was served in courses *à la Russe* style (Figure 15.1).

WINTER

1st course:	Broiled sardines on toast.
Drinks:	Tea, coffee, or chocolate.
2nd course:	Larded sweet breads or cold French rolls (i.e., breakfast pastry). Whichever one was served, it was accompanied by French peas (i.e., English peas).
Drink:	Sauterne (i.e., a white wine).
3rd course:	Small fillets of meat on squares of toast, garnished with mushrooms.

Figure 15.1 Table setting for a breakfast in the early twentieth century.

4th course:	Fried oysters and breakfast puffs.
5th course:	Fillets of grouse (or pigeon) on fried mush (or grits in the South), garnished with small potatoes.
6th course:	Sliced oranges with sugar (these are Seville oranges, which are quite tart and bitter).
7th course:	Waffles with maple or other syrup.

SPRING

1st course:	Orange.
2nd course:	Broiled or fried fish, maitre d'hotel or tartar sauce, and potato chips or shrimp and olive mixture.
Drink:	Coffee, tea, or chocolate.
3rd course:	Lamb chops and vegetables.
Drink:	Claret (i.e., a red wine).
4th course:	Omelet with green peas, thin slices of ham, or shrimp.

| 5th course: | Fillets of beef with accompanying muffins or tomatoes and mayonnaise. |
| 6th course: | Pancakes with maple or other syrup.[2] |

These large breakfasts fell out of favor in the 1880s and 1890s as food faddists and medical reformers—such as Dr. John Harvey Kellogg—advocated lighter meals. Some of these proposed completely doing away with meat. Breakfast cereals as we know them today have their origins in the Battle Creek Sanatorium of Dr. Kellogg. It was there that Dr. Kellogg's brother, W. K. Kellogg, developed the methods of production that would form the basis for both the Post and Kellogg cereal enterprises. It also explains why for years most breakfast cereals were produced in Battle Creek, Michigan.

In the 1890s the following was a typical family breakfast:

Grapefruit;

Wheatlet with sugar and cream;

Beefsteak, lyonnaise potatoes, muffins;

Coffee.

Another sample menu was:

Sliced oranges;

Wheat germ with sugar and cream;

Warmed-over lamb, French fried potatoes, biscuit;

Buckwheat cakes with maple syrup;

Coffee.[3]

The table setting for the long 1877 menus described above was *à la Russe* as these were grand occasions. They were very close in concept to what today is called "brunch." For more everyday breakfasts the service was more casual. The breakfast group would serve themselves from food set out on the table or on sideboards. These essential family meals were served earlier, perhaps as early as seven or eight A.M.

In country homes the breakfast would be a type of buffet. The food would be put out and people would serve themselves as they got up.

If one was invited to a formal breakfast, a woman would wear a walking-out dress and a man, a morning coat. While eating, a woman would wear her hat.

LUNCH

In the United States luncheons have preeminently been a ladies' meal since the the country became industrialized and urbanized. The men have generally been too far away and too busy at work to be a significant part of the luncheon proceedings. As such, the meal has been traditionally one of light and dainty foods.

Today these luncheons either strike us as redolent of the stifling existence that women once had, or exercise an almost forbidden allure. How nice it would be to get dressed up, and eat a leisurely meal without having to keep an eye on the clock.

Lunch during the Victorian period was basically a dinner-type meal for women. The food was lighter and the portions smaller as befitted the smaller food needs of ladies with their dainty proclivities.

The table was set like a dinner table and, unless small and informal, served from the side *à la Russe*.

A centerpiece of flowers or fruit with compotes of fruits, bonbons, small cakes, and so on was set down the center of the table. As lunch is a day time meal candles were never lighted unless the weather was very dark.

In the United States bouillon was commonly served as a first course, and a cup of hot chocolate with whipped cream was typically served as a separate course.

Four different menus from the 1870s follow:

1st course:	Bouillon
Drink:	Sherry
2nd course:	Oysters on half-shell on an oyster plate
Drink:	Sauterne
3rd course:	*Vols-au-vent* with meat centers
4th course:	Cuts of fillet of braised beef and French peas
Drink:	Champagne
5th course:	Chicken croquettes and potato croquettes
6th course:	Cup of chocolate with whipped cream
7th course:	Lettuce salad with dressing

8th course:	Cookies and fruit ices (or sherbet)
9th course:	Fruit
10th course:	Coffee and bonbons

1st course:	Oysters
2nd course:	Bouillon
Drink:	Sherry
3rd course:	*Vols-au-vent* of sweetbread
4th course:	Lamb chops with tomato sauce
5th course:	Chicken croquettes and French peas
6th course:	Snipe and small potatoes
7th course:	Lettuce salad
8th course:	Cheese and toasted milk wafers
9th course:	Chocolate molded in little cups with peach marmalade
10th course:	Vanilla ice cream and fancy cakes
11th course:	Fruit

1st course:	Bouillon
2nd course:	Deviled crabs and olives
Drink:	Claret punch
3rd course:	Sweetbreads
4th course:	Fillets of grouse, currant jelly, and potato chips
5th course:	Roman punch
6th course:	Fried oysters with chow-chow
7th course:	Chicken salad (with mayonnaise)
8th course:	Ramekins
9th course:	Wine jelly with whipped cream
10th course:	Neapolitan ice cream
11th course:	Fruit
12th course:	Bonbons and coffee

1st course:	Mock turtle soup
Drink:	English milk punch
2nd course:	Lobster chops
Drink:	Claret
3rd course:	Mushrooms in crust

4th course: Lamb chops

5th course: Chutney on slices of baked fillet of beef

6th course: Chocolate with whipped cream

7th course: Tongue with spinach, tartar sauce

8th course: Roast quail with bread sauce

9th course: Cheese, lettuce with dressing

10th course: Mincemeat pies

Drink: Champagne

11th course: Ices (sherbet or ice cream) and fancy cakes

12th course: Fruit[4]

A lunch served on the Vanderbilt yacht, *Alva*, a few years later, probably in the mid-1880s, had the following menu:

1st course: Eggs

2nd course: Lobster Newburg

3rd course: Tournedos with marrow

4th course: Potatoes, spinach, and asparagus with hollandaise

5th course: Chicken with watercress

6th course: Salad

7th course: Crepes

8th course: Dessert

9th course: Coffee.[5]

In the 1890s the lunches became lighter, more specialized, and less like a smaller version of dinner. One etiquette book[6] described twenty courses of very small servings—paté the size of a silver dollar and elaborate creations of ice cream in the shape of toadstools, or birds' nests colored to match. Other dishes consisted of strawberries in lilies, or sherbet in the form of a flower or candlestick (with burning wick). Also served were little shish kabobs with slivers of chicken, liver, or pork. The food was dainty and interesting to tempt what the Victorians assumed to be ladies' delicate and tiny appetites. With this goal in mind meals might be all green for St. Patrick's Day luncheons, or red for Valentine's Day.

This tied into the Victorian view that women were ethereal creatures. It was thought that they had little or no appetite and had to be tempted by dainty, beautiful, and interesting food presentations.

The period after World War I saw a definite break with this hot house, artificial, and elaborate type of lunch. Emily Post writing in 1922, but generally harkening back to a generation earlier when she was a young hostess, provided the following menu for lunch:

1st course: Soup in cups

2nd course: Eggs or shellfish

3rd course: Fowl and vegetables

4th course: Salad

5th course: Dessert

She noted that in ultra-fashionable New York the menu was usually limited to four courses with either a soup, the second course, or the dessert being eliminated.

Rather than start with bouillon as was the American custom, the French tradition was to begin with eggs—either hot or cold. These might take the form of deviled eggs, soft-boiled eggs, or hard-boiled eggs cut up and put in a cheese sauce, or with chicken livers. Being a French tradition, the eggs were considered the more formal course.[7]

Invitations

The invitation for a luncheon could be either formal or informal depending on the style of the luncheon. If a formal meal was planned, the invitation would be much like that used for a dinner. Since a formal lunch is a sit-down affair, the invitation had to be responded to immediately. For an informal lunch often a short note in the first person was used and it was more flexible. It was still necessary to reply to the invitation, but there was more room for unexpected drop-in guests or visitors.

Table Setting and Dress

In 1887, Florence Hall, one of the leading etiquette writers of her period, noted that menus were not to be used at luncheons,

Figure 15.2   Table setting for a lunch in the early twentieth century.

and normally candles were not on the table as part of the decoration. If they were on the table they should not be lit unless it
was impossibly dark in the room. (Figure 15.2). The silverware,
glassware, and china for a lunch were the same as for a dinner,
with the exception that it was proper to use a bread-and-butter
plate with lunch.

In the 1880s a normal table setting for a luncheon consisted of
two forks, two knives, one or two spoons, a water goblet, and two
wine glasses—one for sherry and one for claret. But for elaborate
lunches three knives and forks, as well as an oyster fork might be
set out (Figure 15.3). As noted above, a bread-and-butter dish and
butter knife would be used.

In the 1880s hostesses were moving away from colored tablecloths for dinners, but they were still sometimes being used for
lunches. During Edwardian times there was a tendency to show
off the wood of the table at a lunch. Place mats would be used,
with perhaps the addition of a runner down the center of the table.
Sometimes full tablecloths of lace or with alternating squares of
solid cloth and lace, called "Army-Navy" cloths, would be used. It
was said, "We dine on Damask but lunch on lace." Sometimes colored tablecloths and matching napkins were used.

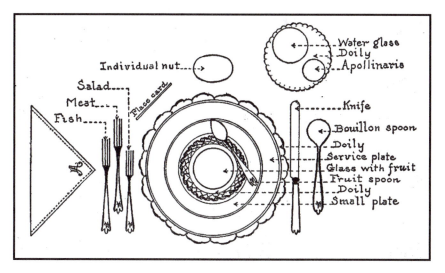

Figure 15.3 Drawing of a lunch place cover in the early twentieth century.

As noted above, menu cards were not used at lunch. Place cards were also not normally used, but if it was a formal meal with a large number of guests, they were sometimes placed on the table as there would be too many guests for the hostess to tell everyone where to sit.

For a formal lunch the men traditionally wore morning dress. By the twentieth century this dress for lunch was limited to Sundays. During the week a man could wear a business suit. The women wore either tailored street dresses or reception dresses. The women would wear bonnets while they ate, but of course would remove their gloves. So strong was the idea of bonnets for lunch that sometimes even the hostess wore one. Emily Post warned against the hostess wearing a hat with a veil.

Etiquette

The men, if present, did not offer their arms to the ladies. The ladies would go into the dining room unescorted, ahead of the men. This was because the women normally outnumbered the men at lunch.

The English tended to have the food put on the table for a lunch and the hostess served the food. This was done by putting a stack of plates in front of the hostess and having her place food on each person's plate from the bowls and platters in front of her. Servants normally were not used for lunch in England.

In the United States the meal was normally served *à la Russe* and servants were necessary. Butlers would not wear tails while serving at a luncheon. Rather, they would wear a black coat, dark but not black trousers, and a black necktie (not a bow tie). The footmen would wear normal footmen's livery.

During the Victorian and Edwardian periods the English did not serve coffee and tea after lunch, but Americans offered them in addition to the wine.

The coffee was served in demitasse cups in the 1870s, but the rule against cream and sugar with demitasse cups was widely broken. The Americans in this period also used finger bowls following the meal, again unlike the British.

Figures 15.4 to 15.11 show the progression of courses for a formal lunch with iced tea in about 1910.

Figure 15.4 Individual place setting for lunch as diner first sees it: two glasses, eight items of flatware, napkin on the plate.

Figure 15.5 Napkin removed and bouillon cup and underplate brought in.

Figure 15.6 Bouillon spoon, bouillon cup, and underplate removed and entree plate brought in. Iced tea has been served and the iced tea spoon used to stir the iced tea. The spoon, after being used, is put on the butter pat which is on the table to keep the wet spoon from either being placed on the table or kept in the glass for the entire meal.

Figure 15.7 Entree plate and one fork removed and meat plate brought in.

Figure 15.8 Meat plate, knife, and fork removed and salad plate brought in.

Figure 15.9 Salad plate, knife, and fork removed and dessert plate brought in. (Knife was used for salad as it is silver plated.) Table is partially cleared—bread and butter set, iced tea spoon, and butter pat are removed. Dessert plate has a finger bowl, doily, dessert fork, and dessert spoon on it.

Figure 15.10 The finger bowl and doily are placed at the top left of the plate by the diner. She also moves the dessert fork and dessert spoon to either side of the plate.

Figure 15.11 The dessert plate, dessert fork, and dessert spoon are removed and the diner moves the finger bowl and doily back in front of her.

NOTES

1. James Trager, *The Food Chronology* (New York: Henry Holt and Company, 1995), p. 233.

2. Mary Henderson, *Practical Cooking and Dinner Giving* (New York: Harper & Brothers, Publishers, 1877), p. 36.

3. Fannie Merritt Farmer, *The Original Boston Cooking-School Cook Book* (1896; reprint, n.p.: Hugh Lauter Levin Associates, 1996), p. 512.

4. Henderson, *Practical Cooking and Dinner Giving*, pp. 37–39.

5. This menu is still at Marble House in Newport, Rhode Island.

6. Florence Howe Hall, *Social Customs* (Boston: Estes and Lauriat, 1887), p. 119.

7. Millicent Fenwick, *Vogue's Book of Etiquette* (New York: Simon & Schuster, 1948), pp. 312–17.

English/French Glossary

SOUPS

Amber or clear soup	*Consomme de boeuf clair*
Soup, with bread	*Potage aux croutons*
Soup, with vegetables	*Consomme aux legumes*
Macaroni soup	*Consomme au macaroni*
Noodle soup	*Consomme aux nouilles*
Vermicelli soup	*Consomme aux vermicelles*
Spring soup	*Potage printanier*
Julienne soup	*Potage a la julienne*
Asparagus soup	*Potage d'asperge*
Ox-tail soup	*Potage aux queues de boeuf*
Chicken puree	*Potage a la puree de volaille*
Chicken soup	*Consomme de volaille*
Mock-turtle soup	*Potage a la fausse tortue*
Oyster soup	*Potage aux huitres*
Bean soup	*Potage a la puree d'haricots*
Onion soup	*Soupe a l'ognon*
Vegetable puree	*Puree de legumes*
Tomato soup	*Potage aux tomates*

Potato soup   *Potage a la puree de pommes de terre*
Sorrel soup   *Soupe a l'oseille*

FISH

Salmon, sauce Hollandaise   *Saumon, sauce Hollandaise*

Salmon, with lobster sauce   *Saumon, sauce homard*
Salmon, with parsley sauce   *Saumon, sauce au persil*
Salmon, with egg sauce   *Saumon, sauce aux oeufs*
Salmon, with potatoes   *Saumon aux pommes de terre*

Slices of salmon   *Tranches de saumon*
Middle cut of salmon   *Troncon de saumon*
Salmon cutlets, with pickles   *Cotelettes de saumon aux cornichons*

Salmon, with cucumbers   *Saumon aux concombres*
Sardines, broiled   *Sardines grillees*
Smelts, fried   *Eperlans frits*
Little trout, fried   *Petites truites frites*
Trout, in shells   *Truite en coquilles*
Salmon-trout   *Truite saumonee*
Trout cooked *au court bouillon*   *Truite au court bouillon*
Codfish, with caper sauce   *Morue a la sauce aux capres*

Codfish, with Bechamel sauce   *Morue a la Bechamel*
Codfish, with potatoes   *Morue aux pommes de terre*

Eels au gratin   *Gratin d'anguilles*
Eels en matelote   *Matelote d'anguilles*
Fresh mackerel, with maitre-d'hotel butter   *Maquereau frais a la maitre-d'hotel*

OYSTERS

Oysters in shells   *Huitres en coquille*
Oysters, fried   *Huitres frites*
Oyster fritters   *Beignets d'huitres*
Oyster patties   *Petits vol-au-vent d'huitres, ou bouchees d'huitres*

SAUCES

White sauce (made with stock)	*Sauce a la Bechamel*
Pickle sauce	*Sauce aux cornichons*
Egg sauce	*Sauce aux oeufs*
Caper sauce	*Sauce aux capres*
Anchovy sauce	*Sauce aux anchois*
Shrimp sauce	*Sauce aux crevettes*
Lobster sauce	*Sauce homard*
Oyster sauce	*Sauce aux huitres*
Parsley sauce	*Sauce au persil*
Cauliflower sauce	*Sauce au chou-fleur*
Madeira-wine sauce	*Sauce au vin de Madere*
Currant-jelly sauce	*Sauce aux groseilles*
Tomato sauce	*Sauce tomate*
Mushroom sauce	*Sauce aux champignons*

MEATS

Roast fillet of beef	*Filet de boeuf roti*
Fillet of beef, larded	*Filet de boeuf pique*
Fillet of beef, with mushrooms	*Filet de boeuf aux champignons*
Braised beef	*Boeuf braise*
Braised beef, with vegetables	*Boeuf braise a la jardiniere*
Beef hash	*Hachis de boeuf*
Beefsteak, with mushrooms	*Bifteck aux champignons*
Beefsteak pie	*Pate de biftecks*
A la mode beef	*Boeuf a la mode*
Pickled tongue	*Langue de boeuf a l'ecarlate*
Mutton tongues	*Langues de mouton*
Saddle of mutton (roast)	*Selle de mouton rotie*
Shoulder of mutton, stuffed	*Poitrine de mouton farcie*
Mutton stew	*Ragout de mouton*
Mutton cutlets, broiled	*Cotelettes de mouton grillees*
Mutton cutlets, breaded	*Cotelettes de mouton panees*
Mutton cutlets, with peas	*Cotelettes de mouton aux petits pois*
Sheep's kidneys	*Rognons de mouton*

Lamb cutlets	*Cotelettes d'agneau*
Lamb croquettes	*Croquettes d'agneau*
Veal cutlets, with mushrooms	*Cotelettes de veau aux champignons*
Veal cutlets, with tomato sauce	*Cotelettes de veau, sauce tomate*
Fricandeau of veal	*Fricandeau de veau*
Liver, broiled	*Foie de veau grille*
Pork cutlets, with pickles	*Cotelettes de porc aux cornichons*
Cold ham	*Jambon froid*
Blanquette of veal	*Blanquette de veau*

SWEETBREADS

Sweetbreads, with macaroni	*Ris de veau a la Milanaise*
Sweetbreads, with tomato sauce	*Ris de veau a la sauce tomate*
Sweetbreads, with peas	*Ris de veau aux petits pois*
Sweetbreads, larded	*Ris de veau pique*
Sweetbread fritters	*Beignets de ris de veau*
Sweetbread croquettes	*Croquettes de ris de veau*

POULTRY AND GAME

Stuffed turkey	*Dinde farcie*
Larded turkey	*Dinde piquee*
Turkey, celery sauce	*Dinde, sauce celeri*
Roast wild turkey	*Dinde sauvage rotie*
Boned turkey	*Galantine de dinde*
Fricassee of chicken	*Fricassee de poulet*
Chicken breasts, with peas	*Filets de poulet aux petits pois*
Roast spring chicken	*Poulets nouveaux rotis*
Chickens, with tomatoes	*Poulets aux tomates*
Chickens, with cauliflowers	*Poulets aux choux-fleurs*
Chickens, with rice	*Poulets au ris*
Fried chickens	*Poulets sautes*
Chicken croquettes	*Croquettes de volaille*
Wild duck	*Canard sauvage*
Pigeon pie	*Pate chaud de pigeons*
Pigeon stew	*Compote de pigeons*

Roast pigeons, with string beans	*Pigeons rotis aux haricots verts*
Roast pigeons, with spinach	*Pigeons rotis aux epinards*
Braised pigeons, with spinach	*Pigeons a l'ecarlate*
Grouse	*Grouse*
Roast woodcock	*Becasses roties*
Roast quails	*Cailles roties*
Prairie chicken, or partridge, cutlets	*Cotelettes de perdreux*
Saddle of venison	*Selle de venaison*
Squabs, with watercress	*Pigeonnaux au cresson*
Pheasant, larded	*Faisan pique*

VEGETABLES

Potatoes, with white sauce	*Pommes de terre a la sauce blanche*
Lyonnaise potatoes	*Pommes de terre a la Lyonnaise*
Potatoes in cases	*Pommes de terre farcies*
Fried potatoes	*Pommes de terre frites*
Parsnip fritters	*Beignets de panais*
Asparagus	*Asperges*
Cauliflowers, with cream dressing	*Choux-fleurs a la creme*
Spinach	*Epinards*
String beans	*Haricots verts*
Mashed potatoes	*Puree de pommes de terre*
Pease, with butter	*Petits pois au beurre*
Stuffed tomatoes	*Tomates farcies*

SHELLS

Chickens in shells	*Coquilles de volaille*
Lobster in shells	*Coquilles de homard*
Fish in shells	*Coquilles de poisson*
Mushrooms in shells	*Coquilles de champignons*

MACARONI

Macaroni, with cheese	*Macarone au fromage*
Macaroni, with tomato sauce	*Macaroni, sauce tomate*

EGGS

Stuffed eggs	*Oeufs farcis*
Poached eggs	*Oeufs poches*
Poached eggs, on anchovy toast	*Oeufs poches aux croutes d'anchois*
Omelet, with fine herbs	*Omelette aux herbes fines*
Omelet, with mushrooms	*Omelette aux champignons*
Omelet, with ham	*Omelette au jambon*
Omelet, with rum	*Omelette au rhum*
Omelet, with preserves	*Omelette aux confitures*
Omelet souffles, with preserves	*Omelette soufflee aux confitures*

SALADS

Chicken mayonnaise	*Mayonnaise de volaille*
Cauliflower mayonnaise	*Mayonnaise de choux-fleurs*
Tomato mayonnaise	*Mayonnaise de tomates*
Salad of vegetables	*Salade de legumes*
Lettuce salad	*Salade de laitue*

FRITTERS

Peach fritters	*Beignets de peches*
Cream fritters	*Beignets de bouillie, or Creme frite*
Oyster fritters	*Beignets d'huitres*

LITTLE VOLS-AU-VENT, OR BOUCHEES

Patties of chickens	*Bouchees au poulet*
Almost any kind of meat patties are called this	*Bouchees a la reine*
Strawberry patties	*Bouchees aux fraises*
Patties, with lemon paste	*Bouchees au citron*
Little tarts of preserves	*Tartelettes aux confitures*
Little tarts of apples	*Tartelettes aux pommes*

PUDDINGS

Cabinet pudding	*Pouding de cabinet*
Rice pudding	*Pouding au riz*

Roly poly pudding	*Pouding roule*
Bread pudding	*Pouding au pain*
Rice pudding, with peaches	*Pouding de riz aux peches*
Apple souffle	*Souffle de pommes*
Apple pie	*Tarte aux pommes*
Chocolate Bavarian cream	*Bavaroise au chocolat*
Coffee Bavarian cream	*Bavaroise au cafe*
Pineapple Bavarian cream	*Bavaroise a l'ananas*

DESSERTS

Blancmange	*Blanc-manger*
Peach compote	*Compote de peches*
Apple compote	*Compote de pommes*
Iced champagne	*Champagne frappe*
Ice cream, vanilla	*Creme glacee a la vanille*
Ices of any kind, generally written in menus	*Glaces*
Chocolate ice cream	*Glace de creme au chocolat*
Madeira-wine jelly	*Gelee au Madere*
Whipped jelly, with fruits	*Gelee fouettee aux fruits*
Champagne jelly	*Gelee au vin de Champagne*
Jelly, with fruits	*Gelee a la macedoine*
Macaroons	*Macarons aux amandes*
Peach marmalade	*Marmalade d'abricots*

NOTE

This glossary is derived from Mary Henderson, *Practical Cooking and Dinner Giving* (New York: Harper & Brothers, Publishers, 1877).

Further Reading

HISTORY OF DINING

American Heritage Cookbook and Illustrated History of American Eating and Drinking. New York: American Heritage Publishing Co., 1964.

Aron, Jean Paul. *The Art of Eating in France*. Translated by Nina Rootes. New York: Harper & Row, Publishers, 1973.

Brillat-Savarin, Jean Anthelme. *The Physiology of Taste, or Meditations on Transcendental Gastronomy*. New York: Alfred A. Knopf, 1972.

Claiborne, Craig, and Pierre Franey. *Classic French Cooking*. New York: Time-Life Books, 1970.

Clair, Colin. *Kitchen and Table: A Bedside History of Eating in the Western World*. London: Abelard-Schuman, 1964.

Cook's and Diner's Dictionary. New York: Funk and Wagnalls, 1968.

Coleman, Feay Shellman. *Nostrums for Fashionable Entertainments*. Savannah, GA: Telfair Academy of Arts and Sciences, 1992.

Cosman, Madeline Pelner. *Fabulous Feasts: Medieval Cookery and Ceremony*. New York: George Braziller, 1976.

Ellwanger, George H. *The Pleasures of the Table: An Account of Gastronomy from Ancient Days to Present Times*. New York: Doubleday Page and Co., 1902.

Grover, Kathryn, ed. *Dining in America 1850–1900*. Amherst, MA: University of Massachusetts Press, 1987.

Hale, William Harlan. *The Horizon Cookbook and Illustrated History of*

Eating and Drinking through the Ages. New York: American Heritage Publishing Co., 1968.

Hammond, P. W. *Food and Feast in Medieval England*. Stroud, Gloucestershire: Alan Sutton Publishing, 1993.

Jeanneret, Michel. *A Feast of Words: Banquets and Table Talk in the Renaissance*. Translated by Jeremy Whiteley and Emma Hughes. Chicago: University of Chicago Press, 1991.

Levenstein, Harvey. *Revolution at the Table*. New York: Oxford University Press, 1988.

MacDonogh, Giles. *Brillat-Savarin*. Chicago: Ivan R. Dee, 1992.

Paston-Williams, Sara. *The Art of Dining*. London: National Trust Enterprises, 1993.

Peterson, T. Sarah. *Acquired Taste: The French Origins of Modern Cooking*. Ithaca, NY: Cornell University Press, 1994.

Roberts, Patricia Easterbrook, and Richard de Rochemont. *Eating in America*. New York: William Morrow and Company, 1976.

Root, Waverley. *Food*. New York: Simon & Schuster, 1980.

Schivelbush, Wolfgang. *Tastes of Paradise: A Social History of Spices, Stimulants and Intoxicants*. Translated by David Jacobson. New York: Pantheon Books, 1992.

Show, Timothy. *The World of Escoffier*. London: Zwemmer, 1994.

Tannahill, Reay. *Food in History*. New York: Three Rivers Press, 1988.

SILVER

Carpenter, Charles H., Jr. *Tiffany Silver*. New York: Dodd, Mead & Company, 1978.

———. *Gorham Silver 1831–1981*. New York: Dodd, Mead & Company, 1982.

Dolian, Maryanne. *1830's–1990's American Sterling Silver Flatware*. Florence, AL: Books Americana, 1993.

Glanville, Philippa, ed. *Silver History & Design*. New York: Harry N. Abrams, Publishers, 1996.

Hood, William P., Jr., Roslyn Berlin, and Edward Wawrynek. *Tiffany Silver Flatware 1845–1905: When Dining Was an Art*. Woodbridge, England: Antique Collector's Club, 1999.

Osterberg, Richard. *Sterling Silver Flatware*. Atglen, PA: Schiffer Publishing, 1994.

———. *Silver Holloware for Dining Elegance*. Atglen, PA: Schiffer Publishing, 1996.

Osterberg, Richard, and Betty Smith. *Silver Flatware Dictionary*. La Jolla, CA: S. A. Barnes & Co., 1981.

Turner, Noel D. *American Silver Flatware 1837–1910*. New York: A. S. Barnes and Company, 1972.

Venable, Charles L. *Silver in America 1840–1940: A Century of Splendor*. New York: Harry Abrams, 1995.

CHINA

Beurdeley, Michel. *Chinese Trade Porcelain*. Translated by Diana Imber. Rutland, VT: Charles E. Tuttle Company, Publishers, 1962.

Gaston, Mary Frank. *Limoges Porcelain*. 2d ed. Paducah, KY: Collector Books, 1992.

Gleeson, Janet. *The Arcanum*. New York: Warner Books, 1998.

Honey, William Bowyer. *Dresden China: An Introduction to the Study of Meissen Porcelain*. New York: Pitman Publishing Corporation, 1954.

Jasper, Joanne. *American Dinnerware 1880's to 1920's*. Paducah, KY: Collector Books, 1996.

Katz-Marks, Mariann. *Majolica*. Paducah, KY: Collector Books, 1992.

Klapther, Margaret Brown. *Official White House China 1789 to the Present*. 2d ed. New York: Harry N. Abrams, Publishers, 1999.

Patterson, Jerry E. *Porcelain*. Washington, DC: Smithsonian Institution, 1979.

Schiffer, Herbert, Peter Schiffer, and Nancy Schiffer. *Chinese Export Porcelain*. Exton, PA: Schiffer Publishing, 1975.

GLASSWARE

Farrar, Estelle Sinclair, and Jane Shadel Spillman. *The Complete Cut & Engraved Glass of Corning*. New York: Crown Publishers, 1979.

Gardner, Paul Vickers. *Glass*. Washington, DC: Smithsonian Institution, 1979.

Hajdamach, Charles R. *British Glass 1800–1914*. London: Antique Collector's Club, 1991.

Lee, Ruth Webb, and James H. Rose. *American Glass Cup Plates*. Northborough, MA: Ruth Webb Lee, 1948.

Long, Milbra, and Emily Seate. *Fostoria Stemware*. Paducah, KY: Collector Books, 1995.

McKearin, Helen, and George S. McKearin. *Two Hundred Years of American Blown Glass*. New York: Crown Publishers, 1949.

Pina, Leslie. *Fostoria: Serving the American Table 1887–1986*. Atglen, PA: Schiffer Publishing, 1995.

Root, Waverley. *Glass of the World*. New York: Galahad Books, 1975.

Savage, George. *Glass and Glassware*. London: Octopus Books Limited, 1973.

Spillman, Jane Shadel. *Glass Tableware, Bowls & Vases*. New York: Alfred A. Knopf, 1982.

———. *White House Glassware*. Washington, DC: The White House Historical Association, 1989.

———. *The American Cut Glass Industry*. London: Antique Collector's Club, 1996.

Truitt, Robert, and Deborah Truitt. *Collectible Bohemian Glass 1880–1940*. Kensington, MD: B&D Glass, 1995.

Weatherman, Hazel Marie. *Fostoria. Its First Fifty Years*. Springfield, MO: The Weatherman's, 1972.

WINE

Brook, Stephen. *Liquid Gold: Dessert Wines of the World*. New York: Beech Tree Books, 1987.

Dorozynski, Alexander, and Bibiane Bell. *The Wine Book*. New York: Golden Press, 1969.

Faith, Nicholas. *Cognac*. Boston: David R. Godine, 1987.

Grossman, Harold J. *Grossman's Guide to Wines, Beers and Spirits*. 7th ed. New York: Macmillan, 1983.

Johnson, Hugh. *The World Atlas of Wine*. London: Mitchell Beazley Publishers Limited, 1971.

———. *Hugh Johnson's Story of Wine*. London: Mitchell Beazley Publishers Limited, 1996.

Markham, Dewey, Jr. *1855, a History of the Bordeaux Classification*. New York: John Wiley & Sons, 1998.

Pieroth, Kuno. *The Great German Wine Book*. New York: Sterling Publishing Co., 1983.

Schoonmaker, Frank. *Frank Schoonmaker's Encyclopedia of Wine*. New York: Hastings House, 1964.

Simon, Andre L. *The Noble Grapes and the Great Wines of France*. New York: McGraw-Hill, 1957.

———. *The History of Champagne*. London: Octopus Books Limited, 1971.

Waugh, Alec. *Wines and Spirits*. New York: Time-Life Books, 1968.

Younger, William. *Gods, Men and Wine*. Cleveland, OH: World Publishing Company, 1966.

DRESS

Buck, Anne. *Victorian Costume and Costume Accessories*. London: Herbert Jenkins, 1961.

Gernsheim, Alison. *Victorian and Edwardian Fashion*. New York: Dover Publications, 1963.

Gibbs-Smith, Charles. *The Fashionable Lady in the 19th Century*. London: Her Majesty's Stationery Office, 1960.

U.S. War Office. *Dress Regulations for the Officers of the Army 1900*. Reprint. Rutland, VT: Charles E. Tuttle Co., 1970.

TEA

Calvert, Catherine. *Having Tea*. New York: Clarkson N. Potter, Publishers, 1887.

Dusinberg, Deke. *The Book of Tea*. Paris: Flammarion, 1997.

Smith, Michael. *The Afternoon Tea Book*. New York: Macmillan, 1989.

TABLECLOTHS AND NAPKINS

Hetzer, Linda. *The Simple Art of Napkin Folding*. New York: Hearst Books, 1980.

Muller, Marianne, and Ola Mikolasek. *Great Napkin Foldings and Table Settings*. English translation. New York: Sterling Publishing Co., 1990.

ETIQUETTE AND ENTERTAINING

Allen, Lucy G. *Table Service*. Boston: Little, Brown and Company, 1915.

Aresty, Esther. *The Best Behavior*. New York: Simon & Schuster, 1970.

Beeton, Isabella. *The Book of Household Management*. London: Ward, Lock & Co., 1861.

———. *Beeton's Every-Day Cookery and Housekeeping Book*. New York: D. Appleton and Co., 1872.

Berriedale-Johnson, Michelle. *The Victorian Cookbook*. New York: Interlink Books, 1989.

Bradley, Julia M. [James Bethuel Smiley]. *Modern Manners and Social Forms*. Chicago: James B. Smiley, Publishers, 1889.

———. *The Correct Thing in Good Society*. Boston: Page Company, 1902.

Briggs, Emily Edison. *The Olivia Letters*. New York: Neale Publishing Company, 1906.

Child, Theodore. *Delicate Feasting*. New York: Harper & Brothers, 1890.

Civil War Etiquette: Martine's Handbook & Vulgarisms in Conversation. Reprint. Mendocino, CA: R. L. Shep, 1988.

Daisy Eyebright [S. O. Johnson]. *A Manual of Etiquette with Hints on Politeness and Good Breeding*. Philadelphia: David McKay, Publisher, 1873.

Davis, Jennifer. *The Victorian Kitchen*. London: BBC Books, 1989.

Devereux, G.R.M. *A Book of Edwardian Etiquette*. 1902. Reprint of *Etiquette for Women: A Book of Modern Modes and Manners*. London: George Allen & Unwin, 1983.

Ellet, Mrs. E. F., ed. *The New Encyclopedia of Domestic Economy, and Practical Housekeeping Adopted to All Classes of Society*. Norwich, CT: Henry Bill, 1872.

Ervin, Janet Halliday, ed. *The White House Cookbook*. Chicago: Follett Publishing Company, 1964.

Farmer, Fannie Merritt. *The Boston Cooking-School Cook Book*. Boston: Little, Brown and Company, 1916.

————. *The Original Boston Cooking-School Cook Book*. 1896. Reprint. N.p.: Hugh Lauter Levin Associates, 1996.

Fenwick, Millicent. *Vogue's Book of Etiquette*. New York: Simon & Schuster, 1948.

Gunn, Lilian M. *Table Service and Decoration*. Philadelphia: J. B. Lippincott Company, 1928.

Hall, Florence Howe. *Social Customs*. Boston: Estes and Lauriat, 1887.

Hathaway, Helen. *Manners: American Etiquette*. New York: E. P. Dutton & Company, 1928.

Haywood, Abraham. *The Art of Dining*. New York: G. P. Putnam's Sons, 1899.

Henderson, Mary. *Practical Cooking and Dinner Giving*. New York: Harper & Brothers, Publishers, 1877.

Hirst, Arlene. *Every Woman's Guide to China, Glass and Silver*. New York: Arco, 1970.

Keim, DeB Randolph. *Hand-Book of Official and Social Etiquette and Public Ceremonials at Washington*. 3d ed. Washington, DC: DeB Randolph Keim, 1889.

Jeaffreson, John Cordy. *A Book about the Table*. London: Hurst and Blackett Publishers, 1875.

Ladies Hand-Book of Etiquette and Manual of Politeness. New York: James Miller, n.d.

Lady Troubridge [pseud.]. *The Book of Etiquette*. 1926. Reprint. Kingswood, Surrey: The World's Work (1913) Ltd., 1958.

Learned, Mrs. Frank [Ellis Craven Learned]. *The Etiquette of New York Today*. New York: Frederick A. Stokes Company, 1906.

McAllister, Ward. *Society as I Have Found It*. New York: Cassell Publishing Company, 1890.

A Married Lady [Mrs. A. L. Webster]. *The Improved Housewife*. Hartford CT: R. H. Hobbs, 1844.

Martine, Arthur. *Martine's Hand-Book of Etiquette and Guide to True Politeness*. 1866. Reprint. Bedford, MA: Applewood Books, 1996.

A Member of the Aristocracy. *Manners and Rules of Good Society or Solecisms to be Avoided*. London: Frederick Warne and Co., 1911.

Miss Leslie. *The Behavior Book: A Manual for Ladies*. Philadelphia: Willis P. Hazard, 1854.

Post, Emily. *Etiquette*. New York: Funk & Wagnalls Company, 1922.

Ranholfer, Charles. *The Epicurean*. 1893. Reprint, New York: Dover Publications, 1971.

Roberts, Robert. *The House Servant's Directory*. 1827. Reprint. Boston: Munrow and Francis, 1969.

Senn, C. Herman. *The Art of the Table*. London: Ward, Lock & Co., 1923.

Sherwood, Mrs. John [Mary Elizabeth Wilson Sherwood]. *Manners & Social Usage*. New York: Harper & Brothers, 1887.

Smith, Eliza. *The Complete Housewife or Accomplished Gentlewoman's Companion*. 1753. Reprint. London: Literary Services and Production Limited, 1968.

Southgate, Henry. *Things a Lady Would Like to Know*. Edinburgh, UK: W. P. Nimmo, 1881.

Waiting at Table. London: Frederick Warner & Co., 1894.

Ward, Mrs. H. O. *Sensible Etiquette of the Best Society*. Philadelphia: Porter & Coates, 1878.

TABLE SETTING

Alexander, Mary Wipple. *The Table and How to Decorate It*. New York: D. Appleton and Company, 1904.

Belden, Louise Conway. *The Festive Tradition: Table Decoration and Desserts in America 1650–1900*. New York: W. W. Norton & Company, 1983.

Coates, Foster. "How Delmonico Sets a Table." *Ladies Home Journal* 8 (November 1891): 10.

Kemp, Jim. *Dining in Style: Fabulous Table Settings for Special Occasions*. New York: Sterling Publishing Co., 1986.

Roberts, Patricia Easterbrook. *Table Settings, Entertaining and Etiquette*. New York: Viking Press, 1967.

Smith, Georgiana Reynolds. *Table Decoration: Yesterday, Today and Tomorrow*. Rutland, VT: Charles E. Tuttle Company, 1968.

Sprackling, Helen. *The New Setting Your Table: Its Art, Etiquette and Service*. New York: M. Barrows & Company, 1960.

GENERAL WORKS

Brimelow, Peter. "All that Glitters." *Forbes* 161, no. 11 (June 1, 1998): 52–53.

Brown, Henry Collins. *In the Golden Nineties*. Hastings-on-Hudson, NY: Valentine's Manual, 1928.

Derks, E. Scott. *The Value of a Dollar. Prices and Incomes in the United States, 1860–1999*. Lakeville, CT: Grey House Publishing, 1999.

Fernandez-Armesto, Felipe. *Millennium: A History of the Last Thousand Years*. New York: Scribner, 1995.

Hibbert, Christopher. *The Grand Tour*. New York: G. P. Putnam's Sons, 1969.

Matthews, Glenna. *"Just a Housewife."* New York: Oxford University Press, 1987.

Mitchell, Sally. *Daily Life in Victorian England*. Westport, CT: Greenwood Press, 1996.

O'Conner, Richard. *The Golden Summers*. New York: G. P. Putnam's Sons, 1974.

Plante, Ellen. *The American Kitchen, 1700 to the Present*. New York: Facts on File, 1995.

———. *Women at Home in Victorian America*. New York: Facts on File, 1997.

Schlereth, Thomas J. *Victorian America: Transformations in Everyday Life, 1876–1915*. New York: Harper Perennial, 1992.

Schlesinger, Arthur M. *Paths to the Present*. Boston: Houghton Mifflin Company, 1964.

Smith, Marie. *Entertaining in the White House*. Washington, DC: Acropolis Books, 1967.

Stearns, Peter N. *Fat History: Bodies and Beauty in the Modern West*. New York: New York University Press, 1997.

This Fabulous Century, Prelude, 1870–1900. New York: Time-Life Books, 1988.

This Fabulous Century, Volume 1, 1900–1910. New York: Time-Life Books, 1988.

Trager, James. *The Food Chronology*. New York: Henry Holt and Company, 1995.

The Victorians. Introduction by Joan Evans. Cambridge: Cambridge University Press, 1966.

Visser, Margaret. *The Rituals of Dinner*. New York: Penguin Books USA, 1991.

Williams, Susan. *Savory Suppers and Fashionable Feasts*. New York: Pantheon Books, 1985.

Wilson, Jose. *American Cooking: The Eastern Heartland*. New York: Time-Life Books, 1971.

Index

About the Authors

WENDELL SCHOLLANDER is a practicing lawyer. He and his wife have collected Victorian etiquette books, silver, and porcelain over a period of twenty-five years.

WES SCHOLLANDER is a student at Wake Forest Law School. In addition to growing up discussing the proper placement of forks at formal dinners, he has backpacked around the world, been named a Presidential Point of Light for conservation work, served as a missionary in Central America, has art work in museums, and speaks four languages.